Management for Professior

More information about this series at http://www.springer.com/series/10101

Nicolas A. Valcik • Meghna Sabharwal
Teodoro J. Benavides

Human Resources Information Systems

A Guide for Public Administrators

Springer

Nicolas A. Valcik
Department of Institutional Research
Texas Tech University
Lubbock, TX, USA

Teodoro J. Benavides
School of Economic, Political and Policy Sciences
The University of Texas at Dallas
Richardson, TX, USA

Meghna Sabharwal
School of Economic, Political and Policy Sciences
University of Texas, Dallas
Richardson, TX, USA

ISSN 2192-8096 ISSN 2192-810X (electronic)
Management for Professionals
ISBN 978-3-030-75113-5 ISBN 978-3-030-75111-1 (eBook)
https://doi.org/10.1007/978-3-030-75111-1

This Springer imprint is published by the registered company Springer Nature Switzerland AG
The registered company address is: Gewerbestrasse 11, 6330 Cham, Switzerland

Information Systems

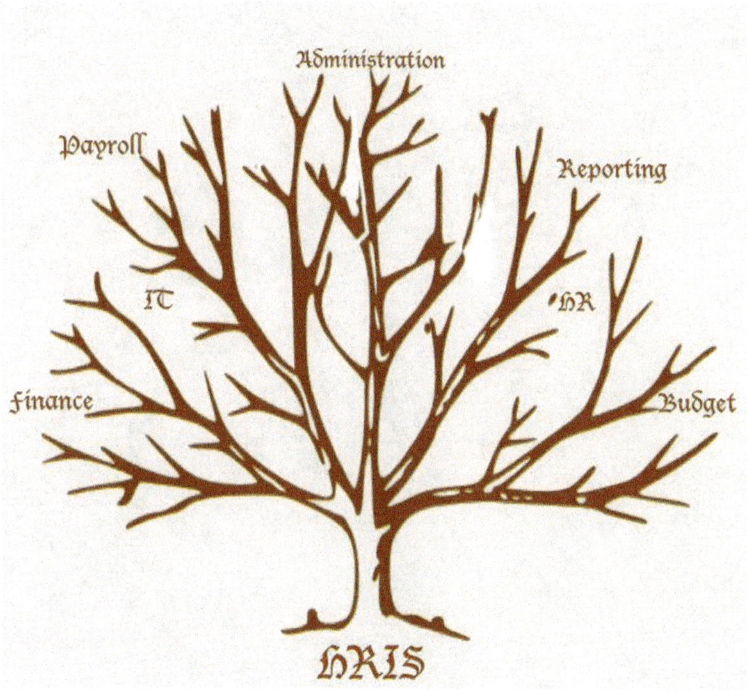

Artwork: Andrea D. Stigdon

Nicolas Valcik: I would like to dedicate this book to Paul E. Tracy, a person who was gone way too early, and to Keith N. Haley, who believed in me to go to graduate school.

Teodoro J. Benavides: I would like to dedicate this book to my mother and father, Maria M. Benavides and Manuel T. Benavides

Meghna Sabharwal: I would like to dedicate this book to my mentor and eminent scholar in public human resources management, Dr. N. Joseph Cayer

Foreword

Having been in public administration for over 30 years, one of the resounding truths I have discovered is that the complexity of data management in a public institution is substantive, and negligent management poses tangible risk to an organization. Because of the quagmire of regulations, coupled with social pressure, human resources data management is arguably the most challenging data source to effectively manage for public administrators. Proficient human resource data management in public administration requires knowledge, collaboration, and detail dedication. Dr. Nicolas Valcik has over 20 years of experience navigating the data management in public administration waters, and I have watched him traverse the complexities of human resource data management and reporting. His mastery of quantitative aspects of human resource data is only surpassed by his understanding of the culture of public administration, the intricacies of the external regulatory requirements. His insights are practical, and will help any public organization navigating the tumultuous waters of human resources data management and reporting.

The present collection of applied chapters aids public administrators in understanding the challenges of the human resource data, including the challenges present in the public administration environment. For instance, many public organizations operate with human resources siloed from data reporting and data management for the organization. In my experience at multiple public institutions, the human resource function typically lacks the information technology, advanced statistical, and reporting expertise resources required for proper data governance and management. Further, the federal and state human resource authorities lack a mature, standardized, and comprehensive data standard for reporting. Although the sector has made strides with the CUPA standards, the industry is a far cry from the other industry sector standardizations, such as IPEDS and the Common Data Set. For example, the notion of "institutional salary" has multiple definitions, and is further complicated by the various information systems used at public organizations. The lack of standardized data elements in the human resource information systems, in the face of ambiguity in reporting against often vague data standards, leads to an infinite, recursive loop of problems, each blaming the other. While many consultation firms have attempted to create human resource data standards by with public institutions can compare human resource data, to date I have not found a true comparative and robust methodology. The institutional cost and ramifications of this scenario are well articulated and discussed in this book, and provide tactical strategies to mitigate the problems.

The present book aids the reader in better understanding the complexities of the human resource climate, warns of the known problems associated with human resource data, and offers a theoretical and applied approaches to raise the success of a public administrator managing human resource data. Experience and knowledge provide a means of success as public administrators face these challenges in the operations of their organization. As a veteran of public administration data management, I am honored to provide an overview of this excellent, applied handbook. The authors provide insightful observations, discussion, and suggestions in an effective, organized, and comprehensive manner. The need for such a handbook has been great, and this reference will not disappoint. The present book is an effective description of the problems, outline of the issues, and delineation of the strategies for human resource and organization data mangers in public administration. In our quest to discover a methodical approach to the challenge of human resource data management, the present work deliveries a resource useful in the workplace, as well as graduate education. To quote my late father, Dr. Larry M. Austin, a management science guru, managers make decisions, models don't (Austin 1993). [Austin, L.M. & Ghandforoush, P. Management Science for Decision Makers, West Publishing Co., 1993).} This handbook helps managers understand human resource data, and master data supported decision-making for the public organization.

Katherine A. Austin, Ph.D.
Associate Vice President
Adjunct Associate Professor
Texas Tech University

Preface

Personnel data are critical to many public organizations for hiring and recruitment, strategic planning and analysis, as well as reporting data to various local, state, and federal bodies in order to remain compliant with myriad legal requirements. Despite its importance to an organization, having access to accurate data is often not given sufficient attention in the public sector literature. There is a dearth of studies examining the reasons for poor quality data in public organizations. However, public organizations often have several obstacles to overcome before they are able to provide accurate data that complies with legislative requirements. These challenges range from information systems, human resources, an organizational culture resistant to change, data ownership, and reporting issues. Studies often discuss the challenges of poor data, but are amiss to discuss what occurs from the time the data are input to receiving an output. Through this study, the authors unravel the various reasons that might lead to inaccurate personnel data and offer solutions for circumventing the challenges of poor quality human resources data.

This book has been designed to provide public administrators, both practitioners and students, with the definition of what a human resources information system (HRIS) is, what the functionality of such a system should be theoretically, and the practical aspects of an HRIS. The book discusses the different aspects of human resources between public, non-profit organizations (NPO) and private corporations, which must be managed in an HRIS database. Throughout the book, topics are brought forth to discuss the pitfalls and advantages to organizations using an HRIS enterprise system and it will discuss how HRIS impacts an entity on an organizational level. Within the text, there is discussion on what public administrators will need to be concerned with in the aspect of data quality in the HRIS enterprise system. Additionally, there is an organizational theory component to the book, which will frame how an HRIS enterprise system and the organization interact both from a functional standpoint and a reporting standpoint. This book uses theoretical approaches and ties in practitioner knowledge to provide a complete overview on HRIS for the public administrator. To achieve this aim, there will be several real case studies of public and/or NPOs throughout the book to illustrate how the theoretical aspects at times may sound ideal, but in reality are not practical for implementation.

From a technical standpoint, this book will explore the issues that public administrators face when HRIS is migrated to newer versions or completely migrated to a different vendor-supported HRIS database. HRIS migrations have several pitfalls that public administrators will need to watch for and to prepare solutions. Since there are so many critical data components for a public organization or NPO, it is essential that all steps are taken to alleviate any type of problems that may arise. If problems do arise, it can impact everything from payroll to retirement benefits, a nightmare scenario for any public administrator who depends upon the information for operational or decision-making purposes.

For small public organizations that employ staff with limited knowledge of HRIS, it only takes one individual to introduce errors through faulty data entry, thus causing work for the rest of the staff as they correct errors in the personnel records. Public organizations connected to larger parent organizations (i.e. an institution connected to a system) can have data integrity issues ripple through the institution and potentially lead to issues with medical benefits, retirement benefits, and so on. For every one individual performing incorrect data entry, it will take additional staff members to correct those issues. This excludes staff required to correct any data issues transmitted to a parent organization.

The purpose of this book is to help practitioners and students understand and contend with these types of data issues with HRIS. In the last decade or so, of greater concern are issues of data security and cyber threat. The book discusses these aspects as it relates to HRIS. Furthermore, the complexity of human resource data and HRIS will be discussed throughout the book along with real life case studies to assist the readers with connecting the theoretical with the realities of HRIS issues. The case studies in particular have been compiled by the authors' own experiences and expertise in interacting with HRIS. To disguise the organizations where these case studies took place, generic names have been used to maintain anonymity.

Lubbock, TX, USA Nicolas A. Valcik
Richardson, TX, USA Teodoro J. Benavides
Richardson, TX, USA Meghna Sabharwal

Acknowledgments

I would like to thank everyone who worked on this project. A project such as this takes time and effort as research has to be first undertaken followed by a high standard of writing fit for publication. I would like to thank my co-authors Ted and Meghna for all of the work they have put into this project. I would like to thank my supervisor Dr. Kathy Austin for writing such a great foreword to this book as well as being very supportive of my role at Texas Tech University. I would like to thank my co-workers and employees at Texas Tech University for support throughout this project. I would like to thank Dr. Maria Flores-Harris for her support and expertise on this project. I would like to thank Andrea Stigdon for providing proofing support for this book and for the amazing artwork for the inside page. Last but not least, I want to thank my mother Jo Valcik and my wife Kristi Valcik for all of their love and support throughout my career. Without their support, this project would not be possible.

Nicolas A. Valcik

I would like to thank my mom and dad, Maria M. Benavides and Manuel T. Benavides, who taught me the love and virtue of public service. My mom, who worked at a nonprofit hospital, and my dad, who worked at the Fire Department of the City of Corpus Christi, lived lives of public service, which enriched the lives of my two sisters and me.

Teodoro J. Benavides

I would like to thank my mentor and advisor Dr. N. Joseph Cayer, who introduced me to public human resources management, and the countless other mentors who helped me in my academic journey. I would like to thank Nick Valcik for adding me to this project, and my co-author and colleague Ted Benavides from whom I have learned so much about local government. I would like to extend a special thanks to my graduate research assistant, Thanh Thi Hoang, who helped immensely conducting literature reviews on this subject. She also provided excellent ideas for graphics. Lastly, I would like to acknowledge my parents, my husband Nikhil Gupta, and my son Aakash Sabharwal Gupta who have been very patient with me as I worked on this project during these tough COVID times. Without their constant support, love, and encouragement I would not be able to make this a reality.

Meghna Sabharwal

General Acknowledgment

There were some parts used in this book that were taken from the chapter previously published:

Valcik, N., and M. Sabharwal, 2018. "Public Personnel Data in Organizations" in Farazmand, Ali (Ed.) *Global Encyclopedia of Public Administration, Public Policy and Governance*. ISBN: 978-3-319-20927-2, Springer, New York, New York.

Contents

Case Studies

About the Authors

Nicolas A. Valcik Nicolas A. Valcik currently works as the managing director for institutional research at Texas Tech University. Previously, Nicolas was the director for institutional research and business intelligence at the University of Texas of the Permian Basin, the executive director for institutional effectiveness at Central Washington University, director for institutional research at West Virginia University, and as associate director of strategic planning and analysis at the University of Texas at Dallas. In addition, Nicolas held an academic appointment as a clinical assistant professor for public affairs at the University of Texas at Dallas. Prior to 1997, Nicolas worked for a number of municipalities, across different of departments, as well as for Nortel. Nicolas received a doctorate degree in public affairs from the University of Texas at Dallas in 2005, a master's degree in public affairs from the University of Texas at Dallas in 1996, a bachelor's degree in interdisciplinary studies from the University of Texas at Dallas in 1994, and an associate's degree in political science from Collin County Community College in 1994.

Nicolas has authored the following books for Taylor and Francis: *Institutional Research Initiatives in Higher Education* (2018) co-edited with Jeffery Johnson, *City Planning for the Public Manager* (2017) co-authored with Ted Benavides, Todd Jordan and Andrea Stigdon, *Case Studies in Disaster Response and Emergency Management: Second Edition* (2017) co-authored with Paul Tracy, *Strategic Planning, Decision-Making and Practical Aspects for Public Sector and Non-Profit Organizations* (2016), co-authored with Ted Benavides and Kim Scruton *Non-Profit Organization Case Study Book* (2015), *Hazardous Materials Compliance for Public Research Organizations: A Case Study* (2013), co-authored with Paul E. Tracy *Case Studies in Disaster Response and Emergency Management* and co-authored with Ted Benavides *Practical Human Resources Management for Public Managers: A Case Study Approach* (2011). Prior to 2011, Nicolas authored *Regulating the Use of Biological Hazardous Materials in Universities: Complying with the New Federal Guidelines*, which was published by Mellen Press in 2006. Nicolas has served as editor for three volumes of *New Directions for Institutional Research* (Volumes 135, 140, and 146 and co-edited with Gary Levy 156) in addition to writing numerous articles and book chapters on institutional research topics and homeland security issues. Nicolas specializes in several areas as both a researcher and a practitioner: higher education, information technology, human resources, homeland security, organizational behavior, and emergency management.

Meghna Sabharwal Meghna Sabharwal is professor and program director in the Public and Nonprofit Management program at the University of Texas at Dallas. Her research interests are focused on public human resources management, specifically workforce diversity, job performance, job satisfaction, and high-skilled migration. She is widely published in public administration journals, and is the winner of two best paper awards. She also has two book publications: *Public Personnel Administration* (6th Ed.) and *Public Administration in South Asia: India, Bangladesh, and Pakistan*. She is the recipient of the 2020 Rita Mae Kelly Distinguished Research Award by the Section for Women in Public Administration (SWPA), American Society for Public Administration, and the 2019 Mary Hamilton Award given by the International Chapter, ASPA. She also received the 2015 Julia J. Henderson International Award by the American Society for Public Administration (ASPA) Section on Women in Public Administration. In 2018, she was chosen as one of the top 20 women in the United States in the field of Public Affairs. She has won several graduate and undergraduate teaching awards. She is also the recipient of two National Science Foundation grants. She serves on several editorial boards and is the incoming associate editor for the *Review of Public Personnel Administration,* the leading human resource journal in public administration. She graduated with a Ph.D. in public administration from Arizona State University in 2008.

Teodoro J. Benavides Teodoro J. Benavides currently serves as a faculty member, Associate Professor of Practice, at the University of Texas at Dallas (UTD) in the School of Economic, Political and Policy Sciences' Public and Nonprofit Management Program. In addition, he serves as the director for the Master of Public Affairs program and the department's internship coordinator.

Teodoro has co-authored a textbook on human resources, titled *Practical Human Resources for Public Managers*, with Nicolas Valcik; has co-authored a textbook on nonprofits, titled *Non-Profit Organizations:*

Real Issues for Public Administrators, with Nicolas Valcik and Kimberly Scruton; and has co-authored a textbook on urban planning, titled *City Planning for the Public Manager*, with Nicolas Valcik, Todd Jordan, and Andrea Stigdon. He is also currently contracted to write two additional books on local government management and human resource information systems.

Teodoro served from 1998 to 2004 as city of manager of Dallas, Texas. From 1996 to 1998, he was city manager of the City of Denton, Texas. Previously, he held several other positions with the City of Dallas, including assistant city manager, director of the budget and research, assistant director of the human services, assistant director of capital budget programs, capital budget administrator, and budget analyst.

Teodoro earned a bachelor's degree in education, political science, and history from Texas A&M University-Kingsville and a master's degree in public administration from Southern Methodist University. Teodoro is a fellow of the National Academy of Public Administration (NAPA).

Introduction

1

Data is the lifeblood of any organization; it constitutes the basis for decision-making at all levels. Inaccurate or poor data can lead to inefficiencies whether in public or private sectors (Oliveira et al., 2005). Despite its importance to an organization, access to accurate data is often not given sufficient attention in the literature. There is a dearth of studies examining the reasons for poor data in public organizations.

Several studies agree that poor and inaccurate data can cost a significant amount to an organization both in terms of monetary and non-monetary losses. Some estimates in the business world indicate the losses due to poor quality data can amount to $10 million a year (Eckerson, 2002). Despite these colossal costs, Kim and Choi (2003, p. 70) suggest, "There have been limited efforts to systematically understand the effects of low quality data." Most efforts are directed at investigating and correcting errors in sophisticated computer and linear models. The impact of low quality data usually depends of the nature and usage of the data (by citizens or end users) (Kim, 2002).

Why is having and maintaining accurate personnel data so difficult for public organizations to achieve? Unfortunately, obtaining and maintaining accurate personnel information is not as easy as it would seem to a person outside a public organization. If the public organization has a large number of employees, the issue of obtaining accurate personnel information becomes more complex not only due to the quantity of information that needs to be captured but also due to the complexity of the organization and legal reporting requirements (Ashbaugh & Miranda, 2002; Abella, 1985; Givan, 2005).

Is there a method for inputting the information in an official information system of record? Are there rules and legal guidelines that prevent such information from being obtained? Do public organizations need leadership and structure in place to ensure the collection of such information? Does the organizational culture support good quality data? In short, all of these questions are pivotal in obtaining accurate personnel information, most of which can be overcome by the organizational actions and business processes that are implemented. However, there will always be

N. A. Valcik et al., *Human Resources Information Systems*, Management for Professionals, https://doi.org/10.1007/978-3-030-75111-1_1

unresolvable difficulties in obtaining some personnel information due to legal statutes that prevent employers from requiring disclosure of certain information, ethnicity for example, from employees.

Normally packaged as a database, many companies sell some form of HRIS and every HRIS has different capabilities. Choosing an HRIS is a major undertaking for any organization. Selecting the options that are best for your needs at your organization is challenging because so many options exist. A robust HRIS can grow with your organization. Does your system accomplish the things that you want done, also do you have the training and support in place to make your system work for your organization? The system must provide information regarding names, titles, addresses, salary and position history, reporting structures, performance appraisal histories, and other critical employee information. Some of the major components that the system must include the following:

- Benefits administration - An ideal system benefits administration system enables employees to review and update their own information including vacation tracking, sign up for benefits enrollment, track status changes and update other personal information.
- Complete integration with payroll - The system will need to include the organization's financial software and accounting systems. These systems must be connected to ensure that paychecks are correct. There must be no disconnect between what the official pay rate is and the information in the system.
- Applicant tracking and resume management – A seamless system enables the recruiter to click a button and all the information from the applicant is transferred to the employee. This saves time significantly by reducing data entry and paperwork.
- Performance development plans - It is not enough to have plans. If performance development plans are recorded in a central system, they can easily follow the employees' career growth. Senior leadership can run reports to see where people are and what their individual bosses are planning in terms of succession planning.
- Disciplinary actions - It is important to keep track of who has been suspended, demoted, or had other negative actions taken against them, even after the employee leaves the organization. When a company calls and asks for a former employee reference, it is easy for an administrator in the human resources department to look up and report back whether the person is eligible for rehire. This is especially critical in an organization where certifications and licenses are required.
- HRIS systems must serve organizations by tracking the following information:
  - Attendance and Paid Time Off (PTO)
  - Pay raises and related history
  - Pay grades and position held
  - Performance development plans
  - Training received
  - Disciplinary action received

- Personal employee information
- Management and key employee succession plans
- High potential employee identification
- Applicant tracking, interviewing and selection

An effective HRIS provides information on just about anything the organization needs to track and analyze of their employees, former employees, and applicants. Organizations need to select a human resources information system and customize it to meet their needs. The system needs to be robust enough to allow non-human resource personnel to access information for themselves.

Human Resources Information Systems in Public Sector Organizations

HRIS and its use is growing among public sector organizations. Organizations must look for ways to manage their internal processes efficiently while preserving the integrity of each practice. In human resources, this involves many transactions affecting people, including the benefits they receive and the ways they are treated by the organization. Tracking Human Resources activities through a human resources information system is efficient and effective for many public sector organizations. For the public sector leaders, it is usually a matter of which system is affordable and suited to the organization's needs. Several uses of public sector HRIS are identified in the next section.

Identifying Manpower Requirements

In the most basic sense, a Human Resources Information System organizes information about every job in your organization. This information might include details such as who is currently in the position, what they are paid and what their job responsibilities, training needs and assigned benefits are. You can use reports about groups of positions or your entire workforce to determine your manpower requirements. To increase productivity, for example, you must ensure there are enough employees to staff the expansion to your schedule or workload. With a computerized system, you can study the impact of program expansion, such as how much it will cost to add the employees that will be needed (Troshani et al., 2011).

Identifying Resources

When making decisions such as how many employees will be required, managers want to determine quickly what resources are already at their disposal. Using an HRIS can help managers make better decisions. Instead of jumping immediately to a plan to recruit and train new employees for organizational program expansion, managers could pull a report from the HRIS, identifying employees who have skills and training required to be promoted to the new positions. Then, less-skilled workers can be recruited to replace them (Workday, 2020).

Compliance

In most organizations, there is a critical need to manage how employees are treated, especially to comply with the requirements of Title VII of the Civil Rights Law of 1964 and other laws such as the Americans with Disabilities Act. This is easier to accomplish when all the ways that applicants and employees are managed and their data, from their application to their termination, is housed in one powerful information system. For example, a Human Resources manager could pull a report about the diversity of the organization, including percentages of employees in each occupation by their race, gender, or national origin. This report would help to show whether the business is complying with Equal Employment Opportunity regulations (BambooHR, 2020).

Meeting Training Needs

An HRIS system can help employers manage training needs, allowing them to complete mandated and optional training. For example, in the HRIS, an employee might go into a description of available training courses and request courses for their personal learning. When that training becomes available, the HRIS notifies them so they can register and complete the training. In this kind of model, the HRIS helps the organization to automatically manage the fulfillment of many training needs. Also, when employees are ready to apply for a promotion, they may already have much of the training they need because they have taken it in anticipation of promotion (Bianca, 2018).

Ways HRIS Can Promote Diversity

Technology is an important tool when creating unbiased protocols to support diversity initiatives. The right software solution helps organizations make strides for diversity in recruiting, performance evaluations, employee collaboration, and social accountability. Here are just a few ways your HRIS can help a diversity-friendly environment:

- Analytics—Past data helps predict future behavior. Monitor metrics like pay increases and bonuses, turnover patterns, recruiting and hiring variables, and the ratio between diversity candidates vs. diversity hires.
- Performance Reviews—There is a shift away from traditional annual performance reviews, and that is a good thing. More frequent evaluations help

managers base ratings on solid data rather than gut feelings. Alerts, journal entries, self-evaluations, and strategic ratings systems all help managers focus on talent and achievement rather than on feelings.
- Recruiting Algorithms—Perhaps not surprisingly, algorithms often make better hiring decisions than humans. That is because the algorithm will assess each candidate based on the same criteria, identifying candidates most qualified for the position. Once there is a short list of candidates, some software programs can hide demographic information to encourage unbiased hiring decisions.
- Blind Assessments—During the screening process, blind assessments can be set up to test candidate skills. This prevents unconscious bias toward a certain kind of candidate.
- Mentorships—Mentoring programs help managers get to know a wide variety of employees and learn to appreciate the contributions of different perspectives. HRIS can help facilitate communication between mentors and mentees through social platforms and feedback reminders.

Diversity is not just about reaching an arbitrary percentage or making everybody happy. It is about making the best use of all available talent to make your organization more successful. The tools available in HRIS can help make smart hiring decisions, facilitate collaboration, and promote inclusiveness in the workplace—and that's good news for everybody. Setting goals is a useful exercise at almost any level of public sector organizations (Hayes, 2012).
Individual employees should also be involved in goal setting. Having goals can motivate team members and encourage them to work harder, especially in remote work scenarios. People are more productive when they have goals to work toward, which helps them grow in their careers. Of course, it is important for people to have realistic and achievable goals to strive for. That is where a human resources information system, or HRIS, comes into play. Here is how an HRIS could assist with goal setting (Hayes, 2012).

Use the HRIS to Track How Employees Spend Time to Start Goal Setting

An HRIS is a tool the HR team can use to track different information for the team. Many people use one to keep track of payroll and benefits administration. It is also helpful for keeping track of hours or even expense reports. HRIS can keep track of projects. The team can record their tasks and the hours they are spending on those tasks as well. This is helpful if there are team members working in remote locations, allowing managers to keep tabs on their schedule, hours, and productivity. With this information, managers can examine which tasks take employees the longest to complete. This could help the manager and the employee identify where they are struggling. Maybe one task is taking up so much of their time that they cannot get to other important items on their to-do lists. They might not have the right skills or training for the time-intensive task, which means it takes longer (Oregon, 2016).

Crunch the Numbers to Set Realistic Goals

Actionable data from an HRIS can enable a manager to evaluate current productivity to set future work goals. How many projects would it be reasonable for an employee to complete? Are there ways to decreases hours on one task, while increasing hours on another? The numbers allow managers to set realistic goals for every employee. If an employee only finished two projects last year, it may not be reasonable to expect them to be able to finish twenty this year. Creating such a high goal, even with proper supports, could be setting them up to fail. Realistic goals encourage employees to strive, which means these goals are not easily achieved. With hard work and motivation, though, they can still be achieved (Oregon, 2016).

Ask the Employee for Their Feedback

Once the numbers are in hand, the manager can discuss with the employee the hours spent on some tasks, especially when their time usage is different from that of other employees. The point of this exercise is to help identify areas where they are struggling and where they need support. If an employee is struggling to meet their productivity goals, the manager may be able to provide them with more training or other supports to help them become more productive. In this way, goal setting can also be focused on skills and development, not just productivity. The manager can ask the employee if there are skills they would like to master that will help make their job easier and then assist the employee in creating a plan to build those skills through the year (Lucerna, 2020).

Monitor, Track, and Adjust Goals

With an HRIS, managers can move from goal setting to goal tracking by keeping an eye on employees' progress toward their goals. Employee progress can be reviewed and goals adjusted as needed. Maybe the stretch goal that was set was not really a stretch goal, or maybe a new set of skills has been discovered that will help the team excel. In short, the powerful data-driven insights provided by an HRIS could help managers and their employees create a better goal setting process (Oregon, 2016).

Potential Methods HRMS Can Reduce Employee Turnover

Human Resource Management Systems (HRMS) are often used to automate administrative tasks and improve return on in investment (ROI). But these systems can also retain an organization's number one resource — employees. Here are three ways that HRMS solutions can help public sector organizations reduce employee turnover.

Improve Employee Engagement

The first step in reducing employee turnover is to improve engagement because engaged employees are less likely to leave their organizations. Organizations should begin by streamlining the onboarding process, as new employees who go through a structured onboarding program more likely to stay with an organization. With HRMS software, onboarding can start even before the new employee reaches the office. Employees can sign administrative documents electronically catch up on organizational news and goals through self-service user portals and join virtual social networks of colleagues. On their first day, employees will have more time to tour the facility, set up their equipment and hit the ground running. HRMS solutions can also boost retention through continuing education. Millennial employees ranked training and development as the most important benefit of working for a company, higher than cash bonuses, free health care and a pension. HRMS software offers a cost-effective alternative for employing learning management systems and e-learning modules allow employees to improve individual skills and performance at their own pace. This type of professional development not only promotes employee engagement, but also prepares future leaders within a company who might otherwise leave (NEOGOV, 2020).

Track Employee Goals, Performance, and Recognition

Employee turnover is not always a bad thing and can be necessary if employees are underperforming. However, measuring an employee's performance can be a difficult task. HRMS solutions allow companies to determine skill sets, assign goals and track accomplishments. The performance data is beneficial to both employees and managers.

Employees are empowered to:

- Monitor their progress
- Seek help and make improvements between scheduled reviews
- Determine their future goals

Managers can:

- Assess employees in quantifiable ways
- Provide more relevant feedback
- Determine appropriate assignments
- Recognize employee achievements
- Develop succession plans to promote exceptional employees

When employees feel that business objectives are aligned with their skill sets, projects are challenging, and accomplishments are properly rewarded, they will be more likely to stay with the organization (Bianca, 2019).

Understand Why Employees Leave

When an employee leaves an organization, HR departments conduct exit interviews or use paper questionnaires to understand why. However, this information may not be accurate. The interviewer may have a bias, the employee may not feel comfortable being honest in person or there may be no exit interview at all. HRMS solutions can communicate with employees even after they leave. Because they have had time to understand their reasoning and now have the space to be direct, their insight can be valuable. This information can be combined with other metrics collected by the software — demographics, performance, promotion wait time and compensation ratio — to create a more holistic analysis of employee turnover. Fully examining why an employee leaves is important because it helps to develop a strategy for reducing employee turnover in the future. Without proper data, HR departments are left to wonder if their assessments are accurate. An HRMS not only records necessary information, but also offers predictive analytics that can give HR departments more certainty in their workforce decisions and a clearer path for future recruitment and retention strategies. With the right HRMS solution, public sector units can follow the entire employee life cycle with a bird's eye view. Governmental agencies can then develop evidence-based strategies to reduce turnover, improve hiring and retain the best talent.

In modern organizations, employee job satisfaction has become an extremely important concern that managers must get right and improve. When employees are satisfied with their job within the workplace, associated benefits such as lower turnover, higher productivity, increased organizational productivity and further employee loyalty may be attained. Interestingly, closely associated with job satisfaction is employee satisfaction. When employees are satisfied in all employment aspects, an increase in associated job satisfaction may be attained. Likewise, critical factors of satisfaction and engagement are of top consideration for managers to ensure employees feel a sense of workplace trust and can enjoy their time working within the organization, which may lead to associated job satisfaction increases. Although, employee job satisfaction needs a specific strategy to ensure you are keeping your employees happy and satisfied with their job. In turn, managers may utilize the following five different ways to improve employee job satisfaction within an organization.

Create a Positive Culture

To ensure employee job satisfaction is being attained managers should consider creating a positive organizational culture. There are a wide variety of positive influencing organizational cultures that may help improve employee job satisfaction. One specific way is through ensuring organizational employees realize that they may communicate truly open and honest to one another. The aim is for managers to work towards creating a culture of open and positive employee interactions. When this is achieved, employees may likely find that any concern that they may have had with the job is easily answered for through the open communication between employees. Furthermore, managers should ensure that a culture of teamwork is being developed within the organization. Employees will find that when they can communicate between team members about any job or task concerns they may have, they will find they can get positive responses extremely efficiently. In turn, the work environment of a positive culture that is built around being open and honest with strong communication and with a team focus will effectively improve employee job satisfaction.

Recognize and Reward

A largely effective way to ensure organizational managers are improving employee job satisfaction is through rewarding and recognizing employees within the workplace. To begin, when employees receive rewards and recognitions that are outside of the classic financial remuneration that they receive working within the organization employees may begin to feel increasingly satisfied with the agency or unit. This satisfaction is largely linked to associated increases of employee motivation and productivity, which is sought out by managers constantly. Likewise, when employees receive rewards such as a bonus for the hard work they have completed or even recognition such as large positive employee feedback statement that is given for the achievement of completing a difficult project, employees will correspondingly likely want to receive the same or similar recognition and reward again. This will, in turn, display an employee's effort of working towards receiving the reward or recognition again which can likely display an association of an increase in job satisfaction as the employee becomes happy with the work, they are completing aiming to continue their driven efforts.

Offer Flexibility

To ensure that managers are attaining an effective increase in employee job satisfaction a large consideration of offering employees work flexibility becomes extremely critical. Managers should specifically consider if an employee will feel increasingly satisfied with the job they are completing if they are given an increasingly flexible work schedule. That is, the employee may be allowed to leave work earlier or start work later due to the associated problems they may find with their daily commute. When this is positively working to ensure employees are satisfied with the work they complete as they have a flexible work schedule, managers may find an increase in employee job satisfaction levels. Moreover, to ensure that an increase in employees' job satisfaction levels is being attained, flexibility is important in ensuring the employee's work-life balance is being attained. Employees may feel that some organizations are extremely inflexible asking them to work outside of the period of work they are scheduled for regularly. Thus, it becomes important for managers to respect employees' time-off work not only for an increase in job satisfaction but ensuring the employee's well-being is being maintained. Through giving the employee work specifically during work hours and not outside, it will ensure employees do not feel stressed and are not experiencing burn-out (People Strategy, 2020).

Career Development

Another extremely valuable way to ensure managers are working to improve employee job satisfaction is through thoughtful career development consideration for employees. When an employee enters an organization, they are working towards the professional development of their careers through gaining the necessary knowledge, skills and tools needed to grow as an employee. Likewise, it becomes extremely important for managers to recognize this and in turn assist employees in developing their careers. One effective method that management may likely want to utilize to ensure they are developing the careers of employees is through investing in training activities. When effectively investing in training activities designed for specific employees, that employee will feel the organization cares about developing their skills and will likely receive an increase in personal job satisfaction (Karikari et al., 2015).

Conduct Surveys

Finally, to effectively improve employee job satisfaction levels, managers may utilize employee surveys. Surveys are an extremely useful tool that may ensure that managers understand what employees' attitudes towards certain organizational activities are. Moreover, surveys provide critical data on specific metrics that managers would likely want to recognize and address within the workplace. Specifically, to effectively improve employee job satisfaction managers may likely want to utilize a survey such as a pulse survey. Pulse surveys are designed to ask employees regularly about a variety of questions that can be used to specifically address any job satisfaction concerns employees may have. Interestingly due to the development of technology, a Human Resource Information System (HRIS) can be utilized to run associated surveys simply all online. Thus, surveys will act as a largely efficient way for managers to collect data, analyze and act in improving employee job satisfaction levels.

Human Resources Information Systems in Nonprofits

Human Resource Information System is of equal, if not more important for meeting the long-term human capital objectives of nonprofit organizations. However, nonprofits need to be equipped with the right tools to help them reach these objectives. That is why HRIS provides the latest human resources technology to develop a motivated, skilled, and engaged workforce. Being a nonprofit organization does not go against adopting a professional approach to human resources management and the adoption of human resources best practices. Only few professional solutions can trigger a passion for work as strongly as in the nonprofit sector. Nonetheless, this enthusiasm does not generally benefit from an optimal support. Without the right foundation and focused attention from management and human resources, employees and volunteers, guided by emotions, will singlehandedly carry missions, which can compromise the strategic development of the organization. Maintaining a talented and highly motivated workforce is a challenge very specific to human resources. With increased pressure from work specific to the nonprofit sector this challenge appears even more complex. HRIS help optimize the processes that contribute to the mutual engagement of the organization, management, employees, and volunteers on one platform (Lucerna, 2020).

Staffing decisions are among the most important decisions that nonprofit organizations make. Just as businesses and organizations of all sizes and areas of operation rely on their personnel to execute their strategies and advance their goals, so do nonprofit groups. Thus, nonprofit organizations need to attend to the same tasks as profit-seeking companies and public organizations do when they turn to the challenges of establishing and maintaining a solid work force. To accomplish this, nonprofit organizations must address the following personnel issues when using a HRIS system which essential for its proper execution:

- Assessing personnel needs
- Recruiting personnel
- Screening personnel
- Selecting and hiring personnel
- Orienting new employees to the organization
- Deciding compensation issues

An effective non-profit manager must try to get more out of the people which can only be done effectively using integrated HRIS. The productivity that a nonprofit manager can extract from their workforce requires the maximization of an entire staff. This is achieved by the basic decisions of whom to hire, fire, where to place people, and who to promote. The quality of these human decisions largely determines whether the organization is being run seriously, and whether its mission, its values, and its objectives are real and meaningful to people rather than just public relations and rhetoric (Paycor, 2020).

A key component of running any nonprofit is to build a quality core of personnel that meets the future internal needs and can accept the external influences that buffet each nonprofit organization. HRIS can help nonprofit organizations track their personnel demands associated with current and planned initiatives, operating budget, and costs, and the quality and quantity of the area worker pool, both for volunteer and staff positions. HRIS allows nonprofit leaders to adhere to general business principles such as sound fiscal management, retention of good employees through good compensation packages and related human resources issues. HRIS systems facilitate use fundamental business principles used in the assessment of personnel needs that apply to nonprofits as well. These principles include:

- Fill positions with people who are willing and able to do the job.
- Providing accurate and realistic job and skill specifications for each position ensures that it will be filled by someone capable of handling the responsibilities associated with that position.
- Written job descriptions are essential to communicating job expectations.
- Employees who are chosen because they are the best available candidates are far more likely to have a positive impact than those who are chosen based on friendship or expediency.
- Performance appraisals, when coupled with specific job expectations, help boost performance.

The process of selecting a competent person for each position is best accomplished through a systematic use of HRIS to allow an analysis of the requirements for each job, including the skills, knowledge, and other qualifications that employees must possess to perform each task. To guarantee personnel needs are adequately specified it requires that the following steps must be followed, (1) conducting a job analysis, (2) developing a written job description, and (3) preparing job specifications (People Strategy, 2020).

Recruiting, Screening, and Selecting Organization Work Force

Recruiting

For many nonprofit organizations, publicizing its very existence is the most important step that it can take in its efforts to recruit staff and volunteers alike. This is especially true if one wishes to encourage volunteers to become involved. Volunteers are the lifeblood of countless nonprofit organizations, for they attend to the basic tasks that need performing, from paperwork to transportation of goods and/or services to maintenance. Management of their staff must be tracked with the assistance HRIS but of even more importance is the management of their volunteers using their HRIS. Nonprofit groups rely on several basic avenues to publicize their work and their staffing needs: local media (newspapers, newsletters, radio advertising, billboards, etc.), social media and other community organizations (municipal governments, churches, civic groups, other nonprofit organizations, etc.) (Everything at Work, 2020).

Screening and Selection

The interviewing process is another essential component of successful staffing for nonprofit groups. This holds true for volunteers as well as for officers, directors, and paid staff. Indeed, HRIS is vital to every nonprofit to assist them in the recruitment and interviewing systematically of all their volunteers the same way you would recruit paid staff. An orderly and professional approach to volunteer management will pay off handsomely for all nonprofit organizations. What is done in the recruitment phase will set the standard for volunteer performance. If the manager is disciplined and well organized, they will often attract more qualified volunteers. Managers of nonprofit organizations should make sure that their HRIS systems are fully engaged in the process of staffing, screening, and selection:

- Recognize that all personnel, whether they are heading your organization's annual fundraising drive or lending a hand for a few hours every other week, have an impact on the group's performance. Certainly, some positions are more important than others, but countless nonprofit managers can attest to the fact that an under-performing, unethical, or unpleasant individual can have an enormously negative impact on organization morale and/or organization reputation in the community. This can be true of the occasional volunteer as well as the full-time staff member.
- Use an application form that covers all pertinent areas of the applicant's background.
- Ensure that the screening process provides information about an individual's skills, attitudes, and knowledge.
- Try to determine if the applicant or would-be volunteer is interested in the organization for legitimate reasons (professional development and/or advancement, genuine interest in your group's mission) or primarily for reasons that may not advance your organization's cause (loneliness, corporate burnout, etc.).
- Objectively evaluate prospective employees and volunteers based on criteria established in the organization's job specifications.
- Be realistic in putting together your volunteer work force. Managers cause most of the problems with volunteers by making unreasonable assumptions about their intentions and capabilities. An organization that sets the bar too high in its expectations of volunteers (in terms of services provided, hours volunteered, etc.) may find itself with a severe shortage of this potentially valuable resource.
- Recognizing that would-be volunteers and employees bring both assets and negative attributes to your organization, nonprofit groups should be flexible in accommodating those strengths and weaknesses.

HRIS permits organizations that pay attention to these guidelines will be far more likely to enjoy positive and lasting relationships with their volunteers and staff than those who fill their human resource needs in a haphazard fashion (Heathfield, 2019).

Orienting Staff and Volunteers to the Organization

Training is a vital component of successful nonprofit organization management. But many nonprofit managers fail to recognize that training initiatives should be built for all members of the organization, not just those who are salaried employees. Specialized training should be designed and cataloged in organization HRIS systems for every person in the organization, including board members and volunteers. If people are selected and trained with well-established and consistently implemented guidelines, organizations greatly increase the potential for team building. Beyond that, a common objective, a commitment to quality, a sincere concern for the team members, and a dedicated leader can cause wonderful things to happen can be achieved with well managed information with HRIS. HRIS ensures that volunteers who are integrated into an organization's processes and well managed to create consistency in services (Juneja, 2020).

Poor Performers

Many nonprofit organizations find that, at one point or another, they must address poor performance by a member of the organization. When that person is a paid member of the staff, dealing with the issue is in many respects is no different than it would be in the for-profit world or in the public sector. Organizations of all types have a right to assume certain standards of performance from paid employees, and if that standard is not met, they should take steps necessary to ensure that they receive the necessary level of performance from that position, even if that means firing a poor worker. Just as with hiring, HRIS comes to the aid of the nonprofit management leader when terminating poor performers. This situation becomes more complex when the person is a volunteer, however. The volunteer worker is an essential element of many nonprofit organizations, and the primary characteristics of volunteerism—selfless service—make it difficult to remove poor performers. In addition, insensitive handling of one volunteer can have a negative impact on other volunteers upon which your organization relies. Nonetheless, HRIS allows volunteers should be held accountable just as though they were being paid to work. This does not mean that a manager can be careless about poor performers discipline. Even for-profit and public sector managers have learned that managing and supervising requires certain social graces and sensitivity to every individual which is facilitated by a well-functioning HRIS system. However, the reluctance of nonprofit managers to hold volunteers accountable to reasonable levels of performance or to terminate bad volunteer relationships will be facilitated by HRIS.

When HRIS works, volunteers can do a great deal for their organizations. Nonprofit executives are often reluctant to let go of non-productive employees (Maier, 2017).

Compensating the Organization's Employees and Volunteers

Tangible Benefits

Nonprofit corporations must establish fringe benefits programs for their employees. People that can be covered under these programs include not only staff personnel, but also directors and officers. The benefits must be attractive as those provided by for-profit business and public organizations. In addition, the benefits can be far more economical for the organization and beneficial to the employees than any program that could be offered by unincorporated organization's HRIS. The nonprofit can establish an employee pension and retirement income plan. It can provide for sick pay and vacation pay. It may arrange for group life, accident and health insurance coverage for its officers and employees. It can elect to cover its employees' personal medical expenses that are not covered by the group insurance plans, provided that the organization can pay all or part of the cost of the various employee benefits it sets up. It can require some contribution from the employees covered by the fringe benefits, as any good HRIS would manage and track.

Nonprofit, public sector and for-profit organizations compete for the same pool of talented persons. This competition extends not only to salaries but also to benefits and retirement programs and HRIS provides a mechanism for ensuring that your compensation and benefits program can deliver and retain the type of employees that nonprofits require to be successful. Experts indicate that although the compensation packages that are offered by nonprofit organizations are constrained by the so-called private inurement doctrine, which holds that the profits realized by a nonprofit organization cannot be passed along to private individuals (as dividends are passed along to shareholders in a for-profit enterprise), they can still offer attractive compensation packages to employees if they are judged to be "reasonable" (National Council of Nonprofits, 2020).

Intangible Benefits

Successful managers of nonprofit organizations recognize that the people who compose their organizations' work force—volunteers, employees, officers, and directors alike—are often participating in the group at least in part for altruistic reasons. Even paid staff in these organizations needs achievement, the satisfaction of service, or they become alienated or even hostile. After all, what is the point of working in a nonprofit institution if one does not make a clear contribution? Leaders of nonprofit organizations need to always be on the lookout for ways in which they can show their paid staff, their volunteers, and their leadership how their involvement in the organization is making a difference, whether the group is involved with ministering to the poor or devoted to protecting a beloved natural resource (National Council for Nonprofits, 2020).

Organization of the Book

The chapters that follow examine HRIS issues in public and nonprofit organizations in-depth. Chapter 2 discusses the history and evolution of HRIS. Specifically, the chapter examines the opportunities and challenges that have emerged with the advancement of technology and the general competencies required for someone seeking employment as an HRIS specialist. Chapter 3 examines the current research in public organizations and highlights the various phases of adoption of HRIS in public organizations. The chapter is followed by providing the readers an understanding of how HRIS enterprise software database architecture is developed. The next few chapters (5, 6, 7, and 8) delve into the practical applications and differences between public and private sector HRIS. Chapter 7 detail the application of HRIS in real world application. Chapters 9 and 10 highlight the obstacles that currently exist within public organization for the use and adoption of HRIS. Chapter 11 uses an example from higher education to demonstrate the various aspects of HRIS discussed in the previous sections. Finally, Chapter 12 summarizes what we have learned and calls attention to future issues faced by public organizations as it relates to HRIS. While private organizations have certain requirements for federal and state data to be kept on employees, the public and nonprofit organizations typically have a more complex data for human resources needing to be utilized for the organization. As will be discussed in the next chapter, the evolution of HRIS is related to the advancement of software technology as well as the formulation of federal and state reporting requirements. There are several case studies provided throughout the text that provide the readers with practical and in-depth understanding of real-world challenges associated with data and information systems in human resources management.

Case Study: "Y2K or KMN"

Often times a migration will need to occur for a public or non-profit organization, which causes a great deal of chaos and confusion as well as a gap of knowledge between the older employees and newer employees working two different types of software that belong to different eras of technology. Such was the case when the Y2K crisis occurred for many different types of public and non-profit organizations. The Y2K crisis essentially forced organizations, both large and small, to upgrade to systems capable of handling a four digit year. Older systems had issues with date capability since there were only two positions for year. Obviously when the year 2000 was approaching, many organizations were ill equipped and unprepared for migrating (or for that matter purchasing) a new system capable for a four digit year. While having a four digit year capability does not appear to be a big issue, this creates a massive problem for any type of date calculation for payroll, years of service or other Human Resources calculated data. Some organizations decided to modify their older systems, which typically used obsolescent COBOL programming languages and ADAbase file structures. This option may have provided a short term solution, but it would be extremely costly to modify and maintain since the older technology required programmers who would be skilled in older technology. The second option would require the organization to migrate to a newer system.

In the case of one public organization (which was a component of a system of public organizations) they made a decision to migrate from an older mainframe technology to a newer mainframe technology since they still had older employees on the payroll who were familiar with mainframe MVS technology, Job Control Language (JCL) and COBOL programming language. While this choice did allow for the organization to "upgrade" to a newer technology, it was still not cutting edge. This led to the organization evaluating and migrating to yet another platform, which was Oracle based that effectively ended the career of many programmers and increased the cost of the programming staff.

The parent organization then interceded with the public organization and ordered the migration to halt pending the determination of evaluation of different software that could be used by several component organizations instead of just by one unit of the parent organization. This action was undertaken as a "cost measure" so one vendor could be used for all of the components of the parent organization as a "shared service". This action resulted in an estimated loss of at least $20 million from the software that the organization was in the process of migrating to from the mainframe to a completely different HRIS vendor. The migration and conversion did not go as planned and payroll, HR information and financial information had several severe issues. In one case employees were not paid for a month, other people were paid half of their monthly salary, in another case employees were paid double the amount of their salaries and employees who were not employed with the organization any longer were paid what their full salaries would have been if they were still employed. Along with these issues, reports could not be accurately generated for state and federal agencies and the entire process became a manual process. The root causes of these issues were poor planning, over reliance on outside consultants and not having the proper resources internal to the organization in terms of personnel with the proper knowledge, skills and experience to undertake such a project. The results of the "shared service" from a cost savings is subject to debate and could be argued that the migration resulted in a significant financial expense that will not be recovered in the years to come.

References

Abella, J. R. S. (1985). General summary from 'Equality in employment: A royal commission report'. *Canadian Woman Studies, 6*(4), 5–7.

Ashbaugh, S., & Miranda, R. (2002). Technology for human resources management: Seven questions and answers. *Public Personnel Management, 31*(1), 7–20.

BambooHR. (2020). *HR software*. Retrieved on December 23, 2020. HR Software I People Data & Analytics I Hiring I Onboarding I Compensation ICulture I BambooHR Software.

Bianca, A. (2018, April 18). *AZCentral*. Retrieved on December 23, 2020. The Importance of a Human Resource Information System (azcentral.com).

Bianca, A. (2019, August 5). *AZCentral*. What Does EE Stand for in HR. retrieved on December 23, 2020. What Does EE Stand for in HR? (azcentral.com).

Eckerson, W. W. (2002). Data quality and the bottom line. *TDWI Report, The Data Warehouse Institute*.

Everything at Work. (2020). *Talent acquisition and recruitment through HRIS*. How HRIS helps the Recruitment Process – Everything at Work Payroll HR Management System.

Givan, K. R. (2005). Seeing stars: Human resources performance indicators in the National Health Service. *Personnel Review, 34*(6), 634–647.

Hayes, J. (2012). Is the nonprofit sector doing enough for diversity. *Profiles in Diversity Journal, 14*(6), 22–23.

Heathfield, S. M. (2019, November 1). What Is a Human Resource? *The balance careers*. Retrieved on December 23, 2020. https://www.thebalancecareers.com/what-is-a-human-resource-1918144

Juneja, P. (2020). *Management study guide*. Retrieved December 23, 2020. Training & Development and HRIS Applications (managementstudyguide.com).

Karikari, A. F., Boateng, P. A., & Ocansey, E. O. (2015). The role of human resource information system in the process of manpower activities. *American Journal of Industrial and Business Management, 5*(6), 424–431.

Kim, W. (2002). On three major holes in data warehousing today. *Journal of Object Technology, 1*(4), 39–47.

Kim, W., & Choi, B. (2003). Towards quantifying data quality costs. *Journal of Object Technology, 2*(4), 69–76.

Lucerna. (2020). *HR software for nonprofit organizations*. Retrieved December 23, 2020. HR Software for Nonprofit Organizations - HR Payroll Systems.

Maier, S. (2017, August 21). *Biz Journals*. Retrieved December 23, 2020. How to identify and change poor employee performance - https://www.bizjournals.com/bizjournals/how-to/human-resources/2017/08/how-to-identify-and-change-poor-employee.html

National Council for Nonprofits. (2020). *Compensation for nonprofit employees*. Retrieved on December 23, 2020. https://www.councilofnonprofits.org/tools-resources/compensation-nonprofit-employees

NEOGOV. (2020). *HRIS*. Retrieved on December 23, 2020. HRIS I NEOGOV's Human Resource Information System.

Oliveira, P., Rodrigues, F., & Henriques, P. (2005). Formal definition of data quality problems. In *Tenth International Conference on Information Quality (ICIQ'05)*. 2005. MIT, Cambridge, MA

Paycor. (2020). *3 unique HR and payroll nonprofit organization*. Retrieved December 23, 2020. https://www.paycor.com/resource-center/articles/3-unique-hr-and-payroll-needs-for-nonprofit-organizations/

People Strategy. (2020). *Selection*. Retrieved December 23, 2020/ HR software your entire company will love in a single platform (peoplestrategy.com).

State of Oregon. (2016, April 28). *HRIS project vision, goals, and objectives*. Retireved on December 23, 2020. https://www.oregon.gov/das/HR/Documents/Workday%20Project%20vision,%20goals,%20and%20objectives.pdf

Troshani, I., Jerram, C., & Hill, S. R. (2011). Exploring the public sector adoption of HRIS. Industrial Management & Data Systems, 111(3), 470–488.

Workday. (2020). *Human resource management for the changing world of work*. Retrieved on December 23, 2020. Global HR Management System I Workday.

The History and Evolution of HRIS

2

Key Points of the Chapter

- Evolution of Human Resource Information Systems
- Human Resource Information Systems – Opportunities and Challenges
- HRIS General Competencies

Evolution of Human Resource Information System (HRIS)

The success of any organization depends on its practices that range from recruitment, training and development, performance evaluation, compensation, and retention. While these are considered core functions of human resources management (HRM), the technology, policies and procedures that enhance the effectiveness of these core functions is termed as Human Resources Information Systems (HRIS). With the advent of technology, the role of Human Resources (HR) has changed. In the past when an employee applied for a job, they were required to fill out a paper application providing information on demographics, employment history and other details like certification, skills, education and so on.

The HR staff was responsible to file these applications in a physical folder and access as necessary. It was not until 1914 that resumes were discussed in academic business textbooks (Popken, 1999). In fact, prior to World War II, employee information was commonly filled out in 3 × 5 note cards (Kavanaugh, Gueutal & Tannenbaum, 1990). A detailed description of how HRIS developed over time is expanded in the next section. It is important to note that HRIS has not developed in a vacuum, it has evolved as the role of HR progressed from a noncore function to playing a strategic partner in organizational functions like workforce planning and forecasting.

N. A. Valcik et al., *Human Resources Information Systems*, Management for Professionals, https://doi.org/10.1007/978-3-030-75111-1_2

Early Twentieth Century to World War II

The early twentieth century was heavily influenced by the *Principles of Scientific Management*, popularized by Frederick W. Taylor. Using time and motion studies, Taylor emphasized "one best way" of creating efficient organizations that focus on scientific ways of managing people and work by creating well-defined chains of command and hierarchies, labor specialization, and division of work. Within this context, personnel management was subject to strict management control with very little emphasis on developing employee-employer relationship. The role of personnel professionals was limited to basic clerical tasks like employee record keeping, with little or no involvement with core organizational functions. There were no computers and technology available to record employee information. All information related to employee name, address, phone number, employment history etc. were recorded on a paper and stored in files (Hendrickson, 2003).

Post World-War II Era (1945–1960)

The shortcomings of the scientific management style are addressed by the Neo-Classical theorists who argued that organizations cannot exist as self-contained islands isolated from their environments. This era initiated the movement away from the overly simplistic mechanistic views of classical organization theory. Neo-classical theories paved the way for the soon-to-follow explosions of thinking from the human relations, "modern" structural, systems, power and politics, and organizational culture perspectives of organizations. Chester Barnard sought to create a comprehensive theory of behavior in organizations that was centered on the need for people in organizations to cooperate – to enlist others to help accomplish tasks that individuals could not accomplish alone. During these times, organizations became aware of human capital issues and began to develop formal processes for employee selection and development (Shafritz et al., 2015).

At the same time, organizations began to recognize the importance of employee morale on the firm's overall effectiveness. The human relations movement focus on employee development and training started to change the landscape of personnel management in the United States. The Government Employees Training Act of 1958 provided federal agencies an authority to manage and conduct their own training programs to address employees' performance and developmental needs. In the 1950s, all states adopted some form of merit based hiring system (Cayer & Sabharwal, 2016). Job description and classification systems emerged in the civil services, with greater focus on designing appropriate compensation and performance evaluation systems. While this period of change in the profession did not result in significant changes in personnel management and information systems (although employee files did become somewhat more complex), it set the stage for an explosion of changes that began in the 1960s.

Emergence of Human Resources Management (1960–1980)

The civil rights era witnessed passage of several laws and regulations to protect employees from discriminatory work practices. With greater focus on employee recruitment, health and safety, benefits, and regulations, the role of personnel gained significance within organizations giving birth to human resources management (HRM). The passage of the Civil Service Reform Act in 1978 created the Office of Personnel Management (OPM), the chief human resources agency responsible for federal recruitment, hiring and staffing. HRM was integrated into the core business mission, with a greater focus on governmental and regulatory reporting requirements for employees (Bhuiyan et al., 2014). With increased demands on HR staff to report employee data, the advent and widespread use of mainframe computers provided a technological solution to the increased reporting and regulation requirements. The Human Resources department started to adopt computing systems, but the size and scope of the usage continued to remain limited to administrative record keeping (Kavanagh et al., 1990).

Emergence of Human Resources Information System (HRIS) (1980–2000)

With increasing technological developments in the 1990s and early 2000s, HR departments came under pressure to find cost effective measures to automate employee data. As computing power increased, several Enterprise Resource Management (ERP) systems emerged; ERPs shifted the role of HR from simple record keeping to serving as part of the core functions (recruitment, benefits, payroll, time management, benefits, training, performance management etc.). An Enterprise Planning System (ERP) is defined as "configurable information systems packages that integrate information and information-based processes within and across functional areas in an organization" (Kumar & van Hillegersberg, 2000, p. 23). These systems make data accessibility and controls easier. The primary function of an ERP is to enhance efficiency of an organization by streamlining the decision-making process (Bingi et al., 1999; Li, 1999). Thus, the shift from employee administration to employee development and empowerment lead to a change in the way HR departments functioned in an organization. HR was beginning to take its place as a strategic partner in organizational decision making rather than being on the fringes.

Rise of Technology and Strategic Human Resources Management (2000-Current)

Over the last two decades, organizations have increasingly relied on the HR function to provide solutions that increase the effectiveness of human capital. While the role of HR continues to focus on the core functions highlighted by Klingner et al.

(2015) in their acronym – PADS (Planning, Acquisition, Development and Sanction), the increased use of technology has led to HR playing a strategic role in decisions related to workforce needs. The role of information technology is central to the evolution from HR to Strategic Human Resource Management (SHRM), which is a "strategic tool for collecting, processing, and managing strategic data and information in order to make strategic decisions for forecasting, planning, recruiting, developing, promotion, evaluation, and developing key human resources at all levels of organizations" (Farazmand, 2004, p. 11). Within this progression, HRIS serves as a tool to manage large amounts of personnel data alongside providing analytical tools in making strategic organizational decisions (Kovach et al., 2002; Mayfield et al., 2003). HRIS is a "system used to acquire, store, manipulate, analyze, retrieve and distribute pertinent information about an organization's human resources" (Tannenbaum, 1990, p. 27).

HRIS is increasingly used to store sensitive personnel information such as social security numbers, compensation information, bank details, medical records and so on. In federal, state and local governments, this presents challenges with security breaches, identity theft and data leaks (Zafar et al., 2017). Overall, human resource professionals are serving as strategic partners with top management (Lengnick-Hall & Moritz, 2003) where HRIS is facilitating this movement toward SHRM. HRIS is an emerging field within the discipline of HR, which is not just limited to computer hardware and software, but includes people, policies, procedures and data to successfully manage the complexity of HR functions (Hendrickson, 2003). More recently, a move towards electronic human resource (e-HR) has allowed the HR functions to not just stay within HR, but available to people outside HR. e-HR allows individuals to apply for jobs, manage employee benefits and take charge of training and development needs (Stone et al., 2006). Table 2.1 summarizes the evolution of HR and HRIS within the broader organizational context.

Human Resource Information Systems

Human Resource Information System is embedded within the broader Enterprise Resource Planning (ERP) system, which is integrated business management software designed to coordinate data across different organizational units such as accounting, finance, development, procurement, human resources and so on. At the most basic level, HRIS is a blend of all the human resource functions and information technology as represented in Fig. 2.1. HRIS integrates people data across all HR functions (i.e. recruitment, selection, training and development, compensation and benefits, performance management, retention). When core HR functions are integrated within a comprehensive data management system, data can be easily managed and retrieved from a central system instead of fragmented information subsystem for each HR function (Bauer et al., 2018). Some of the more commonly used HR software/vendors that provide HRIS solutions include Oracle-PeopleSoft, SAP, HR Soft, and ADP.

Table 2.1 Evolution of HR and HRIS within the broader organizational context

Time period	Development of HRIS
Early 20th – WWII	**Broader Context:** Scientific Management with "one best way." Less influence of government on employee-employer relations **Personnel Management**: Personnel function was characterized by basic clerical record keeping. Personnel department had little interaction with core business mission. **HRIS:** There is no computer technology to support record keeping at this time. Initial efforts to manage personnel data was mostly paper based and limited to basic employee information such as names, address, age or employment history
1945–1960 (Post WWII)	**Context:** Significant number of laws in the U.S. allows employees to set up labor unions/trade unions and redefine their relationship with employers. The role of personnel departments expanded beyond simple record keeping tasks and reporting. The need to establish special divisions such as recruitment, training, benefit, union relations. **HR profession:** Managers became more aware of employees as important contributor to organizations' overall productivity and success. Human issues such as motivation, productivity received more attention. There was a need to develop formal processes for employee selection and development. **HRIS:** Employee files developed more complexity: for example, more complicated job descriptions, job analysis and job classification system. Computer technology started to appear in some organizations and help HR departments' store, retrieve employee information.
1960–1980 Emergence of Human Resources Management	**Broader context:** Significant increase in the number of labor legislations in the U.S. (tax regulation, prohibition of discrimination at work, retirement benefits, occupational health and safety). Personnel departments collect, store, and analyze employee data. **HR profession**: The field of Human Resource Management (HRM) is born. HRM integrated into the core mission, and governmental and regulatory reporting requirements for employees also increased significantly. **HRIS:** Mainframe computers introduced. Widespread use of computers in legislative compliance and record-keeping. HR departments became important users of computing system. HRIS still primarily used for administrative goals.
1980–2000 Emergence of Human Resources Information System (HRIS)	**Broader context:** Focus on cost reduction through automation **HR profession:** The overall goal of HR profession shifts from employee administration to employee development and empowerment. Organizations increasingly relied on HR to provide management solutions that increase the effectiveness of human capital. **HRIS:** Emergence of HRIS. HR departments came under pressure to find cost effective measures to automate employee data.

(continued)

Table 2.1 (continued)

Time period	Development of HRIS
2000 – present Rise of Technology and Strategic Human Resources Management	**Broader context:** Radical changes with wider globalization and deeper integration, information technology breakthroughs (internet, robotic atomization, machine learning, AI, cyber security), knowledge economy. Organizations and firms rely on innovative and creative employees, develop organizational knowledge to develop a sustainable competitive advantage **HR profession:** Increased use and reliance on information technology shifted the focus of HR function to adding values to organization's products and services. HRM needs become more strategic to attract, retain and engage best people. Strategic Human Resource Management (SHRM) become important in management thinking and practice. HR department as strategic partner. Development of different HR tools (balanced scorecard, HR metrics, Six Sigma) **HRIS:** HRIS to provide important information, helping organization to forecast future needs, support the implementation of strategic plans, support organization to make decision about employees and initiatives.

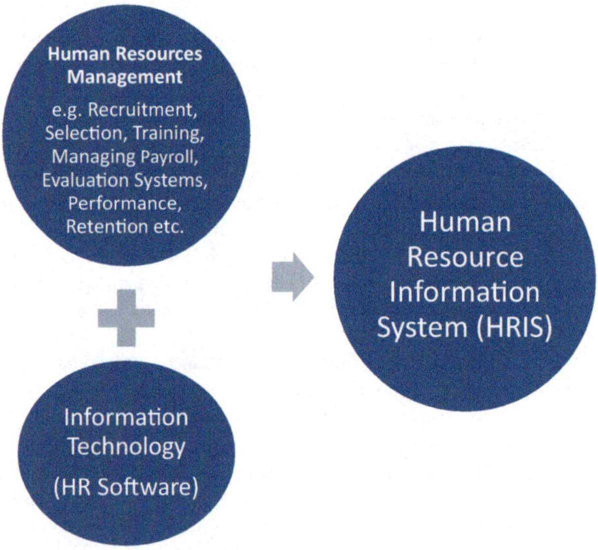

Fig. 2.1 Representation of Human Resource Information System

HRIS Opportunities and Challenges

There are several advantages and challenges in developing and maintaining an HRIS in public organizations. There is consensus that HRIS adoption is challenging in the public sector and remains an under-researched topic (Troshani et al., 2011). Figure 2.2 highlights come of the opportunities and challenges that come with implementing and adopting HRIS in public organizations.

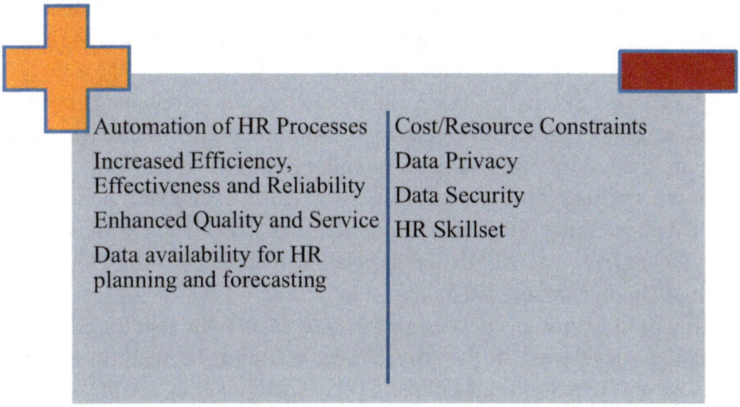

Fig. 2.2 HRIS opportunities and challenges

HRIS Opportunities

A major shift in the role of HR over time has been from serving as the custodian of personnel information to managing and leveraging data for the use of workforce planning and projecting future trends (Beadles II et al., 2005; Troshani et al., 2011). HRIS results in faster processing of data and improves accuracy, planning and development related to human resources. Public sector managers are able to efficiently and effectively transform large amounts to data to "restructure policies, activities, processes, and other procedures" (Roach, 2016, p.2). A study conducted by Beadles II et al. (2005) in public universities in Southeastern United States indicated that 90% of the HR directors at these public institutions believed that HRIS added value to their organizations, while, 80% agreed that HRIS improved their ability to disseminate and provide useful information for decision-making. The city of Virginia Beach, Virginia, home to nearly half a million residents, pioneered a Workforce Planning and Development (WorkPAD) software in 2003 in collaboration with the HR, Communications and Information Technology departments to integrate data from city's HRIS, Virginia Retirement system, and several other databases to plan and forecast for current and future workforce needs (Miracle, 2004). The software allows managers to carefully utilize data for workforce planning. Employees are able to conduct Knowledge, Skill and Abilities (KSA) assessment and identify skills gaps to plan their career goals. Managers are able to use the system to project retirement data, analyze changing demographics and enhance workforce planning.

Some of the key challenges in adoption of HRIS that are unique to public organizations include:

- Multiple Goals: Public organizations have multiple and ambiguous goals that are often difficult to implement and measure (e.g. healthcare, education, poverty etc.).

- Organizational Culture: Bureaucratic culture of public sector organizations hinders technological adoption and is resistant to change. Introduction of innovative solutions is often "reactive" than "proactive."
- Budgetary constraints: Justifying public dollars for purchasing, implementing and maintaining expensive software systems in public sector is challenging. Budgetary cycles are often subject to political priorities.
- In-House Expertise: Public organizations often rely on external consultants for their IT requirements. Staffing and maintaining HRIS projects is heavily dependent on competencies of private consultants adding to the cost conundrum (Roach & Davis-Cooper, 2016).
- Diffusion of Innovation: There is no one-size-fit all approach for adopting HRIS, thus models developed in the private sector cannot be readily adopted in the public sector (Henriksen & Mahnke, 2005; Troshani et al., 2011).
- Data Security: Personnel data is increasingly vulnerable to security breach. Protecting data related to an employees' health, sensitive personal information like social security number, address, hours worked, driver license is critical in preventing identity theft and protecting confidential personal information (Zafar, 2013). Chapter 4 provides more details about the role of HRIS in maintaining data security.

HRIS General Competencies

The public sector has only recently realized the importance of using technology in the HR domain (Selden, 2009). However, the need to manage large amounts of data alongside the need for efficiency and effectiveness prompted government agencies to utilize HRIS in a rapidly changing environment. The Office of Personnel Management (OPM) provides detailed career paths and competencies needed to be successful in HR information systems across various career stages (GS 5–9, GS 11–12, GS 13–15, and GS 15 and SES). For entry-level HR specialists in information systems positions (GS-5/7/9), individuals must possess the knowledge of concepts, basic principles and practices associated with identifying and analyzing HR processes, transforming functional requirements into technical ones and maintaining HRIS. Clearly, working knowledge of managing databases is essential in this role. A list of typical duties of entry-level positions in HR information systems is listed in Table 2.2. At the expert level (GS-13/14/15), there is an expectation that the employees possess expertise in managing HRIS projects and create strategic plans to integrate HR functions with information technology. An example of a job description for the City of Garland's HRIS Manager is provided below. This gives the readers an insight into HRIS position requirements at the federal and local level.

Job Description of a HRIS Manager in City Government
Job Title: Manager HR Information Systems, Reporting & Analytics

Position Summary

Table 2.2 Typical duties of Information specialist in Entry Level Position (GS 5/7/9) in the federal government

Works with senior human resources specialists to:	GS-5	GS-7	GS-9
Perform basic, routine data retrievals from HR systems	X	X	X
Maintain manuals, instructions, and operating procedures for an automated performance management system	X	X	X
Update the organization's automated HR forms based on a new data collection requirement	X	X	X
Specify requirements for automated reports to retrieve HR information requested by staff	X	X	X
Test system modifications using established protocol procedures	X	X	X
Maintain HR databases that support HR business processes using quality assurance principles and practices	X	X	X
Perform basic IT services if necessary	X	X	X
Manage vacancies using automated staffing tools	X	N/A	N/A
Develop selection certificates (reports) using automated staffing tools	X	N/A	N/A
Send selection certificates (reports) to selecting officials via email	X	N/A	N/A
Enter or updates employee data using personnel management tools	X	N/A	N/A

Source: United States Office of Personnel Management, 2021

Functional manager responsible for driving all activities within the scope of data collection, reporting, analytics and technology utilized within the Human Resources department. This position is accountable for ensuring continuity and successful delivery of programs, processes, services, metrics, reporting and time sensitive projects throughout the City of Garland. Typical systems include HR Information System(s), Applicant Tracking System, Benefits Management System(s), Document Control System and various ancillary applications.

Essential Job Functions

Business Partner

1. Collaborate with key stakeholders including Information Technology, Finance, Payroll, related departments and vendors.
2. Continuously identify, evaluate and provide actionable recommendations for process and system improvements.
3. Be able to easily navigate between being a functional leader and an individual contributor depending on the needs of the organization.
4. Be seen as a credible partner, able to effectively outline issues, gain buy-in and execute solutions as needed.

Human Resources

1. Functional knowledge of human resources core programs with the ability to mirror needed processes and outcomes from a technical perspective.
2. General understanding of regulatory practices as it relates to reporting, compliance, employee management, payroll and/or other related areas.

3. Conduct operational and performance audits as assigned by HR and/or City Management

Technology/Database Administration

1. Strong technical acumen, including understanding of database objects and administration.
2. Systems implementation experience.
3. Expert-level knowledge of MS Excel, Word and Access.
4. Experience with an HRMS such as PeopleSoft, Lawson or SAP preferred (direct HRMS experience required)
5. Reporting experience (Knowledge of Crystal Reports or other HRMS report generation tools)

Minimum Education & Work Experience

- Bachelor's degree in business administration, human resources, information technology, or related field
- 3–5 years professional work experience in HRIS or Information Technology administration with demonstrated performance leading process or system improvements
- Demonstrated project management experience
- Ability to identify issues and provide solutions autonomously
- Strong attention to detail and ability to be timely and responsive to the needs of the department and organization
- Proficiency with SQL and creating scripts to automate integrations/interfaces between various systems is required.
- Expert level knowledge of MS Excel, Word and Access or similar database tool
- Or an equivalent combination of education and experience sufficient to successfully perform the essential functions of the job.

Preferred Knowledge – Abilities & Skills
Education/ Experience:

- Bachelor's degree in business administration, human resources, information technology, or related field
- Five or more years professional work experience leading HRIS or Information Technology projects or system improvements.
- Complex project management experience, effectively managing multiple projects on time and on target.
- Prior experience leading or participating in an HRIS or large-scale technology implementation.
- Keen attention to detail, deadline commitments and managing cyclical processes is critical.
- Supervisory experience preferred (1–2 direct reports)

Licenses & Certifications

Valid Class C Texas driver's license

Physical Tasks & Working Conditions

The incumbent works in a typical office environment; relatively free from unpleasant environmental conditions or hazards.

Competencies

Models Organization Values
Customer Focus/Results Focus
Communication
Adaptability/Flexibility/Decision Making
Managing Projects/Managing People

Source: City of Garland, 2020

Case Study: The Employee Who Was "Deadpool" in HRIS

A public organization was on their fifth HR Director in two and a half years when a new employee was hired into the organization. The HR Director themselves were fairly new to the organization and had no technical experience and had no experience with HRIS. The new employee was setup into HRIS with their information and had signed up for health benefits. However, the benefits for their spouse was put on hold until a copy of the marriage certificate was provided. The new employee came to the HR office with the copy of the marriage certificate, which was misplaced by the HR office. The new employee then provided them an electronic copy of the marriage certificate and the employee was told their spouse had their health benefits added in the system.

When the new employee's spouse attempted to obtain medication that they needed for a health condition, the spouse was told they were not covered by benefits. The new employee then went to the HR office to determine what was happening and found out that their spouse's information had been deleted from HRIS. The new employee was then interfacing with the Benefits Manager and the HR Director to determine how the information had been deleted from HRIS. The HR Director was unfamiliar with HRIS or how data was input into the system and had to rely on other personnel to tell them how data could be entered into HRIS as well as how data could be deleted out of HRIS. The Director was unaware of any data entry controls or audit checks that could be performed or should be performed. After pulling up the new employee's personnel record in HRIS, it was discovered that another HR employee had "terminated" and reinstated the employee over seven times to cover for data entry errors. The new employee joked that their name must be "*Deadpool*" in HRIS since they had been "terminated" so many times. In the

(continued)

process the HR employee had deleted the spouse's benefit information from the system. Not only was this occurring to the new employee's records in HRIS, but errors were occurring throughout the entire organization's employees' records in a variety of different areas. The new employees' spouse was eventually reinstated into HRIS for their benefits, and the insurance company had to issue a reimbursement check to the spouse for expenses that were paid out of pocket for their medication. The cleanup process to contend with the data entry issues was time consuming and extensive for the organization, which eventually was just one of the reasons that resulted in the termination of the HR employee responsible for data entry. However, the situation highlights the challenge of not having a Director with a good understanding of how data are entered into HRIS. The organization also lacked data entry controls and training for HR personnel contending with HRIS or for that matter a manual to refer to on how to enter data into HRIS. The level of understanding an HR Director must now possess on HRIS to be successful has increased exponentially over the years and will continue to do so for the foreseeable future.

Summary

With the advent of technology, the role of Human Resources (HR) has evolved from a standalone noncore function to being considered a part of the core organizational mission supporting strategic decision-making. It is within this context that the Human Resource Information Systems (HRIS) has evolved to keep track of data that relates to employee recruitment, evaluation, payroll, benefits, demographics, retention etc. Thus, HRIS allows organizations to manage large amounts of employee data, which further allows in making decisions about workforce planning, compensation, rewards and benefits and performance management. HRIS is an emerging field within the discipline of HR, which is not just limited to computer hardware and software, but includes people, policies, procedures and data to successfully manage the complexity of HR functions (Hendrickson, 2003). Familiarity with the types of HRIS systems and its adoption in the public sector is important as one seeks to better understand the extent to which HRIS systems are employed in the government. There are several challenges that public managers have to be aware of as they adopt HRIS. The public sector, though behind the private sector in its use of technology in HR, is seeking to take advantage of HRIS to meet the growing needs of their agencies and the communities they serve.

References

Bauer, T., Erdogan, B., Caughlin, D., & Truxillo, D. (2018). *Human resource management: People, data, and analytics*. Sage Publications.

Beadles, N. A., II, Lowery, C. M., & Johns, K. (2005). The impact of human resource information systems: An exploratory study in the public sector. *Communications of the IIMA, 5*(4), 6.

Bhuiyan, F., Chowdhury, M. M., & Ferdous, F. (2014). Historical evolution of human resource information system (HRIS): An interface between HR and computer technology. *Human Resource Management Research, 4*(4), 75–80.

Bingi, P., Sharma, M. K., & Godla, J. K. (1999). Critical issues affecting an ERP implementation. *IS Management, 16*(3), 7–14.

Cayer, N. J., & Sabharwal, M. (2016). *Public personnel administration: Managing human capital, 6th Ed.* Birkdale Publishers.

City of Garland. (2020). *Manager HR information systems, reporting and analytics*. Human Resources Department, Garland, TX. Retrieved on January 6, 2021. https://external-garland.icims.com/jobs/6665/job

Farazmand, A. (2004). Innovation in strategic human resource management: Building capacity in the age of globalization. *Public Organization Review, 4*(1), 3–24.

Hendrickson, A. R. (2003). Human resource information systems: Backbone technology of contemporary human resources. *Journal of Labor Research, 24*(3), 381–394.

Henriksen, H. Z., & Mahnke, V. (2005). E-procurement adoption in the Danish public sector: The influence of economic and political rationality. *Scandinavian Journal of Information Systems, 17*(2), 85–106.

Kavanagh, M. J., Gueutal, H. G., & Tannenbaum, S. I. (1990). *Human resource information systems*. PWS-Kent Publishing.

Klingner, D., Llorens, J. J., & Nalbandian, J. (2015). *Public personnel management*. Routledge.

Kovach, K. A., Hughes, A. A., Fagan, P., & Maggitti, P. G. (2002). Administrative and strategic advantages of HRIS. *Employment Relations Today, 29*(2), 43–48.

Kumar, K., & Van Hillegersberg, J. (2000). ERP experiences and evolution. *Communications of the ACM, 43*(4), 22–22.

Lengnick-Hall, M. L., & Moritz, S. (2003). The impact of e-HR on the human resource management function. *Journal of Labor Research, 24*(3), 365–379.

Li, C. (1999). ERP packages: What's next? *Information Systems Management, 16*, 31–35.

Mayfield, M., Mayfield, J., & Lunce, S. (2003). Human resource information systems: A review and model development. *Journal of Competitiveness Studies, 11*(1), 139.

Miracle, K. (2004). Case study: The City of Virginia Beach's innovative tool for workforce planning. *Public Personnel Management, 33*(4), 449–458.

Popken, R. (1999). The pedagogical dissemination of a genre: The resume in American business discourse textbooks, 1914-1939. *JAC: A Journal of Composition Theory, 19*(1), 91–116.

Roach, C. M. L. (2016). Human resource information systems. In A. Farazmand (Ed.), *Global encyclopedia of public administration, public policy, and governance*. Springer. https://doi.org/10.1007/978-3-319-31816-5_2735-1

Roach, C. M., & Davis-Cooper, G. (2016). An Evaluation of the Adoption of the Integrated Human Resource Information System in Trinidad and Tobago. *International Journal of Public Administration in the Digital Age (IJPADA), 3*(3), 1–17.

Selden, S. C. (2009). *Human capital: Tools and strategies in the public sector*. CQ Press.

Shafritz, J. M., Ott, J. S., & Jang, Y. S. (2015). *Classics of organization theory*. Cengage Learning.

Stone, D. L., Stone-Romero, E. F., & Lukaszewski, K. (2006). Factors affecting the acceptance and effectiveness of electronic human resource systems. *Human Resource Management Review, 16*(2), 229–244.

Tannenbaum, S. I. (1990). Human resource information systems: User group implications. *Journal of Systems Management, 41*(1), 27–32.

Troshani, I., Jerram, C., & Hill, S. R. (2011). Exploring the public sector adoption of HRIS. *Industrial Management & Data Systems, 111*(3), 470–488.

United States Office of Personnel Management. (2021). *Human resources specialist (Information Systems) career path guide*. Retrieved from: https://www.opm.gov/wiki/uploads/docs/Wiki/OPM/training/HR%20Career%20Guide/HRIS%20Career%20Path_Final%20508C.pdf

Zafar, H. (2013). Human resource information systems: Information security concerns for organizations. *Human Resource Management Review, 23*(1), 105–113.

Zafar, H., Randolph, A. B., & Martin, N. (2017). Toward a more secure HRIS: The role of HCI and unconscious behavior. *AIS Transactions on Human-Computer Interaction, 9*(1), 59–74.

3 Existing Research on HRIS in Public Organizations

Key Points of the Chapter

- HRIS and its use in public organizations
- HRIS adoption phases
- HRIS and Security Challenges
- Role of HRIS in Maintaining Data Security

HRIS and Its Use in Public Organizations

The utility of Human Resources Information Systems (HRIS) in the public sector remains very much at the functional level; it is beginning to see its use in strategic decision-making. There is a consensus among researchers that HRIS use and its adoption in public and nonprofit organizations is limited. Past studies focused on the adoption of Information Communication Technology (ICT) in public sector (Troshani et al., 2011). There is an increasing reliance on HRIS to fulfill even the most basic tasks (Hendrickson, 2003; Lengnick-Hall & Moritz, 2003) based on the degree of sophistication (Ball, 2001). Payroll management and benefit administration are often considered basic and unsophisticated tasks, while HR planning, recruitment and selection, training and development are considered sophisticated tasks that aid in strategic decision-making (Ball, 2001; Martinsons, 1994). According to Troshani et al. (2011), HRIS adoption in the public sector depends on Technological, Organizational and Environmental (TOE) factors.

1. Technological factors that impact the adoption of HRIS are: integration, user friendliness, accessibility, efficiency, and vendor support.
2. Organizational factors that impact the adoption of HRIS include: organization size, human capability (i.e. training), degree of centralization, and management commitment

N. A. Valcik et al., *Human Resources Information Systems*, Management for Professionals, https://doi.org/10.1007/978-3-030-75111-1_3

3. Environmental factors that impact the adoption of HRIS include: regulatory compliance and successful adoption

The TOE model is widely used to explain the technological drivers and the adoption of HRIS by organizations (DePietro et al., 1990; Pudjianto et al., 2011; Sharif et al., 2016; Troshani et al., 2011). Several studies have adopted this framework to study different aspects of technological uses in the government (Haneem et al., 2019; Roach & Davis-Cooper, 2016; Sharif et al., 2016; Wang & Lo, 2016). For example, a study in Australia employed the TOE framework to study the adoption of social media in local government (Sharif et al., 2016). The authors found several factors influence social media adoption within the TOE framework. The Technological factors include relative advantage and perceived security; Organizational factors include management drive and social media policies and the Environmental Context factors include the demand from the community and the bandwagon effect wherein local governments adopt social media technologies based on success stories from other jurisdictions. Others have applied the TOE framework to identify factors that drive adoption of HRIS in the public sector (Roach & Davis-Cooper, 2016; Troshani et al., 2010, 2011). An in-depth analysis of senior public officials in Trinidad and Tobago revealed the interplay among technological, organizational and environmental factors for the adoption of HRIS (Roach & Davis-Cooper, 2016).

Adoption of HRIS

As the functions of human resources evolved so did the utility of Human Resource Information Systems (HRIS). Adoption of HRIS has been classified into three phases: (a) operational (b) relational and (c) transformational (Kovach & Cathcart Jr, 1999; Reddick, 2009; Thite et al., 2012).

Operational HRIS is focused on the routine tasks of HR that relate to employee record keeping, tracking hours, payroll, benefits, government regulation, and compliance. The use of HRIS to automate some of these labor-intensive tasks is seen as a cost effective and efficient way to improve performance. In a survey of 115 organizations conducted in the United Kingdom by Ball (2001), the author reported that HRIS was used towards administrative rather than analytical ends. Additionally, the author found that smaller organizations are less likely to use HRIS. Overall, HRIS was less likely to be employed in recruitment and training activities as compared to operational tasks. The results of this study were in line with previous findings (Dery et al., 2009; Ngai & Wat, 2006). While most of these studies are conducted in the private sector, the picture is not too different in the public sector. In a study conducted on HR Directors in public universities, HRIS was employed to improve data input and data maintenance rather than recruitment, training and forecasting (Beadles, Lowery, & Johns, 2005).

Relational HRIS is concerned with providing employees and management remote access to databases, improving employee and citizen response time to

Fig. 3.1 Phases of HRIS adoption

requests, and improving service levels. Johnson et al. (2020) in their latest work highlight these three forms of HRIS that they classify as eHRM. According to the authors Relational eHRM concerns recruitment, selection, employee training and development, performance management and rewards. Smaller and mid-size organizations employ operational and relational HRIS (Ruël et al., 2004). According to a report by the Society of Human Resources Management (Johnson & Gueutal, 2011, p.1), e-HR "describes the transformation of HR service delivery using web-based technology."

Transformational HRIS supports strategic human resource functions regarding organizational change, workforce analysis, forecasting, strategic knowledge management, and developing a workforce that integrates organizational goals and strategies with information systems (Al-Dmour et al., 2015; Reddick, 2009; Ruël et al., 2004). Figure 3.1 represents the three phases of HRIS adoption in an organization.

Public Sector Example

The type of HRIS and its use in the public sector was studied by Reddick (2009) in his empirical research on the effectiveness of HRIS in Texas cities in the United States. Of the over 150 cities contacted in Texas, 88 responses were collected from human resource departments in 2006. While the study was conducted more than a decade ago, some of the findings might continue to hold given that the pace of change and adoption of HRIS in the public sector is slower than the private sector. Key findings indicate that majority of employees preferred to contact the HR department either in person or via email (approximately 70%). Web-based applications in HR were overwhelmingly utilized in positing jobs and accepting applications, and less likely to be used in application tracking, automated resume intake or new hire processing. The use of web-based applications in HR was mostly restricted to disseminating information to employees or potential applicants. The results of the survey indicated that over one-third of HR departments agreed that IT increased HR operating efficiency. Assessing the relational impact of IT on HR, the study found that HRIS reduced the response time to customers and clients. The average response rate was highest with the relational aspect of HRIS as compared to operational and transformational. HRIS was not successful in reducing bureaucracy, but improved the quality of services and knowledge management, key aspects of transformational HRIS. The top three barriers inhibiting the adoption of information technology in HR identified by Reddick (2009) are:

1. Inadequate Budget/funding
2. Lack of technical infrastructure
3. Staff resistance to change

Another significant challenge is that data are vulnerable to security breaches and cyber-attack. In the next section, we will discuss these challenges and provide a summary of the various laws and regulations enacted by the U.S. Congress to protect sensitive individual data.

HRIS and Security Challenges

Human resources data are among the most sensitive data stored by organizations, and it is the responsibility of the employers to protect this information from internal and external threats. Information that needs to be protected includes, but is not limited to, employees' social security information, driver license details, home address and phone numbers, and medical information. It is important to choose the right vendor when an organization plans to install an HR information system. The global pandemic has forced most employees to work remotely, causing further concerns related to data protection and security risks. According to the Society of Human Resources Management (2020), Internet related cyber-crimes caused organizations an estimated $2.7 billion in losses. Cyber-crimes have escalated within the last 5 years with the Federal Bureau of Investigation (FBI) receiving 350,000 reports in 2018 (Zeilinski, 2020). The top security threats as it pertains to HR data are (Zeilinski, 2019)

1. **Chatbots or digital assistants**: These are computer programs that use machine learning algorithms and artificial intelligence to mimic human conversations. The United States Citizenship and Immigration Services (USCIS) developed a virtual assistant, Emma, to respond to thousands of immigration related questions a month. Similar virtual assistants help potential employees apply for jobs

or answer frequently asked questions. The potential for phishing and creating fake bots that mimic the original are possible security threats. These imposter chatbots can trick a person into relinquishing secure information, resulting in compromised personal data. In 2018, the U.S. Department of Justice indicted two Iranians on several counts of fraud and computer hacking of data from several hospitals, municipalities and public institutions for a total of $30 million in losses and damages (Tobenkin, 2019).

2. **Phishing and Malware:** Public and private sector employees regularly receive phishing emails from hackers to steal personal and organizational information. Hackers have realized that it is easier to scam humans than machines; emails seem legitimate and appear to come from known contacts within organizations. Thus, it is now incumbent both on the organizations and the employees to protect their information and not fall prey to scammers. Policies at work should secure personal devices since mobile devices continue to pose the highest security risk. Multi-Factor Authentication (MFA) should be required when logging into devices from work or home to confirm one's identify thus reducing threat from malware. Malware is a "broad class of attacks that is loaded on a system, typically without the knowledge of the legitimate owner, to compromise the system to the benefit of an adversary" (Jang-Jaccard & Nepal, 2014, p. 974). Some examples include viruses, worms, Trojan horses, spyware, and bots.
3. **Internal Threat:** Protecting organizations and employees from internal threats is as important as providing safeguards from external security risks (e.g. phishing, malware etc.). The role of HR is critical in developing a company culture that values and ensures organizational and employee security. HR must work closely with the information technology department to protect against data vulnerabilities. For example, in universities there are policies prohibiting staff and faculty to respond to emails from students that are sent from non-university emails. Employees bringing personal mobile devices at work should be required to login to the organization's Wi-Fi system with MFA to reduce security breaches. Monitoring internal data usage by conducting regular audits is an important safeguard that HR can put in place to protect sensitive employee information. HR technology leaders are faced by the paradox of ensuring employees have timely and accurate access to data while protecting vulnerable data.

Public and nonprofit organizations are often strapped for resources and issues of data security are often allocated the least priority in the budget. However, in current times securing data from both internal and external threats must be a priority. In a recent national survey of local governments conducted on issues of cybersecurity, it was found that most municipalities are under regular, if not constant, threat of data breach. The top three things required to ensure cybersecurity in local governments as identified by the Information Technology Directors and Chief Information Officers include greater funding for cybersecurity, better cybersecurity policies, and greater cybersecurity awareness among local government employees. The greatest barrier to cybersecurity was also related to costs, the ability to pay competitive salaries to IT and cybersecurity professionals who are often lured by much higher compensation from the private sector (Norris

Table 3.1 Relevant laws and regulations protecting employee privacy

Year	Laws/Regulation	Purpose	Implications to HRIS
1970	Fair Credit Reporting Act (FCRA)	FCRA aims to ensure the accuracy, fairness and privacy of the information in consumer credit bureau files. The law directs how credit reporting agencies can access, use and share the information from consumer reports.	FCRA helps employees to protect the privacy of their background information. It regulates organizations and employers to get written consent from prospective employees before obtaining consumer reports. Employees should be notified if obtained information leads to adverse action on the part of employers.
1974	Privacy Act 1974	The Privacy Act consists of code of fair information practices that governs the collection, maintenance, and dissemination of personal information maintained in federal record system	The Privacy Act mandates federal agencies to follow strict record-keeping requirements that protect personal information. It allows employees to access their own records, learn whether those records have been disclosed, and request corrections or amendments to those records.
1986	Electronic Communication Privacy Acts (ECPA)	ECPA was an amendment to the Wiretap Act of 1968. The law was designed to prevent third parties from unauthorized access or disclosure of electronic communications.	ECPA protects federal employee communication, especially those held in electronic storage. Employers or third parties must obtain employee consent or have search warrant before accessing such data.
1996	Health Insurance Portability and Accountability Act (HIPAA)	HIPPA protects personal health information and set standard for health care providers that use, disclose personal health information and conduct health care transactions electronically	HIPPA requires organizations and user of health information to have written policies and procedures regarding how personal health information is used and protected.
2002	Sarbanes Oxley Act 2002		Sarbanes Oxley Act protects employee privacy and prohibits any adverse employment actions against employees as whistle-blowers. The law requires organizations to establish internal procedure by which employee reports about fraud can be taken/ reviewed without hurting employee privacy and safety

(continued)

Table 3.1 (continued)

Year	Laws/Regulation	Purpose	Implications to HRIS
2003	Fair and Accurate Credit Transaction Act 2003 (FACTA)	FACTA is an amendment to the Fair Credit Reporting Act for the purpose of protecting consumers against identity theft.	The Act mandates requirements for information privacy and accuracy, the use and disclosure of consumer information. It requires entities that maintain or possess consumer information from consumer reports for business purpose to have a proper process of disposing or compiling such information.
2003	Security Breach Notification laws	Security breach notification laws require individuals or entities affected by a data breach to inform their customers and other parties about the breach and take specific steps remedy the situation based on state legislature	Employers are required to notify employees of potential or real data breach
2008	Genetic Information Nondiscrimination Act (GINA)	Title II of GINA prohibits the use of Genetic Information in making employment decisions and also prohibits requesting, disclosing or purchasing genetic information of employees.	It is unlawful for employers to disclose genetic information about applicants, employers. It is the responsibility of the employer to keep the genetic information of employers confidential, unless requested by a court order.
2009	The Health Information Technology for Economic and Clinical Health (HITECH) Act,	The Act promotes the adoption and meaningful use of health information technology. Subtitle D of this Act addressed the privacy and security of individuals when health information is transferred electronically.	HITECH Act further strengthens HIPAA by imposing significant penalty for unlawful electronic transmission of patient health information thus securing health information exchange.
2010	Social Security Number Laws	Social security number laws restrict and prohibits the dissemination of society security number	Social Security Number Laws prohibit organizations from releasing an employee's Social Security number (SSN). Additionally, employers should not use SSN as employee identifiers and keep the SSNs as narrowly distributed as possible.

(continued)

Table 3.1 (continued)

Year	Laws/Regulation	Purpose	Implications to HRIS
2015	Cybersecurity Information Sharing Act	The law allows for sharing of cyber threat information among public and private sector organizations without fear of liability	When sharing cyber threat information with organizations, the sharing agency cannot reveal personal protected information e.g., health information, human resource information, consumer information, education history, financial information, property ownership information, and identifying information of children.

Data source: Battaglio (2015), Brooks, (2019), US, EEOC (n.d.)

et al., 2019). Given the myriad external and challenges faced by organizations and employees, there are several laws and regulations passed by the Congress to ensure protection of sensitive information (see Table 3.1).

Example of a Large-Scale Data Breach in the Public Sector-Office of Personnel Management

Cybercrime has become a big business worldwide, and there have been several notable data breaches reported in public and private organizations. The largest data breach in the U.S. government in recent times was in 2015 when sensitive data of over 20 million federal employees was stolen from the Office of Personnel Management (OPM). OPM is the chief personnel arm of the federal government responsible for storing and maintaining data of federal employees and potential applicants. A cyber-attack of this magnitude has not been experienced by the government before, accelerating the passage of the Cybersecurity Information Sharing Act that helped reduce barriers to information sharing from private to federal agencies and vice versa. Sensitive information about current and former employees, potential applicants, contractors, and individuals requiring high security clearance was compromised. Social security numbers, birth dates, performance ratings, training information, and fingerprints of millions were stolen (Finklea et al., 2015). The cyber attackers made multiple attempts at hacking the OPM data from 2013 to 2015.

Multiple lawsuits were brought forward against OPM after the data hack, which eventually resulted in two consolidated lawsuits: one, brought forward by the American Federation of Government Employees (AFGC) and the other by National Treasury Employees Union (NTEU) claiming violation of individual privacy rights under the 1974 Privacy Act. The case was dismissed by lower district court, which alleged that the plaintiffs could not establish concrete injury or specific losses resulting from the data breach (Steffel, 2019). However, the D.C. circuit court reversed the decision by lower courts based on future harm that could be caused by identify theft. The appellate court ruled that "OPM effectively left the door to its records unlocked by repeatedly failing to take basic, known, and available steps to secure the trove of sensitive information in its hands" (Katz, 2019). The case hass now returned to the district court for establishing merit of the claims made, thus allowing plaintiffs to sue the government. The Supreme Court has not provided clear precedence on cases of identity theft resulting in split decision across lower and appeals courts.

In June 2019, the Appeals Court ruled that OPM had various flaws (AFGE v. OPM, p.30) as listed below:

- Severely outdated security policies and procedures;
- Permitting employees to leave open, or to not terminate, remote access;
- Understaffed and undertrained cybersecurity personnel;
- Failure to implement or enforce multi-factor identification in any of its major information systems;
- Declining to patch or install security updates for its systems promptly;
- Lacking a mature vulnerability scanning program to find and track the status of security weaknesses in its systems;
- Failure to maintain a centralized information security management structure that would continuously monitor security events and controls;
- Lacking the ability to detect unauthorized devices connected to its network; and
- Failure to engage in appropriate oversight of its contractor-operated systems.

Role of HR in Maintaining Data Security

Human Resources departments play a crucial role in maintaining data security. Some of the common approaches include strengthening security measures, training employees about policies, laws and procedures related to data security, and emphasizing a work culture that places security issues as paramount.

Strengthening Security Measures The majority of data breaches occur due to human errors (Alavi et al., 2013). Hence, it is important to emphasize strengthening technology and security measures. Employees must use strong passwords that are not written down in a document, stored on computers, or shared with others. Human Resources Information Technology should emphasize not just the use of strong passwords but stress avoiding the use of the same password across several accounts. Longer passwords with more than eight characters that include letters, both upper and lower case and numerical and special characters are some key consideration that must be emphasized to employees in creating passwords (Bauer et al., 2018). Organizations must regularly install security patches and invest in updating outdated security technologies. HR should work closely with the IT department to ensure the confidentiality of sensitive employee and organizational data while maintaining employee privacy. However, public employees are subject to Freedom of Information (FOI) laws and open record requests that may have bearing on an employees' expectation of confidentiality.

Employee Training Regular trainings that emphasize an employee's role and responsibility in maintaining data security should be considered. Providing key information about how to handle sensitive data and the ethical and legal obligations for new and current employees is critical in ensuring data security. Employers are required to establish procedures and processes that not only safeguard confidential employee data, but also inform employees when a data breach occurs. Thus, HR plays an instrumental role in communicating the policies that safeguard employee data and at the same time maintain employee privacy. In HR trainings, the emphasis should be on ways public sector employees can serve as good stewards of public data.

Culture of Security While most changes instituted by HR to maintain data security are technological in nature, changing the culture of an organization that emphasizes data protection and compliance of laws and procedures is a challenging task. Ensuring data security is more of a human issue and not solely a technological issue (Alavi et al., 2013), regular training, support from senior management and fostering attitudes that commit to organizational security goals has positive impact on information security compliance (Abdullah et al., 2014; Ifinedo, 2014). Thus "in order to have a positive information security culture, organizations must ensure a mix of technical systems and human behavioral aspects of information security management." (Glaspie & Karwowski, 2018, p. 277).

Case Study: The Big Database That "Couldn't"

An organization purchased a software application for HR that contains personnel data, resumes and is required to perform a statistical analysis to decide on how personnel should be allocated and hired. The software application is extremely expensive and is manpower intensive in inputting data as well as extracting data for decision-makers. The effort is so labor intensive that not only is there no one qualified to obtain the information from the software, but it has now been determined that the software is not capable of being able to produce the statistics needed to make operational decisions.

The Director at the organization's location 'A' decides to take matters into their own hands and hire someone with technical and statistical abilities to obtain data and perform analysis. What the employee is initially told is that they need to gather data for location 'A' and provide statistical analysis to determine what applicant should be recruited based on the types of applicants who were receiving multiple offers. The employee comes back with a disturbing report, which indicates the data inside the software is flawed and that the software itself has serious limitations. The Director understands there is a political aspect within the organization to using the software since the organization has paid millions of dollars to the vendor for the software and

(continued)

upper administrators made a unilateral decision to purchase the software. The Director then asks the employee to devise a way to produce accurate data and provide the statistical model needed for predicting how the Director's department should go about recruiting on limited budget. The employee decides to use a $300 Filemaker Pro application to develop a database with data entry controls and very basic statistical capability to produce what the Director needs for their decision making. Within a couple of weeks the employee produces the information that the Director is able to use for the upper Executive Administrators, which provides not only the information on who should be targeted for recruiting, but also what locations for the organizations are to be expanded. The employee's role is then expanded from location 'A' to all of the locations for the organization. The organization, based on the new information provided by the employee, then decides to expand a new location for new college graduates. The original software essentially becomes unused for any type of statistical analysis. This is unfortunately how many organizations will buy software for statistical analysis without having a clear understanding on what resources are needed to support a specific type of software or how to employ the analysis to make decisions for the organization.

Summary

HRIS adoption in the public sector depends on Technological, Organizational and Environmental (TOE) factors highlighted in this chapter. Familiarity with the types of HRIS systems and its adoption in the public sector is important as one seeks to better understand the extent to which HRIS systems are employed in the government. The public sector, although behind the private sector in its use of technology in HR, is seeking to take advantage of HRIS to meet the growing needs of their agencies and the communities they serve. It is the responsibility of both employers and employees to protect sensitive employee and organizational data from internal and external threats. To protect sensitive information, the U.S. Congress passed several laws and regulations that HR needs to be aware and to educate employees about. Thus, HR departments play a crucial role in maintaining data security by avoiding data breaches. The next chapter will focus on more detailed aspects of the architecture of HRIS and how that architecture has evolved over time.

References

Abdullah, H., Uli, J., & Mohamed, Z. A. (2014). Relationship between organizational characteristics and information security knowledge management implementation. *Procedia-Social and Behavioral Sciences, 123*, 433–443.

Alavi, R., Islam, S., Jahankhani, H., & Al-Nemrat, A. (2013). Analyzing human factors for an effective information security management system. *International Journal of Secure Software Engineering (IJSSE), 4*(1), 50–74.

AFGE v. OPM, No. 17-5217, US Court of Appeals. See https://www.cadc.uscourts.gov/internet/opinions.nsf/156665FF486A73F085258420004F2BA4/$file/17-5217.pdf

Al-Dmour, R. H., Love, S., & Al-Debei, M. M. (2015). Measuring the effectiveness of HRIS practice in business organisations: A study in the context of a developing country. *International Journal of Business Innovation and Research, 9*(5), 507–525.

Ball, K. S. (2001). The use of human resource information systems: A survey. *Personnel Review, 30*(6), 677–693.

Battaglio, R. P. (2015). *Public human resource management: Strategies and practices in the 21st century*. Sage Publications.

Bauer, T., Erdogan, B., Caughlin, D., & Truxillo, D. (2018). *Human resource management: People, data, and analytics*. Sage Publications.

Beadles II, N. A., Lowery, C. M., & Johns, K. (2005). The impact of human resource information systems: An exploratory study in the public sector. *Communications of the IIMA, 5*(4), 39–46.

Brooks, R. (2019). *United States data protection laws: State-level approaches to privacy protection*. Retrieved July 15, 2020 from https://blog.netwrix.com/2019/08/27/data-privacy-laws-by-state-the-u-s-approach-to-privacy-protection/

DePietro, R., Wiarda, E., & Fleischer, M. (1990). The context for change: Organization, technology and environment. In L. G. Tornatzky & M. Fleischer (Eds.), *The process of technological innovation* (pp. 151–175). Lexington Books.

Dery, K., Grant, D., & Wiblen, S. (2009, August). Human resource information systems (HRIS): Replacing or enhancing HRM. In *Proceedings of the 15th World Congress of the International Industrial Relations Association IIRA* (pp. 24–27).

Finklea, K., Christensen, M. D., Fischer, E. A., Lawrence, S. V., & Theohary, C. A. (2015, July). Cyber intrusion into US office of personnel management: In brief. Library of Congress Washington DC Congressional Research Service.

Glaspie, H. W., & Karwowski, W. (2018). Human factors in information security culture: A literature review. In D. Nicholson (Ed.), *Advances in human factors in cybersecurity* (AHFE advances in intelligent systems and computing) (Vol. 593, pp. 269–280). Springer.

Haneem, F., Kama, N., Taskin, N., Pauleen, D., & Bakar, N. A. A. (2019). Determinants of master data management adoption by local government organizations: An empirical study. *International Journal of Information Management, 45*, 25–43.

Hendrickson, A. R. (2003). Human resource information systems: Backbone technology of contemporary human resources. *Journal of Labor Research, 24*(3), 381–394.

Ifinedo, P. (2014). Information systems security policy compliance: An empirical study of the effects of socialisation, influence, and cognition. *Information & Management, 51*(1), 69–79.

Jang-Jaccard, J., & Nepal, S. (2014). A survey of emerging threats in cybersecurity. *Journal of Computer and System Sciences, 80*(5), 973–993.

Johnson, R. D., Carlson, K. D., & Kavanagh, M. J. (Eds.). (2020). *Human resource information systems: Basics, applications, and future directions*. SAGE Publications, Incorporated.

Johnson, R. D., & Gueutal, H. G. (2011). Transforming HR through technology: The use of eHR and human resource information system in organizations. *SHRM Effective Practices Guidelines Series*, pp. 32–45.

Katz, E. (2019). Federal employees suing OPM score win in lawsuit over data hacks. *Government Executive*. Retrieved December 13, 2020 from https://www.govexec.com/pay-benefits/2019/06/feds-suing-opm-score-early-win-lawsuit-over-data-hacks/157970/

Kovach, K. A., & Cathcart, C. E., Jr. (1999). Human resource information systems (HRIS): Providing business with rapid data access, information exchange and strategic advantage. *Public Personnel Management, 28*(2), 275–282.

Lengnick-Hall, M. L., & Moritz, S. (2003). The impact of e-HR on the human resource management function. *Journal of Labor Research, 24*(3), 365–379.

Martinsons, M. G. (1994). Benchmarking human resource information systems in Canada and Hong Kong. *Information & Management, 26*(6), 305–316.

Ngai, E. W. T., & Wat, F. K. T. (2006). Human resource information systems: A review and empirical analysis. *Personnel Review, 35*, 297–314.

Norris, D. F., Mateczun, L., Joshi, A., & Finin, T. (2019). Cyberattacks at the grass roots: American local governments and the need for high levels of cybersecurity. *Public Administration Review, 79*(6), 895–904.

Pudjianto, B., Zo, H., Ciganek, A. P., & Rho, J. J. (2011). Determinants of e-government assimilation in Indonesia: An empirical investigation using a TOE framework. *Asia Pacific Journal of Information Systems, 21*(1), 49–80.

Reddick, C. G. (2009). Human resources information systems in Texas City governments: Scope and perception of its effectiveness. *Public Personnel Management, 38*(4), 19–34.

Roach, C. M., & Davis-Cooper, G. (2016). An evaluation of the adoption of the integrated human resource information system in Trinidad and Tobago. *International Journal of Public Administration in the Digital Age (IJPADA), 3*(3), 1–17.

Ruël, H., Bondarouk, T., & Looise, J. K. (2004). E-HRM: Innovation or irritation. An explorative empirical study in five large companies on web-based HRM. *Management Revue, 15*(3), 364–380.

Sharif, M. H. M., Troshani, I., & Davidson, R. (2016). Adoption of social media services: The case of local government organizations in Australia. In *Social media and networking: Concepts, methodologies, tools, and applications* (pp. 900–916). IGI Global.

Steffel, J. (2019). The time between the theft and the injury: Standing requirements based on a future risk of identity theft after a data breach. *University of Cincinnati Law Review, 88*(4), 1189.

Thite, M., Kavanagh, M. J., & Johnson, R. A. (2012). *Human resource information systems: Basics, applications, and future directions*. Sage.

Tobenkin, D. (2019). The cybersecurity challenge. Society of Human Resource Management. Retrieved December 12, 2020 https://www.shrm.org/hr-today/news/all-things-work/pages/the-cybersecurity-challenge.aspx

Troshani, I., Jerram, C., & Gerrard, M. (2010). Exploring the organizational adoption of Human Resources Information Systems (HRIS) in the Australian public sector. In *Proceedings of the 21st Australasian Conference on Information Systems* (ACIS2010). Brisbane, Queensland.

Troshani, I., Jerram, C., & Hill, S. R. (2011). Exploring the public sector adoption of HRIS. *Industrial Management & Data Systems, 111*(3), 470–488.

U.S. Equal Employment Opportunity Commission (EEOC). (n.d.). *Genetic information discrimination*. Retrieved August 11, 2020 from https://www.eeoc.gov/genetic-information-discrimination

Wang, H. J., & Lo, J. (2016). Adoption of open government data among government agencies. *Government Information Quarterly, 33*(1), 80–88.

Zeilinski, D. (2020). How next-gen technology can keep HR data safe. *Society of Human Resource Management*. Retrieved December 12, 2020. https://www.shrm.org/resourcesandtools/hr-topics/technology/pages/next-gen-technology-can-keep-hr-data-safe.aspx

Zeilinski, D. (2019). 5 top cybersecurity concerns for HR in 2019. *Society of Human Resource Management*. Retrieved December 12, 2020. https://www.shrm.org/resourcesandtools/hr-topics/technology/pages/top-cybersecurity-concerns-hr-2019.aspx

The Architecture of HRIS

4

Key Points of the Chapter

- HRIS enterprise software database architecture is reviewed from the beginning of mainframes to contemporary cloud architecture.
- What is a data warehouse and why are they important?
- The aspect of information security and functional area capabilities are discussed.

Importance of Understanding Database Architecture

While this is a very technical chapter for public administrators, it is critical for public administrators to understand what HRIS is and how it works. As stated by SHRM:

> Research shows that organizations that successfully adopt sophisticated HR technology tools outperform those that do not. But the simple automation of HR processes can no longer guarantee a competitive advantage. I-nstead, organizations must determine how to use technology to transform their HR practices and market their HR brand. (SHRM, 2015)

To successfully implement and use HRIS, the organization has to embrace the concepts of why and how HRIS will work with their organization. To understand the basics of HRIS, it is important to understand the evolution of how HRIS came to be developed so administrators in the public and non-profit organization sector can comprehend why data can be incorrectly input or extracted for reporting or functional purposes. Only when a public or non-profit organization administrator understands the architecture of HRIS and the interactions HRIS has with other systems and personnel, does an administrator know how to identify problems and implement corrections.

N. A. Valcik et al., *Human Resources Information Systems*, Management for Professionals, https://doi.org/10.1007/978-3-030-75111-1_4

Evolution

Why is the architecture important to an HRIS system and ultimately a public organization? Over the decades, database architecture has evolved and, with the advent of new technology and a different perspective on how public and non-profit organizations are so supposed to function, the database architecture will continue to advance and evolve.

Mainframes

With the exception of pen and paper, the earliest technology used by public and non-profit organizations to manage HR data was based on a mainframe, which only the wealthiest public and non-profit organizations could afford. The mainframes utilized early programming languages such as COBOL and FORTRAN to produce applications for HRIS as well as extracting reports. An example of this centralized architecture is seen in the diagram below (Fig. 4.1):

These early programming languages utilized punch cards to input information into the mainframe in a systematic method. Punch cards have been used to manually sort information before the age of modern computers and so they were adapted to be used for the new electronic age. When computers became more affordable and could be used by public and non-profit organizations, the punch card, typically used for financial data or for calculations, was quickly adapted to input human resources information into a computer. For many applications, punch cards had to be input in a specific sequence to ensure the computer could process the data correctly. Other uses of punch cards by organizations such as municipalities included elections, which could be randomly fed into the system to compile results quickly during election cycles. Some punch cards were still used in elections as late as the 1990s.

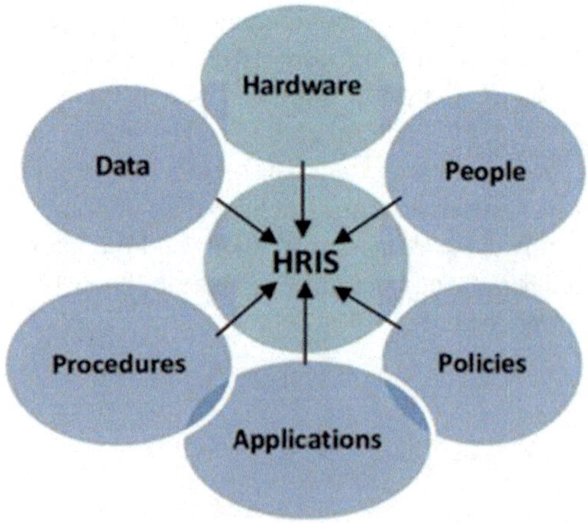

Fig. 4.1 Mainframe HRIS interaction components. (Source: Qadir & Agrawal, 2017)

These early mainframe computers were gigantic in size compared to modern computers. They had to be housed in their own area, needed air conditioning, had limited processing power and storage capabilities compared to modern PC's, and used Job Control Language (JCL) to run programs in batch mode (Fig. 4.2).

Utilities which are taken for granted today, (e.g. disk defragger) had to use utilities written in JCL and run in batch to "compress" disk space in development areas (also referred to as libraries) where programming was developed as well as submitted to run programs. For example, when a program was submitted in TSO (or a similar operating system) a copy of the program would be kept in the memory of the mainframe (Fig. 4.3).

This required a utility program to effectively "delete" the copies from the mainframe to gain the storage space back on the mainframe.

In addition, mainframe systems required staff dedicated to mounting cartridge or tapes (the next evolution from the punch card system) when data was needed for use in a program or to save data to an external storage mechanism. The only other way in which tapes and cartridges could be mounted without computer operators was with a very expensive robot to mount and dismount tapes and cartridges. Only public and non-profit organizations with significant financial resources could afford such a system. These early systems also typically had dummy terminals (later replaced by terminal emulators on PC's) and line printers.

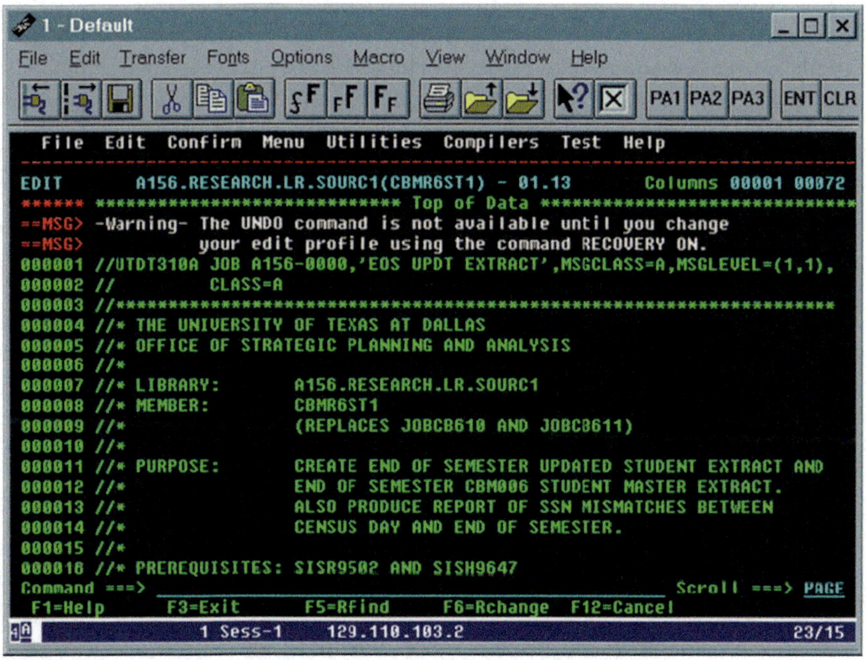

Fig. 4.2 Example of Job Control Language (JCL) mainframe interface

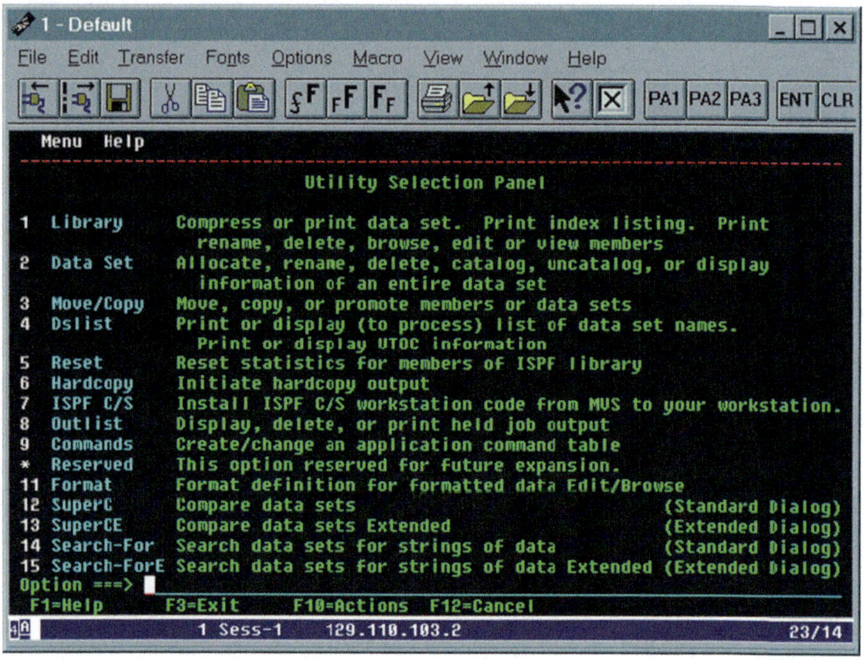

Fig. 4.3 MVS utilities interface

The file structures on these early systems were called ADAbas file structures, which were essentially large file structures that could be either plaintext or binary in nature. The relationship is shown in Fig. 4.4:

Later, mainframes were adapted to use relational table structures (IBM DB2 – Fig. 4.5), which could be joined through programming code to make programs run more efficiently and effectively.

The HRIS user interfaces, however, were command line prompted and were not user friendly in either inputting data or extracting data for reporting. To obtain any type of report from HRIS, users typically had to be programmers and understand the table structure to ensure that meaningful and accurate reports could be produced. The mainframe interfaces also made it more difficult and expensive to modify HRIS to accommodate new system or business requirements. Additionally, users typically would need extensive training on how to use the HRIS interface through a dummy terminal (or later an emulator), which could be quite costly to an organization. These early HRIS applications were often siloed and did not interact with finance, facilities, budget, or, in higher education institutions, student information systems. Therefore, a change in HRIS did not automatically generate similar changes other areas of operation. For example, an employee's social security number might exist in HRIS and finance but if it is modified in HRIS it will not automatically update in finance. This disconnect can result in a data integrity problem with one employee having two different social security numbers in HRIS and in finance. While older

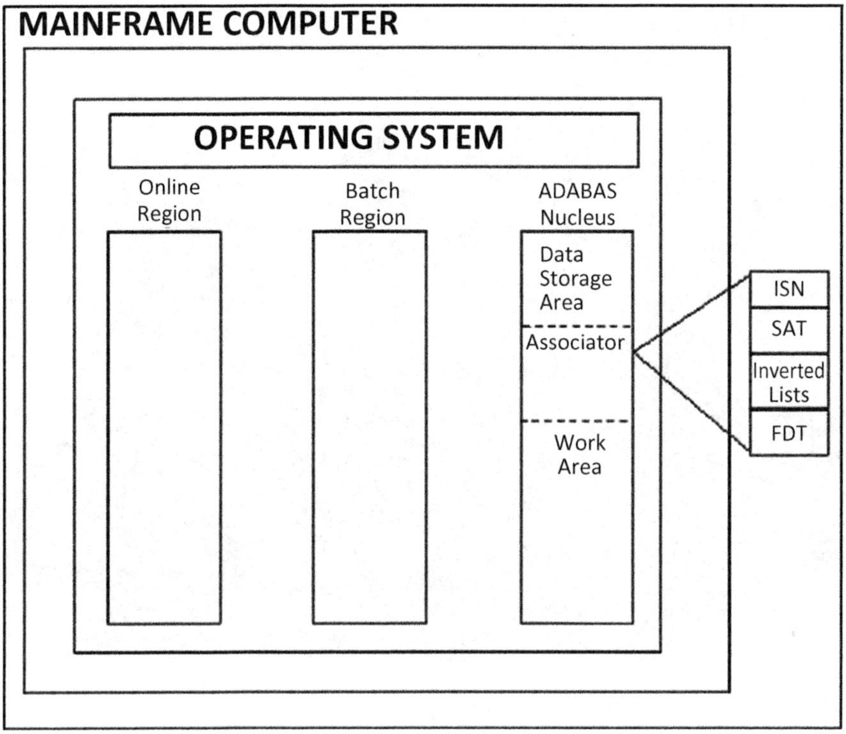

Fig. 4.4 File structure diagram with MVS and operating system. (Source: Information Builders Inc., 2020)

languages such as COBOL began to be phased out, newer programming languages such as C and FOCUS were developed to use on the mainframe systems with Time Shared Option (TSO), which was the operating system for mainframes (e.g. MVS OS/390).

Server Based HRIS

In the late 1990's and early 2000's, mainframes, which were susceptible to the Y2K date bug, were phased out for more advanced technology in the form of servers, which could store more information, operate at a faster pace and could be networked to form a powerful Information Technology (IT) infrastructure. HRIS applications, which had been originally designed with ADA file structures on mainframes, were re-designed to operate with a relational table structure and then re-engineered once again to work with servers and a web interface. Transitioning to server architecture also allowed for client-based processing power not realized on mainframe systems of the past. This allowed for the server to process programming more efficiently and

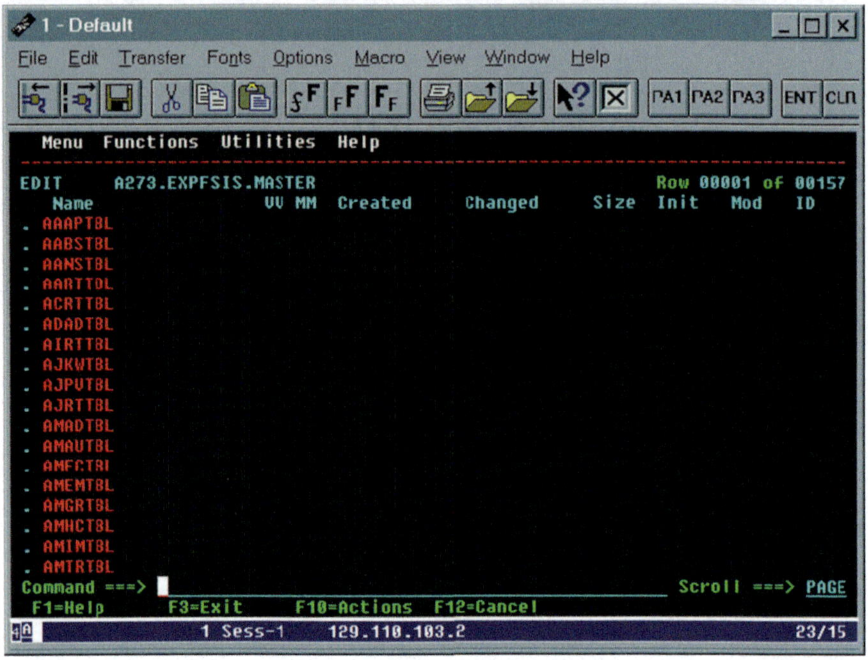

Fig. 4.5 MVS IBM DB2 interface table structure example

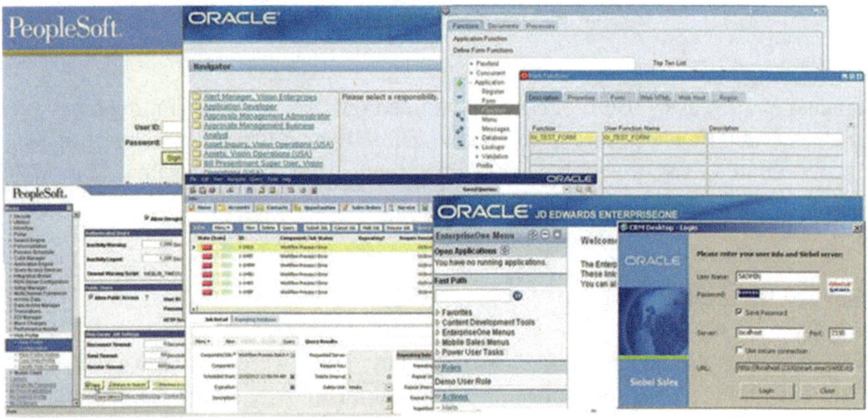

Fig. 4.6 Examples of Graphical User Interfaces (GUI) for HRIS. (Source: Thakker, 2015)

effectively since the clients' machines are also using their processing power to input and extract data for reports.

The interfaces for HRIS on servers have evolved to become web based with improved graphic user interfaces (GUI) that allows for more efficient data input (Fig. 4.6).

A GUI has a number of advantages, not the least of which is being able to add more control for data input on the front (web) data entry pages. Additionally, this allows for navigation to be easier for end users as well as adding capability that, while it may have been possible for mainframes to interface with web portals for client data entry, it would have been difficult and costly to enable those features. With a server environment, an integrated approach for HRIS can be implemented with a relational table structure design, which, in theory, can eliminate siloed operations. As stated by Oracle:

> An HRIS is built on two pillars that create the foundation for managing people and policies to support overall organizational effectiveness.
>
> - **Organizational design:** From a structural perspective, HRIS includes roles, functions, and reporting hierarchies. By defining the organizational structure, HRIS provides recognizable accountability and a pathway for operational functionality and consistency.
>
>   The right HRIS helps you address business challenges by helping you put the right talent in place. Through the consistent, automated management of acquisition and recruiting data, your HRIS can help you build a workforce that has the right people with the right skills, working in the right functions and under the right structure, to meet your strategic goals.
>
> - **Employee data management:** Similar to customer relationship management but within an employer/employee setting, the HRIS provides a comprehensive view of every employee including name, address, date of hire, compensation, benefit selections, and much more. With the right data, you'll be better able to connect with your employees, help them develop career plans, find the right training, and take their performance to the next level.
>
>   The HRIS enables automated and standardized record keeping, reporting, and self-service functionality. This can lead to more accurate and up-to-date information management that drives greater efficiency while providing convenience and ease of use for employees. (Oracle, 2020)

While this approach certainly has many advantages, it also has a major disadvantage – an increased vulnerability to security breaches. As stated by Secureworks:

> Cybersecurity, a subset of information security, is the practice of defending your organization's networks, computers and data from unauthorized digital access, attack or damage by implementing various processes, technologies and practices. With the countless sophisticated threat actors targeting all types of organizations, it is critical that your IT infrastructure is secured at all times to prevent a full-scale attack on your network and risk exposing your company' data and reputation. (Secureworks, 2017)

Because mainframes were centrally controlled with few external ports to attack security weaknesses, mainframes have traditionally been behind the security firewall with limited telecommunication access. Modern servers and the network environment have a multitude of access points, which necessitates the entire network and every machine to be equally secure to defeat potential attackers. Security technology has improved with newer forms of encryption, but hackers have also become more sophisticated in their methods of gaining access. Unlike the mainframe environment, the new server environments in most public organizations have more employees with increased access to computer services as opposed to the old mainframe environment with fewer employees to access the mainframe environment.

With the push for public and non-profit organizations to become more efficient and effective by using technology, this has now opened the door for more non-technical employees to access computers to do tasks such as performance evaluations and time cards, for example. While this may reduce costs in certain areas, it will also increase costs, liability and risk to the organization. Therefore, public and non-profit organizations have to decide how much money to budget toward IT infrastructure security and staff training and what policies and procedures should be in place so that the organization can function while maintaining secure enterprise systems.

Cloud Based HRIS

Due to the costs of HRIS and systems of that nature, a public or non-profit organization of any size will need to assess whether they host HRIS on their own servers using their locations or whether they use a service on the "cloud" (Fig. 4.7).

The term "cloud" is used casually by individuals who do not understand what exactly a cloud-based system means. Essentially, an HRIS cloud-based system is an HRIS that is hosted on a vendor or third party's servers instead of the client's servers. While in theory IT expenditures can be reduced with a cloud-based system, there is an increased risk of the organization's data being breached or rendered less accessible to the organization's employees because the server is not controlled by the organization. An organization has to vet a vendor thoroughly before committing

Fig. 4.7 Abstract image for HRIS in the cloud. (Source: Grones, 2020)

to a cloud-based system due to the risks and access issues involved. If HRIS is breached by a hacker, a public or non-profit organization's sensitive data can be accessed, sold and used illegally, which will cause the organization to lose credibility among other potential consequences.

The advantages for using a cloud-based HRIS enterprise system is that the organization does not have to pay personnel to modify the system (depending on the contract with the vendor), updates can be carried out by the vendor in a timely manner, and the organization does not have to provide facility space for servers. Companies have established entire server farms to provide cloud-based solutions for public and non-profit organizations, which indicate a high demand for those types of services. With public and non-profit organizations paying vendors for these types of services, there is an expectation of rapid response times when issues arise, for example an error in payroll processing. However, technology from the server-based method is no different. What has changed is the business model on who pays for the services, who hosts the services and who assumes liability if an issue arises.

Data Warehouse

"The data warehouse will solve all our problems." This quote, stated by a number of information technology professionals and consultants, is too inaccurate for any public or non-profit organization to rely upon. A data warehouse can greatly assist and add value to the capability of any organization for reporting purposes if the correct architecture is employed. As stated by Johnson and Gueutal:

> Data warehouses provide a centralized repository of selected HR data that is managed separately from live data. Data mining tools with advanced statistical data analysis techniques can then be employed to discover relationships among policies, procedures, practices and organizational outcomes that may not be readily apparent. Common uses of data mining techniques include questions related to manpower planning, predicting turnover, validating tests and monitoring HR practices for disparate impact. (Johnson & Gueutal, 2011)

A data warehouse is not a plug-and play system. A data warehouse must be carefully planned to maximize its value to the organization. How will an organization use the data warehouse? Is the data warehouse to provide additional reporting capability, assist users submitting data queries, and provide a snapshot in time or will it supply minimal industry standard capability? The organization must assess what it needs to fulfil operational and reporting requirements before it can determine how the data warehouse should be designed and what types of data should populate the data warehouse structure. Figure 4.8 depicts a data warehouse that is connected to a dynamic production HR database:

Should the data warehouse use static or dynamically updated data? Is the data warehouse to be employed to mirror the HRIS enterprise application or is the purpose to provide operational reports using data that is not up-to-date through a streaming feed? If the data warehouse is going to need dynamic data, then the ETL's from HRIS should be designed to feed tables accordingly. If the answer is no, then

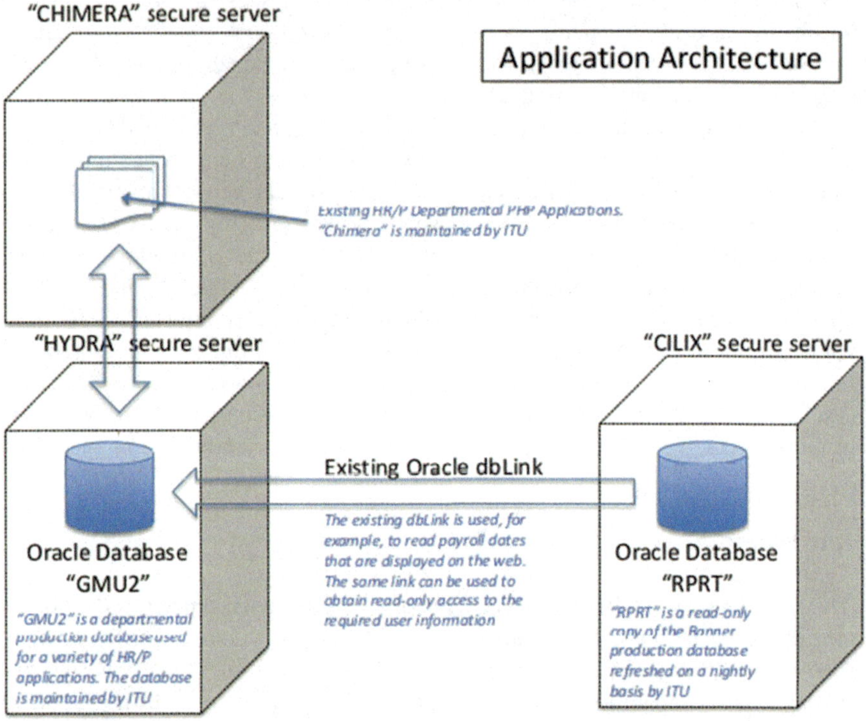

Fig. 4.8 Diagram for data warehouse interactions with HRIS. (Source: Slideshare, 2020)

a static solution needs to be employed by creating a series of tables to house flat files for given data characteristics (e.g. facilities information, financial information, payroll data etc.). A static file architecture allows for official reporting to be consistent and, if programming is employed correctly, edit checks can be developed for a series of audits on the system that will also assist data clean up not only on the host HRIS application but also with the files stored in the data warehouse. The static files allow for not only consistent reporting that can be duplicated for official reports, which allows organizations to pass external audits, but static data also enables reliable trend analysis.

For a number or organizations, both dynamic and static data are used in the table structure design. This type of design allows for an organization to produce official and operational reports. A data warehouse design should take a system approach so that it can interact with the host HRIS enterprise application along with the required specified reports. If a system approach is not taken, a data warehouse project will either fail or have severe shortcomings. Personnel need to ensure proper documentation is available to map variables from HRIS to the data warehouse so that reports can be properly programmed and developed.

Functional Area Access and Data Entry

A question every data owner should ask is, "Who in the organization needs access to HRIS and what type of information do they need?" For public and non-profit organizations who are more centralized, the access will be limited to what employees will need to perform processing, reporting or data entry. As stated by Bedell, Canniff and Wyrick:

> Some users simply input data and information, a few simply look at data and information provided in the form of reports, while a few others analyze the data and information to make decisions. What these users all have in common is that all the information is about potential and current employees with a focus on managing the organization's human capital to achieve strategic organizational goals. (Bedell, Canniff, & Wyrick, 2007)

For organizations that have the HRIS capability and want their employees to have more control over data entry, reporting and processing personnel as well as payroll data, policies and procedures will need to be formulated to ensure data integrity and adhere to security protocols. As alluded to earlier in the chapter, the more distributed HRIS capabilities and functionality is in the organization, the more policies and procedures need to be formulated to ensure data is correctly being input, reported and secured. As stated by Bedell, Canniff and Wyrick:

> Security needs to be maintained at a variety of levels. First, physical access to the DBMS and application server needs to be limited so that machines cannot be destroyed or logged into directly. Network, operating system, and DBMS access must be limited so that tools outside the HR application cannot be used to query sensitive data. (Bedell, Canniff, & Wyrick, 2021)

With a distributed approach, questions will need to be asked on what type of central oversight must be provided to ensure data integrity is being kept within a certain degree of acceptable tolerance.

There will need to be a number of decisions made on how data integrity will be achieved for the organization. Not all of these decisions will be policy or procedure based. For example, training employees is not just a policy decision, but also a budgetary decision. How many resources will be required to achieve the necessary data integrity standards? While decentralizing certain HRIS functionalities to the department level is possible, doing so might take time away from the departments' core functions while incurring additional training costs in using HRIS. While a departmental director may be able to perform certain HRIS tasks, is this how the organization wants a high salaried employee to spend their time, or would their time be better spent doing more specialized tasks? These are important questions the upper administrators of public and non-profit organizations should be asking when implementing HRIS across the organization.

How much access should lower level employees have? This cuts across two different areas: security and ability. How will the organization maintain security while providing access for the employees who need or should have it? Does the employee have the knowledge, skills and abilities to successfully use HRIS? For example, does a police officer have the technical computer skills to access more specialized areas of HRIS to use the system effectively? Does the police officer really need to access every single piece of data in HRIS? Would the organization rather have the police officer behind a desk using HRIS and training them, or would their time be better spent patrolling and keeping the public safe? The organization will need to determine what resources should be allocated to use HRIS and how the data in HRIS should be restricted to those who need it to perform their job duties.

Data Control

There are a number of ways that data entry can be controlled and updated. The HRIS application on the front pages or forms can have selection buttons or drop-down menus that provide only valid data entry options for inputting data. These types of input control mechanisms reduce the amount of data entry errors an employee can put into the system since there is no free form text typing that would be either inconsistent with other data that is entered into the system, or incorrect data (e.g. non-existent choices, special characters, numbers that should be letters etc.). Data entry can be controlled in the table structure as well. Fields can be restricted to only accept certain data types (e.g. nvarchar, date etc.), which will reduce the amount of incorrect data that can be accepted by the HRIS. For systems that are segregated from other functional areas (e.g. Finance, Student etc.), batch processes can be developed to input data directly into the table structure of the database so manually typing the same information into HRIS is avoided.

However, there are still a couple of areas that cannot necessarily be controlled through technology. Human Resources departments frequently have problems updating biographical information on employees. Examples of biographical information would include marital status, visa, job title, contract status, number of dependents, and number of years with the organization. Effective data collection and maintenance should be the first problem to be addressed with any HRIS application. Gathering current employee data can be accomplished through a biographical webpage completed by the employee when benefits are renewed or when a new employee is hired. This should be mandatory and should be completely updated within a month of the new enrollment period for benefits. The system should also be updated every week to reflect employees who have a status change.

To ensure that the HRS system is kept accurate and updated, the Human Resources department must make it mandatory to update biographical information when benefit enrollment begins each year for existing employees. The Human Resources department must then ensure that the system is updated by the employees by the end of the month after benefits enrollment is closed. Employees who have status changes should be entered into the system by a deadline in order to keep the database current and in sync with payroll. Error reports designed to catch inconsistencies should be run weekly on a production schedule.

Reporting Capability

Public and non-profit organizations should set clear goals and objectives for the software vendor when selecting or designing a robust reporting tool. The reporting tool should be supported by the vendor for a given length of time and should have associated training for the organization's employees. Reporting tools should take into account the different skill sets of the organization's employees. In fact, the organization might wish to consider more than one reporting tool. Some users, for example, will need a simple reporting tool to produce lists or queries from HRIS. Other users will need high-level functions such as advanced statistical analysis (e.g. SAS) while other users will need dashboards (e.g. WebFOCUS, OBIEE+ etc.). While this adds to the complexity of training and maintenance, adopting multiple tools also adds capability and flexibility to the organization's reporting abilities. The main goal for reporting should be to provide accurate data in a timely fashion. If the reporting tools fail in either aspect, then the organization is at risk for using faulty information for making decision-making, which can lead to severe consequences.

A reporting goal for any public or non-profit organization is to empower their employees to obtain data without the aid of a programmer. It is more efficient when data can be obtained directly by the end user to facilitate the decision-making process. First, it will be faster if the employee can extract the data correctly themselves instead placing a request for a department to provide that data for them. Secondly, the employee will not have to translate what they want to a programmer with the hope that what they will receive is what is needed for the task. In addition, an organization should seek to automate as many reports as possible that will require a minimal amount of staff time to produce accurate data.

Besides training employees on how to use these types of reporting tools, there will need to be extensive documentation on not only the reporting tools themselves but also documentation on the HRIS table structure, variables and business logic in order to use the reporting tools correctly. Reporting tools will need to be configured differently depending upon the license agreement the organization has with the vendor as well as cost considerations. For example, Central Washington University and West Virginia University opted to use SAS on a server while The University of Texas at Dallas used SAS on the client machine for administrative uses. The SAS license agreement for The University of Texas at Dallas was more economical since SAS had an agreement with The University of Texas System for software whereas Central Washington University and West Virginia University received better pricing on a server-based SAS application.

Case Study: Failure to Launch

A public organization had a data warehouse. The incoming Director of reporting was told by upper administration that the organization was "expanding the data warehouse". Based on the information the Director received, it appeared that the design and information in the existing data warehouse was accurate. Two weeks after the Director started the job, an employee presented the Director with a perplexing problem: a federal report that was produced last year contained different numbers than the current report that was pulling data for the same time parameters. The Director first looked at the code that extracted and produced the report. The code was unchanged from the previous year. Then the Director assessed the table structure and determined that the table structure was exactly the same. This lead to only one reasonable explanation: the data was being dynamically updated from the root HRIS production extracts on a daily basis. When files are not saved as static files, there is no way to prevent the root data from being changed, which results in a report that cannot be reliably reproduced from year to year. The Director drafted a new design that had worked at their previous place of employment in an effort to produce reliable data. Unfortunately, the organization decided to put a Vice President and a consultant in charge of the redesign, neither of which understood the HRIS system or the reporting requirements. The data warehouse project ultimately failed.

The case study also illustrates the concept of Organizational Drift between what is ideal (theoretical) and what is occurring in reality. The gap between what could be accomplished by the data warehouse and what ultimately occurred where basic accurate reporting could not be conducted illustrates how disastrous Organizational Drift can be for a public organization. Another reason the project failed was the personal objectives of the Vice President (power) and the consultant (money). Lack of accountability by the Vice President and the consultant ensured that there was little oversight into their activities, which led to serious negative ramifications for the data warehouse project and ultimately the organization. While technically the data warehouse project was viable, it was not politically feasible for the Director to succeed due to political issues in the upper administration.

Case Study: "Houston, We Have a Problem."

A public organization is still on a MVS 370 mainframe in the late 1990's even after it has been out of support by IBM for over 8 years. The architecture for the HRIS is siloed and does not communicate or cross data with the other ERP systems for the organizations, thus making updates dependent upon the functional areas across the organization. This ultimately leads to data in three different ERP systems to be out of synch with data updates and causes massive problems compiling state and federal reports. Worse, the interface used to interface with the mainframe system is a TN3270 emulator using COMPLETE, that programmers must use to perform programming or data entry on the HRIS (or other ERP) systems, which crashes frequently. To use the mainframe was costly in a number of other areas such as training personnel, costs of the hardware and the costs of the facility space itself.

The programmers must save their programming code on a frequent basis causing the programmers to take double the time to develop programs, which is a cost to the organization. The problem becomes so acute, that one employee required to program asks for a hardwired terminal to be installed in their office so they can complete work assignments in a timely fashion. In addition, because the COMPLETE operating system is being used by the organization, to obtain a file to use on a PC, a programmer would have to go to the Operations room and ask one of the computer operators to download a file on a disk. Not only does this take time, but this also increases the risk of data being lost or compromised if the person loses the disk or does not secure the data properly. While the data is secure on the mainframe, it is not secure between the mainframe and the programmer's office, nor is there a guarantee the data is necessarily secure on the user's PC. Ultimately, the architecture of this HRIS makes obtaining accurate data in a timely manner extremely difficult and problematic.

In addition, the ability to use the data electronically was discouraged since almost all output was routed to a large green bar printer. Any historical data created for federal or state reports could not be kept on the disks for the mainframe and instead had to be saved to tape or cartridge. If historical programs had to be compiled for any type of longitudinal study (e.g. payroll analysis), the program while it was running, would often be paused while tapes were physically mounted by an employee working in the operations area of the mainframe. If there was an error on the program, those tapes would have to be physically remounted when the program was rerun. Another issue that was problematic for the organization was the capacity of the mainframe itself. Since the mainframe was frequently at maximum capacity for processing or running basic programs, the limited capacity did not allow for a large number of programs to be run concurrently or have a complex program running during peak hours. Thus information needed for the upper administrators to make operational decisions was slow in getting to the decision-makers, which in many cases had consequences since timely information could not be obtained to make data driven decisions. The majority of these issues were not alleviated until the migration to an IBM 390 mainframe with a

TSO interface and an IBM DB2 relational table structure. This allowed for more capacity, files to be downloaded by employees at their desk and the ability to update information with all three ERP systems through batch program processes.

Summary

This chapter has been a review of the evolution of HRIS architecture from mainframe to server to cloud system. While it is necessary to understand the different aspects of HRIS architecture, it is also important to see what the changes have been and why these changes have occurred. Over time, the HRIS architecture has changed to meet the more complex legal aspects of Human Resources and the requirement that information be stored in a system for record retention, self-reporting, salary structures, tax codes and compliance reporting with state and federal agencies. With this complexity comes the need for a database structure that has also evolved over time. With mainframes, flat files were a standard practice (e.g. ADAbas file structure). The need then arose for a more complex table structure that could be relational in the HRIS database to reflect the ever-evolving legal and operational requirements (e.g. IBM DB2). As technology evolved, this allowed those types of database structures to be married with evolving hardware that eventually saw the obsolescence of the mainframe and the rise of the servers as they are known today. With the increased capability of the Internet and the requirements of data being able to be secured and encrypted through new methodologies, this movement gave rise to the cloud computing along with the potential to decrease costs to public organizations. The next evolution of HRIS will remain to be seen, but what is certain is the need to keep even more information on employees in the foreseeable future. The next chapter will focus on the role of HRIS in the public organization and discuss the critical nature of HRIS for not only capturing data, but also being able to utilize the data for analysis and for the decision-making process for upper administrators.

References

Bedell, M., Canniff, M., & Wyrick, C. (2007). System considerations in the design of an HRIS. *Human Resource Information Systems*. Sage, Los Angeles, California. Retrieved on June 28, 2021. https://www.sagepub.com/sites/default/files/upm-binaries/25451_Ch3.pdf

Bedell, M. D., Canniff, M., & Wyrick, C. (2021). Introduction to HRM and HRIS. In *Systems considerations in the design of an HRIS*. Sage.

Grones, G. (2020). HRIS systems: What you need to know. *Human Resources Director*. January 23, 2020. Retrieved from: https://www.hcamag.com/ca/specialization/hr-technology/hris-systems-what-you-need-to-know/211249

Information Builders Inc. (2020). Adabas overview. *WebFocus*. Retrieved from: https://webfocusinfocenter.informationbuilders.com/wfappent/TL3s/TL_srv_adapters/source/adabas22.htm

Johnson, R. D., & Gueutal, H. G. (2011). Transforming HR through technololgy. In *Transforming HR through technology: The use of E-HR and HRIS in organizations* (shrm.org) (p. 6).

Oracle. (2020). What is an HRIS? *Oracle*. Retrieved from: https://www.oracle.com/human-capital-management/what-is-hris/

Qadir, A., & Agrawal, S. (2017). Human Resources Information System (HRIS): Re-engineering the traditional human resource management for leveraging strategic human resource management. *Journal of Market-Focused Management*. Retrieved from: https://www.researchgate.net/publication/342716764_Human_Resource_Information_System_HRIS_Re-engineering_the_Traditional_Human_Resource_Management_for_Leveraging_Strategic_Human_Resource_Management

Secureworks. (2017). Cybersecurity vs. Network Security vs. Information Security. *Secureworks*. March 17, 2017. Retrieved from: https://www.secureworks.com/blog/cybersecurity-vs-network-security-vs-information-security

SHRM. (2015). Designing and managing a human resource information system. *SHRM*. August 25, 2015. Retrieved from: https://www.shrm.org/resourcesandtools/tools-and-samples/toolkits/pages/managingahumanresourceinformationsystem.aspx

Slideshare. (2020). Hris architecture. *Slideshare*. Retrieved from: https://www.slideshare.net/jcreuzig/hris-architecture

Thakker, T. (2015). Understanding Oracle fusion applications interface. In *Pro Oracle fusion applications*. Apress. Online ISBN: 978-1-4842-0983-7. Retrieved from: https://link.springer.com/chapter/10.1007/978-1-4842-0983-7_11

Application of HRIS in Public Organizations

5

Key Points of the Chapter

- High level viewpoint on what HRIS can potentially do for an organization.
- Discuss how HRIS stores data along with data entry controls
- Gains for the organization and employees using HRIS.
- Costs considerations for implementing and maintaining HRIS.

There are many HRIS software solutions for public and non-profit organizations that have different capabilities. HRIS's importance and usefulness will vary from organization to organization due to technical capabilities or limitations of the system and personnel. HRIS enterprise software is not as critical to small public and non-profit organizations as it would be to a major municipality, for example. The additional requirements that public and non-profit organizations will need for an HRIS system to be effective will depend upon what type of reporting is required by each entity at the federal, state and local levels for compliance purposes.

For non-profit organizations, reports for stakeholders and board members will be essential. Operational reporting will be key to making decisions since it will impact budget and financial areas of concern for the organization (Pynes, 2009). With higher education institutions, there will be many different operational aspects where data will need to be captured due to the specialized workforce (e.g. tenured faculty) that is different than public organizations (e.g. cities, state agencies etc.) and non-profit organizations. For entities who have unionized segments of their workforce, data will need to be accurate for capturing those who are in the unions, which unions they belong to and what benefits they are receiving that are specific to those employees.

N. A. Valcik et al., *Human Resources Information Systems*, Management for Professionals, https://doi.org/10.1007/978-3-030-75111-1_5

Payroll

A critical area of operation for any organization is payroll. Not only are organizations legally bound to pay their employees according to civil service or contracts that are issued, but employees can become unified against the upper administration if there are payroll errors. Additionally, employees receive incorrect pay, or no pay at all, can file lawsuits or report to the media. If the media does obtain information on a public organization not paying employees properly and it is a pattern, the credibility of the organization will be damaged. This type of damage can extend to impacting upper administrators' ability to interact with their employees, the public and with any type of oversight board.

A trend that has occurred over the last few years is upper level state agencies taking control of payroll systems, as well as other HR functions, from lower level agencies. In the state of West Virginia, most state agencies have had their payroll centralized to a state system called OASIS (2021) (State of West Virginia, 2021). In theory, this system was developed to reduce the number of personnel that work on payroll production for state employees. OASIS did not work well for the two main higher education institutions (West Virginia University and Marshall University) because of their unique accounting structures and the nuances with how faculty were paid. Economies of scale may have some benefit, but also have some disadvantages with regard to customization to unique organizational structures.

While there may be an overall personnel cost savings for a public organization to use a centralized HRIS solution, there are problems inherent with that model of operation which include loss of local control, inability to address specific concerns locally (e.g. software purchased to address specific local organization's issues), potential loss of responsiveness by overall information system and the costs to house as well as operate a centrally located HRIS enterprise solution. There is also the issue of training personnel at a central area of control to understand payroll data at all of the various sub-units of the organization. While some arrangements may be fairly straight forward, other organizations linked to an overall public entity could be extremely complex where the personnel in the central area of control may not have the knowledge, skills and abilities to successfully resolve specific issues.

On newer HRIS architecture, the table structure is often linked with other enterprise systems or links payroll with other modules within the HRIS software. While the integration is better overall for accuracy, accountability of data and the ability to operate in a more decentralized manner, this also opens up HRIS for issues if data is incorrect in one area of the table structure. Problems can ripple throughout HRIS causing multiple problems for the HR staff. There can be issues if a person has more than one job in the organization or has assignments to multiple departments. This is a common situation in higher education institutions where salary can be a stipend, a traditional salary, or a contracted amount. Another area that can further complicate the payroll system is payment of individuals from different types of accounts by the percentage of their salary (e.g. state funds, restricted (research) funds, designated funds and auxiliary funds).

The role of the HRIS software is to ensure that the employee is paid correctly, ensure that the accounting is correct for the organization and to some extent have a record in the form of payment on what the person is supposed to do for the organization. From an accounting perspective, the role of HRIS should be to assist in auditing payroll and to ensure the data is accurate for compliance reporting perspectives. Another role of the payroll module in HRIS is to provide upper administrators with data that can be used to make operational decisions. Often payroll data is used because of its reliability: everyone in the organization has a vested interest in data accuracy if they want to be paid.

Benefits - Sick Time, Vacation Time, Health and Retirement

Benefits are an important component of an employee's compensation. Often employees are drawn to work for public and non-profit organizations because of the benefit packages even if the salaries are not competitive with their private industry counterparts. HRIS is critical in the role of keeping track of the different benefits as well as standard benefits that all employees are entitled to for their classification (e.g. faculty, staff, classified etc.). Almost all benefits are monetary for public and non-profit organizations and need to be seen in that light by upper administrators. Without an accurate accounting of benefits, the organization can lose money if benefits are being claimed that an employee or dependent is not entitled to receive for their employment. As can be seen in the following case study, the inaccurate accounting of benefits can also hamper employees or their dependents from receiving proper medical care that should be covered by their place of employment.

Sick and vacation time is labor hours that the employee is taking from work, which is translated into hours the organization pays the employee while not receiving work output during that timeframe. Some organizations will pay the hours for sick time or a portion of them when the employee leaves the organization while others bank those hours for the employee that can be used later if they are re-employed with the same organization at a later date. Vacation time however, is paid out when the employee leaves since this is part of their compensation package. If an organization is unable to track vacation or sick time successfully, the organization can lose money if vacation or sick time is not accurately accounted for in HRIS. For employees who have come from other public or non-profit organizations and can transfer their vacation and sick time balances to another organization, HRIS plays a pivotal role in ensuring both the organization and the employee have accurately transferred in the leave balances from the previous organization.

Health benefits can be complex if an organization is large enough to offer several different options for employees. With large state agencies or municipalities, the rates can vary highly from one provider to the next with an overwhelming multitude of choices and combinations (e.g. eye insurance, health insurance, dental insurance, FLEX accounts). HRIS is essential for tracking health benefits for each employee, keeping track of how much each employee is deducing from his/her paycheck and determining how much money the organization is spending for each employee on their health care benefit. With more advanced HRIS software, the employee has the ability to select and submit their choices for benefits with minimal interaction with HR staff members. If instructions are clear on the benefits forms, employees interacting with those forms directly can be more efficient and effective than older methods of paper forms or having to interact with HR staff members. This feature of newer HRIS software frees up HR staff members to do other job functions and responsibilities, which may not have been given priority before because resources could have been limited.

Retirement is another area where HRIS can be used to accurately account for money spent towards employees. It is critical for strategic and operational planning for a public or non-profit organization to understand what funds need to be committed for retirement in order to avoid financial hardships for the organization. In 2013, the City of Detroit filed for bankruptcy due to a number of factors including a loss of population and industry over the past six decades (Davey & Walsh, 2013). The pension plan was an underlying issue for the City of Detroit as well as bad investments used to prop up the pension plan (Davey & Walsh, 2013). In addition to the City of Detroit, underfunded pension plans have proven to be an Achilles Heel for a number of public organizations over the years (Graham, 2015).

If upper administrators have an understanding of what retirement funds are encumbered, they can plan how much funding should be secured to cover retirement and pension plans in the future. This allows policy to be set by the organization, which can dictate, for example, how much each employee has to contribute for their retirement out of their paycheck (e.g. 6.7%). A public or non-profit organization, in theory, should be able to recruit and retain high quality employees based on an organization's benefits. If there is no confidence in how viable these benefits are, then how does an organization expect to compete with private industry that can pay higher salary amounts?

Compliance Data (EEO etc.)

HRIS has the capability to capture, track and report demographics for compliance reporting purposes (McCormack, 2004). If designed properly, HRIS can be used to accurately report the number of employees, their demographic profiles and how long they have been employed with the organization so that upper administrators can address recruiting, retention and promotion issues to achieve a diverse workforce. To stay in compliance with federal and state reports, it is critical that information is stored correctly in HRIS so the data can be extracted and reported correctly. However, issues can exist because the data is self-reported, for example gender, race and ethnicity. An organization has to be comfortable with the fact that the data can only be as accurate as the employee or applicant chooses to report if the employee or applicant chooses to report anything at all. Missing data will be a reality for the organization since most organizations cannot mandate that employees and applicants provide that information due to existing non-discrimination and privacy laws. Furthermore, there is no way an organization can verify if the information is truly accurate since it will be up to the employee or applicant to report how "they see themselves".

Federal and State Reports

Many organizations report employee data to the state; among these are public universities and colleges. State agencies can require public organizations (e.g. higher education institutions) to report directory information, salary information, position title, work percentages for different roles and tasks, date of birth, social security numbers, employee identification numbers, race, ethnicity as well as overtime worked for the organization (THECB, 2021). Universities and colleges can be compelled to report tenure status, faculty rank and contracted payments (THECB, 2021, NCES, 2021). While reporting paid amounts is usually more straightforward, contracted payments can prove to be problematic if HRIS cannot capture that type of information. Data such as contracted information will be very different from what is captured in HRIS for payout amounts.

There is also the issue of coding information that is unique to public on non-profit organizations. For example, certain administrators at one public organization appeared to be hiding payment to upper administrators by coding their payments in HRIS as 0% and using a certain code to denote a stipend in lieu of a standard payout. The issue was noticed when the top administrator of the organization was making only $60,000 when they should have been making well over $300,000 per year. The state agency wanted to know what the administrator was actually paid, which resulted in the correct full amount being reported. By using the definition of "stipend", the organization had a slew of extra payments being disbursed as "additional duties" that were effectively not known unless the coding scheme was known. This type of coding scheme was also problematic when attempting to extract information for public records requests.

Operational Reports

Operational reports are important for any organization, not just public or non-profit organizations, for the decision-making process. Money allocated for salaries will be one of the largest, if not the largest, expense the organization has to budget and expense Personnel costs not only include salaries, but also benefits and the management of payroll and benefits administration. For budgeting purposes, it is critical to accurately calculate the organization's expenses compared to incoming revenues (or donations) that the organization relies on for operation. Operational reports enable administrators to understand what resources the organization has in the different functional areas to determine if the organization is properly staffed and budgeted. Most public organizations and non-profit organizations have a segment of public service, which are either directly or indirectly associated with operational aspects.

Most public and non-profit organizations are judged on how efficiently and effectively they deliver public services to meet the needs of their service community.

Recruitment and Retention

Human resources, as a strategic business partner, drives an organization's recruitment and retention to create a workforce that is productive, fully engaged and highly motivated. In addition to HR strategy, empowering line management and communicating with employees are key elements to sustaining an employee base. Although some turnover can cause businesses to infuse new talent and bring new perspectives to the organization, basic recruitment and retention are the concern of HR and company leadership.

Recruiting costs are a component of cost-per-hire measurements, which employers strive to control by considering how they attract applicants and which applicants the company is most eager to attract. Social media and networking are popular and typically low-cost methods for recruiting candidates. However, recruiters must sift through hundreds, sometimes thousands of online applications to determine which applicants have the requisite skills for the job. Reducing the cost to attract applicants, yet finding a source that produces well-qualified applicants, is a constant challenge for HR (Everything at Work, 2020).

It is no secret that communication is necessary for employers to achieve recruiting and retention goals. However, communication between HR and line managers is critical for talent acquisition and talent management. Talent acquisition and talent management refer to the life cycle of recruiting qualified applicants, selecting candidates deemed suitable in terms of qualifications and company culture, and sustaining an engaged workforce. HR -- and, particularly, recruiters -- need a constant and open communication path with hiring managers throughout the recruitment process as well as throughout the employee's career. Therefore, line managers, supervisors and HR together are responsible for recruiting and retention (Everything at Work, 2020).

An employer of choice is the company people want to work for -- these companies are the ones that make the "Best of Employers" lists year after year because they treat their employees well. Employers of choice have low turnover, coveted positions, excellent benefits and a sound business reputation based on the company's success and how they treat their customers. Consequently, employers of choice usually receive an overwhelming response to their recruitment advertisements. Becoming an employer of choice also is a recruiting and retention issue; however, it's an issue that every department in the company works to achieve (Conway, 2020).

Retaining employees doesn't mean hiring an employee who is going to stay in the same position until he or she retires. Employees need challenges to keep them motivated. Provided the employer offers work that continually challenges employees' skills and aptitude, retention should not be difficult. Encouraging employees to aspire to roles with more responsibility instead of looking for advancement opportunities outside the company is a retention strategy that Watson Wyatt consultant

Brian Wilkerson recommends in a November 30, 2007 article titled, Tech Company Stems Departures by Listening to Employees' Needs, in "The Wall Street Journal." Opportunities for professional development, succession planning and training that gives employees options for taking on additional responsibilities or cross-functional assignments can improve retention and minimize turnover. Employers should focus on retaining high-performing employees and not simply retaining employees -- regardless of how they are performing -- to say the company's turnover is low (Mayhew, 2020).

Employee Interface

Employee self-service, or ESS, is an available feature with most modern HRIS. ESS allows employees to take care of many different human resources-related and job-related tasks that would otherwise need to be completed by human resources personnel or management. Employee self-service can help many companies save labor hours and increase efficiency. ESS is a self-service portal is a part of the software that all your employees have access to, not just HR professionals. Employees can access their payroll, schedules and benefits information, make updates to their own details, and more. But why is this an important part of your HRIS? Evolving organizational cultures require that HR systems evolve, too. It has taken a long time for HR systems to evolve from the piecemeal manual process that was used for decades. With the introduction of self-service HRIS, the landscape of HR is now making fast strides toward a more logical and efficient system. Most employee self-service systems allow employees to change personal information such as an address, contact information, and banking information – though approval may be needed. Some ESS systems also allow employees to view scheduling and payroll information. Even the most rudimentary self-service systems generally allow employees to submit time-off requests and allow managers to approve these requests (Scroggin, 2020).

If there are any issues that employees are not authorized to directly change using ESS, some HRIS allow employees to correspond electronically with the human resources department. This allows employees to send messages outside of regular office hours, which saves time and hassle for both employees and human resources professionals. Many organizations find benefits in using ESS to allow employees to make changes for the benefit of information during open enrollment or when life changes have occurred. Many employees prefer this method, as it allows them to control their own information. This method also allows more time for researching different benefit options without the time pressures that may be present when working with human resource professionals (Appointment Plus Blog, 2015).

Human resources professionals, managers, and employers typically enjoy open enrollment self-service options. Labor time is saved for all parties and the disruption that open enrollment presents to many companies is avoided. Depending on the HRIS and the insurance company, the process of applying may also be simpler and the information provided may be more thorough due to the interactive format. Virtually any organization can benefit from employee self-service. Small and medium public and nonprofit sector organizations may also benefit from ESS. Before investing in the software to enable self-service options, however, all organizations should weigh the pros and cons and conduct both internal and external research. Self-service HRIS can transform the HR system of an organization, but it is necessary for human resources managers and the managers of other departments to work together to make employee utilization as common and widespread as possible. Employees should be trained to use the system as part of the standard job training process. Managers should ensure that employees feel as comfortable using the self-service HRIS as performing any other aspect of the job prior to the completion of training. When ESS has been successfully implemented, an organization may see immediate increases in productivity and efficiency. Managers and human resources personnel may save labor hours and frustration daily when not faced with working through scheduling issues, time-off requests, and open enrollment questions. Employees may be able to access scheduling and other information from home, which saves employees time and can boost feelings of empowerment (County of Sonoma, 2020).

Additionally, entry errors and other mistakes may be avoided by allowing employees to enter their own information. If recruiting and onboarding are available through the HRIS and directly tie into the self-service portal, entry errors can be prevented as early as the application phase. By eliminating the need for double entry and allowing employees to evaluate their own information, the chances of inaccurate information may be greatly decreased. Employees are no longer content to have a "middleman" that speaks for them. As companies grow, however, it can be difficult for each voice to be heard. Self-service HRIS is now making it easier for employees to be heard directly by the relevant departments, helping public organizations to meet employee expectations Once upon a time, all HR data had to be entered into the system by an individual that was trained specifically to do so. Payroll data entry was often completed by another department or possibly a third party and other revenue information was the responsibility of yet another department or entity. Self-service HRIS is helping to streamline all these processes by linking these systems together and making the information accessible by those who need it (BambooHR, 2020).

Another benefit of a self-service portal is that it is typically cloud-based. Employees can access the portal from anywhere, whether that is from home, on a mobile device, or in another office building. No one must wait until they're next in the main office to log into the self-service portal. In addition, your employees can access their information at any time. They do not have to wait for work hours or for a member of your HR staff to be available. Employees can get their questions answered or update their information as soon as they need to. Along with making data entry and transfer faster and more efficient, self-service HRIS is also helping to eliminate errors. Human error has always been a major factor when information is entered manually. Self-service HRIS virtually eliminates errors in data transfer and makes it much easier for human resources managers to spot errors in employee or applicant information that has been recently added. The functionality of human resources departments can be greatly improved with the addition of a self-service

HRIS. HR managers can completely focus on issues that require a human touch. HR managers' time is no longer taken up with data entry or researching simple inquiries for employees. A significant advantage of making some HR processes self-service is that it reduces the workload of your HR staff. HR departments are notoriously busy, so anything that employees can do for themselves can save labor hours. Self-service portals allow employees to view their own schedules, check payroll, clock in and out, adjust timesheets, update benefits, change their personal information, and more (ServiceNow, 2020).

Without an HRIS, all of this would require employees to ask the HR staff to assist them. These are day-to-day tasks that would quickly consume a lot of HR time, especially in organizations with many employees. Self-service HRIS allows employees to access and make changes to their own personal information. Some of the information that employees can access or make changes to on self-service HRIS from any computer with Internet includes:

- Sick leave hours
- Vacation hours
- Pay rate information
- Performance appraisals
- Information about HR inquiries or reports
- Requests for paid leave
- Address and personal information changes

Having direct access to and more control over their information improves employee satisfaction and engagement. They can also see information about opportunities for training and advancement, which will give them more control over their own careers. More engaged employees tend to be more loyal to their company as well as more productive. Many may seek out opportunities to improve themselves and their skills, making them more valuable employees and helping to reduce employee turnover. With the ease of data entry and the improved efficiency of HR functions, data has become easier to audit. This has improved data integrity, ensuring greater compliance with both organizational policies and laws. The biggest drawback to investing in ESS options is the required amount of time taken to ensure that each employee understands how to use the system. The rollout process can cost an organization huge amounts of time and money, thereby taking these resources away from regular operations. ESS must also be used frequently by employees for an organization to see a benefit from adopting the system (Pribanic, 2018).

Communication gaps can occur if employees do not completely understand how to use ESS options. In addition, some employees may attempt to use the new system while others use older systems and manual processes as workarounds, which result in even more hindrances to processes. If a company decides to utilize self-service options for common HR tasks, it is important to make sure that all personnel is on the same page and is ready for the transition before moving forward. Self-service portals also have access to a cloud-based database of all HR-related documents. These can include training materials, HR policies, and more. Employees can access these from anywhere at any time whenever they need them. If an employee is out of the office but needs more information about company travel policies and reimbursement, they can access that without involving HR. The available benefits options can also be included in the database so that employees can examine different benefits plans long before open enrollment occurs. Before purchasing and implementing ESS, employers should find out how frequently employees anticipate using the system. While there may be a certain amount of reluctance to conform to new systems in any workplace, certain factors may hinder employees' ability to use the system. Doing internal research may also help an organization to determine which HRIS would be best. If most employees do not have Internet access at home, purchasing an HRIS that has an emphasis on mobile access can be a waste. It may be possible to purchase kiosks so employees can access the system in-house. Nevertheless, this will dramatically change the expectations for the system and the way that it must be rolled out. If the organization is not in the technical field and most employees do not identify as tech-savvy, ESS may not be right for the company (Workday, 2020).

Organizations should conduct external research to compare HRIS pricing for budget purposes and to figure out the intricacies of implementing an ESS system from several different vendors. Organizations may also benefit from doing research to find out how ESS implementation has affected similar public or nonprofit sector organizations with similar operations. Self-service portals can increase employee autonomy, making employees feel empowered and saving managers and HR professionals' time. Self-service options may take time to set up, but the time spent can be worth it if it helps to improve engagement with the system and streamline the way your team communicates. Some HRIS software allows you to set up onboarding through self-service portals. Introducing self-service at this early stage will make it a part of life for new employees, especially if they must use the software for more tasks immediately after onboarding. Allowing employees to acclimate themselves to the company using this option encourages them to take charge of their own career within your company and helps foster user adoption. Self-service portals should be rich with options. Some offerings within self-service portals include schedules, time off requests, pay history, social feeds, peer-to-peer messaging, organizational information libraries, benefits, and personal information change requests. By offering as many of these options as possible, you increase the value of self-service for your employees and encourage them to be even more autonomous (Lucerna, 2020a, b).

Social media can be fun to use, so employees may be drawn to this option if you offer it. Using organizational social feeds can help bring your team together and make it easier to communicate organization wide news instantly. It may also encourage brainstorming and collaboration. If it makes sense for your organization, you may wish to assign job tasks within self-service portals. This is an easy way for you to keep track of employees' accomplishments while allowing them to view and update their own progress. Simply delegating and holding employees accountable may not be reasonable, however, make sure it is possible for two-way communication so that employees feel free to ask questions and request assistance. When HRIS self-service is brought up, it is usually thought of as an option that is available to employees. Employee self-service generally gets all the attention because it takes time to ease the workforce into adoption and can make some groundbreaking changes. Whenever a policy change occurs, it can be difficult to alert all employees using manual methods. Handouts are generally more likely to be thrown away than read. With self-service, sharing policy changes – or even simply highlighting existing policies that are relevant to recent occurrences – is as simple as cutting and pasting text into a message and sharing via the HRIS. Frequent feedback is a rising star in the HR world, with many publications extolling the virtues of weekly, monthly, or even more frequent feedback (increased productivity, improved employee satisfaction, etc.). Messaging options available through HRIS can make it easy for managers to interact with employees in an instant when there is feedback to provide (Pedroncelli, 2020).

Posting schedules on public forums that are available to all managers and employees or in self-service portals can save managers time while allowing employees to see schedules instantly and re-check as needed. Being able to make schedules available online can reduce errors, no-call-no-shows, and overall absences. If online scheduling is available through manager self-service, this option can add to HRIS value. Time-off requests may seem to be easy to handle from an outside perspective but can become rather troublesome at times. Hand-written time-off requests may become lost or may be tough to read. Scheduling in time-off requests and figuring out employee PTO balances adds extra complexity. Manager self-service may make time-off requests much easier to handle by keeping the requests electronic and organized in one place. If scheduling software is integrated with self-service, time off requests can be checked for feasibility in an instant and denied, approved, or passed on to other departments for approval. The status of the request can be communicated to the employee every step of the way. HR matters like training, employee compensation, and turnover concerns affect the way that employees work for managers, so being able to find out information about these issues through self-service can help managers to better control the workforce. Having the ability to pass workflows (like merit increase requests) along to HR using the HRIS can also relieve bottlenecks and save time. To facilitate adoption and encourage managers to take advantage of the opportunities that self-service options offer, it is important to drum up enthusiasm and carefully manage the change. Taking the same care with promoting manager self-service options as with employee self-service options can help your company to get the most from your HRIS. When time-off requests are submitted manually and employees must retrieve their schedules from a piece of paper that is in the workplace, the potential for errors and conflicts is high. Employees may write their schedules down wrong or fail to see changes made after the schedule is released. Time-off requests may also be missed or improperly communicated, leading to dissent (Lucerna, 2020a, b).

Introducing self-service options that allow employees to see their schedules and request time off may help to streamline processes and reduce scheduling issues. This may be as beneficial to management and employers as it is to employees. When employees can easily retrieve their schedules from any mobile device, it can help to increase accountability and reduce the potential for errors. Employees cannot say that the schedule has been changed or that they wrote down the wrong days or times. Employees are both accountable for their own schedules and empowered to retrieve the information at will. Time off processes can be messy when they are handled using paper and scheduling books. Requests may be lost, managers or HR professionals may forget to put requests in, and approvals or denials for requests may not be communicated in a timely manner. Using self-service for time off requests allows employees and managers to interact over a request in seconds from any location and severely decreases the likelihood that the request will be overlooked. When schedules are released using the manual method, employees often swarm to the schedule board or book. This can distract employees from their work, decreasing productivity. Releasing schedules using the HRIS self-service allows employees to access their schedules on their own time, reducing the disturbance during work hours. There are likely to be changes to the schedule sometimes when employees call out or when unforeseen emergencies happen. If the HRIS self-service portal allows instant messaging, this option can help to speed communication up when these events occur. After effective communications, managers can also alter the schedule in the system immediately to reduce confusion and ensure that all shifts are covered adequately. Depending on the type of workplace, it may be possible to use self-service portals for attendance and absence tracking. This may be particularly helpful if some or all the employees work from remote locations. Allowing employees to "clock in," track hours, and report absences using a self-service portal can make payroll and compliance reporting easier and can further empower employees. If necessary, information entered through self-service portals may also be saved and used to assess and back up rewards, performance reviews, and discipline. Having the scheduling and attendance information all in one place can make it easy to identify a pattern of absences or pinpoint which employees are providing the best customer service or performing the best. Using HRIS self-service for schedule distribution, communication, and tracking can improve the scheduling process in many ways (Lucerna, 2020a, b).

When the Bough Breaks: Case Study

A public organization has been requested by the media to report all public official salaries for a given year. This usually would not be an issue for the public organization except that the organization is going through a HRIS migration and is in between information systems. In addition, the former payroll director has resigned from the organization and taken a job at another public higher education institution. The former payroll director was the only one who knew how to code the organization's personnel into the HRIS application to obtain the correct results for personnel who were on less than 12-month contracts.

The person tasked with compiling the report asked Human Resources personnel to verify the top salaries on their list and were told the salaries are correct. Unbeknownst to the person submitting the requested data to the media, the new HRIS database had switched some personnel from 9-month contracts to 12-month contracts internally to ensure their benefits would be active throughout the year. In addition, some of those personnel who were on nine-month contracts elected to take payouts over a 12-month period. To make this salary payout accommodation work, the new payroll director changed those contracts from 9-month to 12-month contracts and adjusted the salaries to reflect a 12-month payout. Thus, the information reported to the media made it appear that several employees had larger salaries, some by approximately 30 percent.

The issue came to light when several employees contacted the top administrator of the public organization to state that the media has over reported their salary by a large margin. The person who compiled the report was initially reprimanded by their supervisor who incorrectly assumed the person submitting the report did not follow procedure. The employee was then ordered to find out what the issue was and to fix the damage. The person analysed the data and had discovered through previous file extracts that the length of contract and salary amounts had been changed for those on nine-month contracts. Unfortunately, the report had to be manually corrected and resubmitted to the media for correction.

This case study illustrates the danger of knowledge transfer failure when personnel resign, assumptions that information compiled from the HRIS is correct, and the lack of an audit process to catch reporting errors if the root data source is incorrect. In this organization, the personnel in Human Resources were not held accountable for changing information in the source system that should not have been modified. The human resource personnel were looking for shortcuts to circumvent the processes in the HRIS when they lacked the institutional knowledge to properly input benefits and payroll data. This case study demonstrates how important HRIS is to the credibility of an organization. The media reported what the organization reported to them, and the organization lost credibility with not only the public, but also the employees within their own organization.

Case Study: "How Much Money is This Going to Take?"

A public organization is attempting to determine how much salary rates are increasing even when there is a mandate to not give raises throughout the organization. This also becomes an increasing problem on trying to determine how much of the organization's revenue will need to be used to cover increases in salary. To resolve this issue, the idea of performing a payroll forecasting model is used to predict how much the salary increases are going to be, if everything remains constant, to determine the fiscal health of the organization.

The office in charge of performing statistical analysis and reporting for the organization is then tasked with developing a statistical model to predict the payroll needs for the organization and determine why payroll is going up at all when there is a mandate to freeze all raises throughout the organization. The employee given the assignment uses SAS to do a forecast on the payroll increases over the last 5 years and their model is proven to be 99.8% accurate the following year, thus providing the organization a useful tool in predicting payroll for the upcoming year.

When performing the research using HR payroll data for monthly salaries for each employee, the employee discovers that raises are not given throughout the organization, but promotions are being given that also includes a fairly hefty salary increase with those promotions. With the freezing of regular salary increases, the thought with the upper administration was that the cost increases would be kept in check. However, with the policy implementation, upper level administrators and mid-level managers were giving promotions to employees to "get around" the new rules that actually caused a larger increase than usual due to the policy of a pay increase minimum with a promotion. Once these issues were discovered using HRIS data, the upper level administrators were then in a position to determine another method to keep costs down by tightening down the loop hole for promotions.

Summary

It is critical to understand how HRIS functions within an organization as well as how HRIS should be utilized by an organization to fulfill the functional areas need of operations. It is also important to understand that often times Organizational Drift occurs of what the ideal situation states should be the case versus the reality of the situation creating a gap of capabilities. The gap created can cause a number of functions to either not be performed or a secondary system can potentially be developed or bought to address a need that is in actually already in reality capable of being performed by the existing HRIS.

The complexity of legal statutes, benefits and employment have evolved over the years and with it HRIS's capabilities and functionalities. With this increase in capabilities and functionalities, it has required more skill level and understanding with human resources functions in relation to the information systems designed to house the data and report the data. With the advent of more automation, the need to understand how the data is stored and retrieved for either end users or compliance/operational reporting is critical. As will be seen in following chapters, it is imperative for Human Resources staff to have a technical background of the HRIS they work with in order to make the organization they work for efficient and effective in regard to staffing. Recruitment in the aspect of applications and self-reporting modules for employees, have changed much of the duties and responsibilities of the traditional Human Resources professional. Instead of interacting with potential employees or employees, the human resources professional is now required to assess data for reporting and analytical predications instead of performing duties as a data entry clerk. In theory, the new HRIS applications should free up time for Human Resources employees to interface more with employees and provide data analysis to upper administration on hiring decisions. Thus, culturally, no how capable or functional an HRIS may be, the Human Resources personnel will have to be just as capable as the systems they interact with to realize this outcome. The next chapter will discuss how the roles in theory should work and utilize HRIS.

References

Appointment Plus Blog. (2015, November 15). *What's in it for you: The benefits of self service technology*. Retireved November 21, 2020, What's in it for you: The benefits of self-service technology l AppointmentPlus BambooHR HR Software l People Data & Analytics l Hiring l Onboarding l Compensation l Culture l BambooHR Software.

BambooHR. (2020). *Automated operations*. Retrieved November 21, 2020. HR Software l People Data & Analytics l Hiring l Onboarding l Compensation lCulture l BambooHR Software.

Conway, B. (2020). *Employer of choice: How to be an employment hero, employee connect*. Retrieved November 21, 2020. Employer of Choice: How to be an Employment Hero - EmployeeConnect HRIS.

County of Sonoma. (2020). *Employee self service*. Retrieved November 21, 2020. HRIS Employee Self Service l Human Resources l County of Sonoma (ca.gov).

Davey, M., & Walsh, M. W. (2013, July 18). Billions in Debt, Detroit Tumbles Into Insolvency - The New York Times (nytimes.com)

Everything at Work. (2020). *Payroll HRIS benefit – Employee retention*. Retrieved November 21, 2020, Payroll HRIS Benefit - Employee Retention - Everything at Work Payroll HR Management System.

Graham, L. (2015). Detroit bankruptcy lesson: Underfunded pension funds could trip other municipalities. *Michigan Radio*. Retrieved from: https://www.michiganradio.org/post/detroit-bankruptcy-lesson-underfunded-pension-funds-could-trip-other-municipalities

Lucerna. (2020a). *What is employee service*. Retrieved November 21, 2020. What is Employee Self-Service? – HR Payroll Systems.

Lucerna. (2020b). *Benefits of implementing employee scheduling software*. Retireved November 21, 2020, Benefits of Implementing Employee Scheduling Software (hrpayrollsystems.net).

Mayhew, R., Chron, 2020, *HR issues: Recruiting and retnetion*. Retrieved November 21, 2020. https://work.chron.com/hr-issues-recruiting-retention-11623.html

McCormack, J. (2004, March 1). HR technology: Compliance tools. *SHRM*. Retrieved on January 6, 2021. https://www.shrm.org/hr-today/news/hr-magazine/pages/0304mccormack.aspx

NCES. (2021). *IPEDS*. Retrieved on January 6, 2021. https://nces.ed.gov/ipeds/

Pedroncelli, P. (2020). *Jobcast, The importance of social media for HR*. Retireved November 21, 2020. The Importance Of Social Media For HR l Jobcast Social Recruitment App.

Pribanic, E. (2018, February 21). HR management systems: Benefits of HRIS you can't ignore. *Tech Funnel*. Retrieved November 21, 2020. HR Management Systems: Benefits of HRIS You Can't Ignore (techfunnel.com).

Pynes, J. E. (2009). *Human resources management for public and non-profit organizations*. ISBN: 978-0-470-33185-9. Wiley. www.untag-smd.ac.id/files/Perpustakaan_Digital_2/PERSONNEL MANAGEMENTHumanresourcesmanagementforpublicandnonprofitorganizations.pdf

Scroggin, C. (2020). *CompareHRIS. 2020, HRMS system and yayroll interfaces defined*. Retireved November 21, 2020. Payroll HRMS System Interfaces (comparehris.com).

ServiceNow. (2020). *Transform how you provide employee service*. Retrieved November 21, 2020, New Message! (servicenow.com).

State of West Virginia. (2021). *WVOASIS*. Retrieved on January 6, 2021. https://www.wvoasis.gov/

THECB. (2021). *CBM reporting manuals*. Retrieved on January 6, 2021. http://www.txhighered-data.org/index.cfm?objectId=96F8EE70-D880-11E8-BB650050560100A9

Workday. (2020). *Human resource management for the changing world of work*. Retrieved November 21, 2020. Global HR Management System l Workday.

6 Public and Non-Profit Organizations Versus Private Industry Needs

Key Points of the Chapter

- Public and non-profit organizations have more requirements for government compliance than does private industry.
- Civil Service is unique to public organizations
- Benefits plans can be extremely complex in public organizations.

HRIS systems need to be flexible and adaptable to allow human resources professionals to enable public, non-profit human resources, and private sector organizations to manage various personnel records to fully serve their organizations. The range of needs for public and non-profit organizations include Civil Service, Compliance Reporting, Pension Plans, Benefits and Types of Employees.

Human resource information systems help organizations use an integrated set of human resources modules to automate the multi-faceted complexities of human resources processes. HRIS has gained a considerable amount of traction with organizations of all sizes for their centralized approach to managing human resource management needs whether it is in private, public, or nonprofit sector. It collects, stores, manages, and interprets employee-related data from various operating units to eliminate data duplication and provide a single source of truth. An HRIS is an ideal solution for private, nonprofit, and public organizations when dealing with automation, streamlining, and optimization of human resource processes.

Yet, with an array of HRIS options available that can be tailored with various features, selecting the right HRIS to suit the needs of private, public, or nonprofit organizations can be a challenge. Here is a list of must-have core functionalities that all private, public, and nonprofits organizations can look for in a potential HRIS software solution to deal with civil service, compliance reporting, pension plans, benefits, and the various types of employees that organizations hire. (Heathfield, 2019).

N. A. Valcik et al., *Human Resources Information Systems*, Management for Professionals, https://doi.org/10.1007/978-3-030-75111-1_6

Centralized Storage

With an automated database that collects, stores, and displays up-to-date, consistent information about the personnel, policies, and procedures in an organization, human resource leaders from all types of organizations can finally dispense with spreadsheets and paper files. A centralized database that is seamlessly integrated with other human resource modules will ensure accessibility to all end-users regardless of what sector the organizations operates in to accomplish its mission. Storing confidential employee information in a centralized cloud-based HRIS Software is essential for organizations in all three sectors and will eliminate redundancy and promote data integrity. Any updates or changes made to the master database will reflect immediately across all modules, saving a considerable amount of time and effort the human resources department puts into matching and duplicating all records manually. While small organizations can operate without this feature, it can improve their operational efficiency and set them on the right path towards success. (ZingHR, 2020).

Recruitment Management

Attracting, hiring, and retaining employees is essential regardless of what sector the organization operates. Obtaining the right talent quickly and efficiently is the cornerstone of an organization's success. Successful recruitment relies solely on building long-term relationships with potential and current employees. The ideal applicant tracking system can not only streamline traditional recruitment functions but also simplify talent relationship management. An automated recruitment process integrates seamlessly with the inbuilt reporting module to analyze trends and patterns in recruitment. It also seamlessly integrates with job-portals, internal websites, and employment-service providers to make hiring chaos-free. Organizations that are looking for ways to reduce their recruitment costs and accelerate their recruitment efforts can streamline their recruitment process and align it better with their overall public, private and nonprofit strategy using the right applicant tracking system. (ZingHR, 2020).

Employee Onboarding

A user-friendly employee onboarding process will set up new hires for immediate success and ensure that they start off on the right foot. With an automated onboarding process employer such as private, public, and nonprofits can:

- Minimize the chaos made by paperwork
- Shorten the employee onboarding lifecycle
- Reduce manual interventions and human errors
- Offer a consistent experience to all new hires
- Facilitate a transparent onboarding process

What is more, with an automated onboarding process, human resources managers do not have to chase after new hires and managers to complete the onboarding documentation. The system will send automatic notifications to the people who cause a delay in the workflow and ensure that it keeps flowing as smoothly as possible. Regardless of whether they are startups or well established, organizations that are having trouble with their onboarding checklists and forms can eliminate manual dependency in their onboarding process with automation. (b; Lucerna, 2020a).

Talent Management

Employees are the most valuable resources in any organization. However, the process of talent management, such as attracting, recruiting, engaging, developing, and retaining employees, is a complicated process. Employee turnover can be expensive. An HRIS with an exclusive talent management system will help any type of organization take better care of their employees. An ideal talent management module will help employees get through every phase of their employment, from recruitment through training, development, and retention. Best of all, it will allow employers to get a single view of their talent profile across the organization and align their talent management efforts with overarching organization objectives. Organizations that have difficulty spotting talent gaps and predicting performance shortfalls could benefit from the use of a robust talent management module to refine their talent management strategies, improve decision making, and plan ahead for future talent needs. (Kopolus, 2016).

Performance Management

Performance management modules are tasked with monitoring the performance of employees consistently and measurably. It allows the organization to ensure that employees and departments across the organization are working effectively towards achieving the strategic goals. Successful entities gain an advantage from having employees better aligned with organizational goals. It enables line managers and human resource teams to spend less time on the manual administration of performance appraisals and instead focus on more value-adding parts of the process, such as coaching, supporting, and training employees. However, a performance management module will not only standardize employee performance review but also align team and individual goals with organizational goals. Organizations can make their appraisal process bias-free, tie employee performance with compensation, and establish a performance-oriented compensation system. Organizations that use online forms and paperwork to manage their performance management process and enterprises that use standalone systems for appraisals need to find an HRIS that comes with a robust performance management module. (b; Lucerna, 2020a).

Public, private, and nonprofit organizations can find it difficult to keep their employee-related data updated. Employee Self-Service (ESS) is an effective way to manage this problem. Giving employees access to view and manage their personal information (profile, time off, benefits, or payroll) can reduce the time HR staff spend on mundane clerical tasks. Employees do not have to engage in a mail chase to retrieve their leave balance or pay slips. With a self-service portal, every human resource process from employee onboarding to reporting will become more efficient. If the HRIS has multi-channel accessibility, employees can view, edit, and retrieve all work-related information right from their mobile phones. Organizations of all kinds that are outgrowing their startup size processes and are thinking about expanding the human resources team to combat the increasing workload can rely on HRIS tools that come with a self-service portal to reduce the workload of human resource processes and empower their employees to manage their own profile. Public, private, and nonprofit organizations need their employees to be engaged in the management of their personal information. (van Vulpen, 2020).

Time and Absence Management

Managing employee timesheets, schedules, and tracking attendance manually involves an immense amount of human resources labor. Keeping up with leave request emails and tracking employee absence while sketching out a schedule to manage the changing workload is a huge ordeal. On top of that, exporting all attendance data to the payroll system is time-consuming and tedious. An HRIS will solve the problems associated with leave and time management with a comprehensive set of features such as:

- Auto-capture and submit timesheet entries
- Workforce scheduling
- Leave management
- Drill-down and drill-through analytics
- Integrations with payroll, accounting, etc.

If not handled properly, timesheets and vacation requests have the potential to create conflict. Mishandled time-off requests can leave a bad impression on the quality of life in the organization and reduce employee satisfaction. Streamlining the timesheet management and time-off process with an HRIS can control the manual errors and prevent possible disasters. Organizations where employees still rely on human resource managers to manage attendance reports and create authorizations for leave and time-off need to invest in an HRIS that comes with a self-service enabled, time management module. (Basic, 2020).

Training Management

A training management module will enable organizations to offer blended training experience to their staff to improve engagement, job satisfaction, and retention. It enables organizations to identify employee skills gaps to structure, tailor, and deliver training programs that are in sync with individual training needs. Organizations in all sectors of the economy can use the training management module to assess, track, and measure the impact of employee training programs to ensure effectiveness. It accelerates employee performance, decreases performance gaps, and stimulates employee collaboration to create a high-performing workforce that is engaged and motivated to deliver their best efforts. Companies, public and nonprofit entities that are looking for ways to deliver convenient and easy to use training can use these modules to improve employee performance and increase the return on investment of their training programs. (Juneja, 2020).

Workforce Analytics

Visual-rich reporting modules provide real-time insights into an organization's workforce. Businesses and public entities can use their existing employee data to identify employee trends, retrieve actionable insights, and make informed decisions to get more out of their human capital. It can help businesses and public entities do everything from predicting future talent needs to performing human cost accounting analysis. An HRIS tool that comes with pre-defined reports can help organizations create a collaborative environment that thrives on action and make a seamless connection between insights, activities, and results. Businesses and public entities that are looking to drive strategic human resources initiatives for skill set management, career development, and succession planning need a visualization tool to ensure sustainable performance. (Zeepedia, 2020) Choosing the right HRIS system that is flexible enough to deal with the varying needs of private, public, and nonprofit sector organizations is vital to having a system nimble to deal with the multifaceted needs of these organizations. (Arun, 2020).

Civil Service

While the HRIS system will not encounter civil service issues in private and nonprofit organizations, it will certainly have to do so in public organizations in all levels of government. It can be assumed that public-sector employees may enjoy more employee rights than their private counterparts. Public-sector employees are hired by government agencies typically on a permanent basis and the constitutional law automatically grants them their rights. This is not necessarily the case with private or nonprofit employees. Private sector employees are hired to boost the profits of private businesses, unlike public-sector employees who discharge official functions and render public service. The only thing that can curb exploitation is union activity and speech, because these employees hold positions of trust in the society. There are some rights and restrictions on both private sector and public-sector employees.

Private sector employees can be terminated for any reason except for their race and/or gender, for their rights under workers' compensation or for testifying in court. On the other hand, a public-sector employer requires a cause for disciplining, demoting, or firing an employee, which may include poor performance, misconduct, dishonesty and/or violation of work rules. Even for this, the employer is required to give a show cause notice to the employee to enable him or her to respond to the charges leveled against them.

- **Freedom of Speech - P**ublic-sector employees are protected under the First Amendment of the United States Constitution for openly airing their views under freedom of speech. However, their views should not hamper the government's ability to function. In contrast, private sector employees are under no such government protection and can be demoted or terminated if they express their views not in agreement with the policies of the organization they work for.
- **Creating or Joining Unions - P**rivate sector employees are at liberty to create or join unions under the federal law. This is to enable such employees to redress any grievance they have against employers about wage or working conditions. This also give them the right to go on a strike if their grievance is not addressed or demands not met.

Private sector employers are restrained from disciplining or cutting wages or firing employees for these acts, for joining the union, or for collective bargaining. Although public-sector employees enjoy no such right, many states have permitted them to join unions, under the provisions of the federal or state law. (**Acharyya,** 2017)

- **Submitting to Interrogation or Investigation -** The Federal Court of Appeals for the Second Circuit in its recent decision held that the services of a private sector employee can be terminated in case he or she refuses to be interviewed by the employer conducting an internal investigation. However, a private sector employee can use a union representative during his or her investigation by the employer.

The public-sector employees' rights are protected under the Fifth Amendment from self-recrimination. This means that a public-sector employee cannot be compelled by the employer to say anything that can be used against him or her in criminal prosecutions. A case in point is Garrity vs. New Jersey case in the United States Supreme Court that upheld the retention of a police officer who refused to speak with the investigators in a case where his deposition was important. The difference between the rights of public-sector employees and private sector employees is based on the nature of government and private sector jobs. While a government job is protected by the constitution, a private sector job is not, but it enjoys some rights that public-sector employees do not. Your HRIS system must be able to track and distinguish between private sector and civil service employees. In addition, it must distinguish between civil service and non-civil service employees within public organizations. (Raines, 2019).

Compliance Reporting

From recruiting to retirement, HRIS Systems handle a variety of compliance issues related to employees. It is important to stay abreast of action at the federal level, state, and local levels. Keep in mind, however, that these laws set the floor beneath which you cannot go. State and local governments have been very active as well and employers also need to know about any requirements that go above and beyond federal law whether you are a government, nonprofit or a private organization. Federal anti-discrimination laws prohibit employment discrimination based on race, color, sex, ethnic origin, disability or age, as well as because of genetic information or veteran status. In general, these laws prohibit employers from taking adverse employment actions based on these factors.

In all facets of human resource management, organizations must have excellent information on each employee to ensure that no discriminatory acts are being committed or allowed by the organization. For example, every time there is a downsizing, the organization must make sure the layoffs do not have a negative impact on any segment of the workforce. Title VII of the Civil Rights Act of 1964 (Title VII) outlaws discrimination based on race, color, sex, or ethnic origin and applies to organizations with fifteen or more employees. Sexual harassment, so prevalent in the news, is prohibited by Title VII because it is a form of sex discrimination.

The Americans with Disabilities Act (ADA) prohibits discrimination against individuals with disabilities and limits the questions employers can ask workers. It also protects those who have a record of a disability, are regarded as having a disability or are associated with an individual with a disability. The ADA, which applies to employers with fifteen or more employees, also requires companies to provide covered individuals with reasonable accommodations. The Age Discrimination in Employment Act (ADEA) protects workers who are 40 years or older from discrimination based on age. To guard against this type of discrimination, employers should avoid making assumptions about what an employee can or cannot do based on age.

Title II of the Genetic Information Nondiscrimination Act (GINA) guards against employment discrimination based on genetic information. GINA restricts employers from asking, requiring, or using genetic information to make employment decisions. The Uniformed Services Employment and Reemployment Rights Act (USERRA), which is enforced by the U.S. Department of Labor (DOL), prohibits discrimination based on military service and provides job protection while individuals are serving, under certain circumstances. Human Resources Management professionals will use their HRIS systems to keep abreast of the lasts changes to employee compliance requirements to keep their organizations safe and free of legal challenges.

Wage and Hour Statutes

Wage and hour laws include requirements for minimum wage, overtime, hours worked, child labor, and meal and break time requirements can all be monitored with integrated HRIS systems as well. The Fair Labor Standards Act (FLSA) is a federal law that establishes minimum wage and overtime requirements, but many states have adopted stringent requirements, the federal minimum wage is something organizations must stay alert to any changes in this level of compensation. However, most states have their own minimum wage and increases to those rates can take place throughout the year. You need to make sure you are paying the correct rate for each of the states in which you operate. It is also recommended that employers note any other applicable rates, such as tip credit maximums for the hospitality industry. HRIS systems also should note related state and local wage and hour laws. Individual jurisdictions are increasingly adopting salary history bans, predictable scheduling laws, and more.

Family and Medical Leave

Many local jurisdictions are requiring businesses within their boundaries to provide sick leave to private sector employees. The Family and Medical Leave Act (FMLA) is a federal law that allows workers who have met certain requirements take 12 weeks of unpaid leave each year without losing their jobs. This leave is granted for the birth and care of an employee's newborn, bonding time with an adoptive child or with a child from foster care, to provide care of an immediate family member or for the employee's own serious health condition. While few federal changes are anticipated, the trend in employment is to expand the amount of time allowed for leave, and making the leave paid instead of unpaid. Several states currently offering paid leave. It will eventually require some income replacement for all 12 weeks covered by the FMLA (phased in over 4 years) and will pay for a greater percentage of the employee's salary in comparison to the other states' plans. (b; Lucerna, 2020a).

Immigration Statutes

Immigration laws, including the Immigration and Nationality Act (INA), the Immigration Reform and Control Act of 1986 (IRCA), the Immigration Act of 1990 and the Illegal Immigration Reform and Immigrant Responsibility Act of 1996 (IIRIRA), serve, among other things, to ensure that employers only hire candidates who are eligible to work in the U.S. Eligible candidates include citizens, noncitizen nationals, lawful permanent residents, and aliens authorized to work. Employers must verify candidate eligibility through documentation while also ensuring they do not run afoul of anti-discrimination laws. Immigration has been a hot button issue during the Trump administration. The Trump administration increased workplace visits. Deeper vetting of visa applications, along with an increased focus on hiring

U.S. workers and an expectation that the government will review visa programs were all signs that immigration policies will continue to fluctuate in the future. Human resource leaders and their HRIS systems will need to make sure their I-9 process is up to par and watch for changes to immigration requirements. It is certain that more changes are on the horizon with the impending start of the Biden administration. (Jenns, 2017).

Benefits

Although the Affordable Care Act (ACA, also known as "Obamacare") no longer includes an individual mandate, most of the plan is still in effect. Experts caution that all employers should remember that reporting deadlines are also still in place and should not be ignored or overlooked. Other major employee benefits law, including the Employment Retirement Income Security Act of 1974 (ERISA), the Health Insurance Portability and Accountability Act (HIPAA) and the Consolidated Omnibus Budget Reconciliation Act (COBRA) are not expected to change. (Lucerna, 2020a, b).

Safety Statutes

The Occupational Health and Safety Act (OSH Act) was created to ensure employees had safe working conditions and is administered by the Occupational Health and Safety Administration (OSHA). While several OSHA initiatives remain in limbo in light of the administration change, Human Resources may want keep a careful eye on new recordkeeping and reporting requirements. (Lucerna, 2020a, b).

Union Statutes

It may be tempting to ignore the National Labor Relations Act (NLRA) if your workplace is not unionized, but that would be a mistake. Several employers have faced claims alleging that they interfered with workers' rights to work together to improve their working conditions. Of particular note are claims involving workers taking to social media to air grievances and employer trainings and policies that, for example, prohibit negativity at work. The National Labor Relations Board, which is made up of members appointed by the president, decides labor cases, and because of that, decisions can shift politically especially with the coming Biden administration. "Over the past decade, we've seen dramatic expansion for protections of employees, empowerment of unions," Human Resource leaders would do well to stay tuned as the landscape continues to shift must update their HRIS systems to stay abreast of legal changes. Human Resources leaders are expected to be experts in every area of compliance. "HR professionals are the absolute front line of defense for every governmental unit, nonprofit organization or company to make sure it treats people fairly, legally and keeps the organization out of danger." (BLR, 2020).

Public V. Private Pension Plans

Not all pensions are made the same. Public and private are two types of pensions available to help people to create a nest-egg for their retirement. These major differences may help you discover which retirement fund is helping you plan for your future. Only certain people have access to each of these pension plans. A public pension is available to individuals that work for state and local governments—this includes law enforcement officers and firefighters. These programs are referred to as defined-benefit retirement plans where participants receive a regular monthly or weekly check, which is determined by past wages and tenure.

Managing pension plan contributions for every eligible employee requires extensive tracking. Considering each employee becomes eligible at different times throughout the year. A private pension plan is one offered by employees that work for a company, but not every business offers private pension plans. Those who have a private pension contribute their earnings, which will begin dispersing after retirement. A private pension plan may also be referred to as a defined-contribution concept because the beneficiary must contribute to their own retirement pension. Many people consider public pensions better than private because the benefits are substantially better. According to the Center for Retirement Research at Boston College, benefit plans for public pensions are determined by multiplying an employee's final average salary (usually final three or 5 years) by a factor for each year of service. If an employee retires with an average salary of $50,000, he or she will receive a benefit of $20,000. Private sectors rely on the employee contributing to their own 401(k) plan, although some businesses match contributions up to a certain amount. Boston College determined that an employee that had a private pension would have to accumulate about $260,000 to purchase an annuity that would provide about $20,000 per year for life. An employee that is enrolled in a public pension plan is essentially trusting the government to provide them with funds once they retire. It has become an issue in the past that states can mismanage public employee pensions and some experts have begun to wonder if there should be more federal regulation for state and local pensions. Private pensions are protected by the Employee Retirement Income Security Act (ERISA) of 1974, which is designed to protect private pensions from being mishandled. ERISA was enacted to protect beneficiaries by:

- Requiring the disclosure of financial and other information concerning the plan to beneficiaries
- Establishing standards of conduct for plan fiduciaries
- Providing for appropriate remedies and access to the federal courts

ERISA only protects pension plans in the private sector, but it does not require an employer to create a pension for employees. It only requires that those who establish the plans must meet certain minimum standards. Employees in the private sector are automatically enrolled and covered by Social Security, whereas state and local governments have the option of not choosing Social Security coverage for their employees if a public pension plan already includes them. The reasoning for this is that the public pension plan can be more generous when compared to private plans because it replaces Social Security benefits. (Sanford, 2020).

Types of Employees

There are several classifications of employees and companies can hire one or many types of employees to perform work. The most common employee classifications include:

- Part-time employees
- Full-time employees
- Seasonal employees
- Temporary employees
- Leased employees
- Contingent employees
- Public safety employees
- Military employees

Part-Time Employees

Part-time employees are individuals who work less than 40 hours a week and are typically paid by the hour rather than salaried. These employees are still considered legitimate employees of a company but may not be eligible for benefits. For public organizations, employees are typically in Parks and Recreation departments, physical plant departments as well as libraries.

Full-Time Employees

Full-time employees are those that work an average of 40 hours a week and are eligible for benefits. Because the Fair Labor Standards Act does not provide a definition for part-time or full-time employees, employers are given the liberty to decide how they classify full-time employment within their organizations. Employers with fifty or more full-time employees must offer health care coverage to their full-time employees and their dependents. In public organizations, full-time employees can also be potentially in unions for collective bargaining purposes.

Seasonal Employees

Seasonal employees are those who are hired based on the seasonal needs of a company. For example, a retail company may hire ten seasonal employees to cover the increase in business during peak seasons such as the summer months and holidays. For public organizations, these types of employees will typically be seen in Parks and Recreation departments, which can oscillate during the different months as facility usage increases for specific types of recreation. This type of employee is not eligible for Social Security and unemployment benefits as they are not considered permanent employees.

Temporary Employees

Temporary employees are those that are hired on a temporary basis, often for a set period such as 6 months. They may also be hired to work on a specific project and stop working for the company when the project is complete. Employers can hire temporary employees directly or can go through a staffing agency to find employees that fit their needs. Temporary employees in public organizations are typically in the areas of information technology or even public health departments (e.g. COVID-19).

Leased Employees

A leased employee is an individual who is hired by a staffing agency and then "leased" out to an organization to complete a specific job. Leased employees typically work with the company they are leased to for a year or longer. While still considered an employee, leased workers are on the payroll of the staffing agency and receive any benefits through the employment agency rather than the organization they are working for on a particular project. Typically employees in this category for public organizations can be potentially working on information technology areas.

Contingent Employees

Contingent workers are individuals who are outsourced by a business to perform specific duties on a non-permanent and non-employee basis. They may work remotely or in the office but are not considered an employee of the company. Contingent workers are typically experts in their field and are sourced to complete certain projects based on their skillset. Examples of contingent workers include freelancers, consultants, and independent contractors. These types of workers can also be referred to as consultants.

Contingent workers often perform under a statement of work provision that is agreed upon at the onset of the relationship with a company. Once a project is complete, the worker will no longer work for the company at that time. However, companies may utilize the same contingent workers on recurring projects if the company was satisfied with the worker's performance. For public universities, these types of employees are frequently working on migrations and upgrades to a variety of information technology systems (e.g. PeopleSoft, BANNER etc.).

Contingent workers are different from traditional employees in a few keyways, including:

- Contingent workers do not have access to fringe benefits such as health insurance through the company
- Contingent workers are not salaried
- Contingent workers are required to pay for and file their own taxes with the IRS
- Contingent workers have control over how and when they perform their work

The following are the common types of contingent workers hired by individuals and companies:

- Contract workers
- Independent contractors
- Interns
- Consultants
- Student Workers

Contract Workers

A contract worker is a person who is retained by an organization for a set period to perform a specific task or duty. How much the contract worker will be paid is also pre-determined and may be paid before, during or after the worker has completed their job.

Independent Contractors

An independent contractor is a person or firm sourced by a company to perform work or services. Independent contractors may work on a permanent basis for the company or they may work on a single project or as needed. These workers are responsible for paying their own taxes and are not eligible for benefits through the companies they work with. Independent contractors may also be referred to as free-lancers, subcontractors, or contractors. Examples of an independent contractor include actors, freelance writers, and auctioneers.

Interns

An intern is a person who performs work for a company on a paid, unpaid, or partially paid basis in exchange for the work experience gained. Many high school and college students participate in internships to prepare for their careers after school. Internships typically last for a few months and after this time some interns are asked to become permanent employees by the company.

Consultants

A consultant is a self-employed person who offers professional advice in their area of expertise. For example, a consultant may specialize in education, law or marketing and provide companies with expert advice in attempt to help the company improve in these specific areas. Consultants provide their services on a temporary basis but may be utilized repeatedly by a company based on the organization's consulting needs.

Student Workers

Many universities hire and utilize student workers as temporary employees during their time at the institution when they are a student. Some student workers receive payment as part of Federal financial aid and others are paid from a particular department. Other student workers who are graduate students can be categorized as graduate assistants for either research or teaching duties. These students frequently are paid for their services and in addition, they are provided tuition and fee waivers to attend the university.

Public Safety Employees

A Public Safety Officer (PSO) is defined as: "an individual serving a public agency in an official capacity, with or without compensation, as a law enforcement officer, as a firefighter, as a chaplain, or as a member of a rescue squad or ambulance crew."

Military Employees

Military personnel are members of the state's armed forces. Their roles, pay, and obligations differ according to their military branch (army, navy, marines, air force, space force, and sometimes coast guard), rank (officer, non-commissioned officer, or enlisted recruit), and their military task when deployed on operations and on exercise. (Indeed, 2020).

Case Study: SOCS Are a.O.K.

Federal compliance reporting for public universities and colleges are difficult and complex under the best circumstances. However, when an institution is going through a migration to a new HRIS on top of federal deadlines, it can be chaotic. In this case study not only was a migration occurring to PeopleSoft, but the federal government was changing the reporting requirements from EEOC codes to a new Standard Occupational Classification (SOC) code category for all institutional employees. Since the institution is required to report this information in IPEDS to receive federal Title IV funding (Financial Aid), it is imperative that the information is input into HRIS correctly. This action took a number of collaborations with the reporting staff of the institution, HR personnel, and IT staff members to determine how the information was going to be populated correctly in HRIS and what SOC codes were going to be assigned to certain employees in job specific categories.

This required that the HR staff to not only understand what the new SOC codes represented, but also where those codes were located in a new system. The HR staff had to verify with the IT staff that the new SOC codes were populated as valid choices in the new PeopleSoft system. In addition, the personnel from the institution had to coordinate with other institutions within their state to ensure that the codes were being used by other institutions as a verification process. Once the new SOC codes were in the system correctly, the HR staff then had to work to assign every employee a SOC code in order for a report to be developed and tested. Once the report was developed, the reporting staff ran the report and worked with HR to audit the report. For employees who appeared to be in a questionable SOC category, the reporting staff and the HR staff would work with the department the employee was working for to verify or modify the information in the system for that particular employee. Once the report had run clean and accurately, the information was submitted to the federal government.

Case Study: Hold on to 18

The City of Rocket, Texas had an employee group that proposed to the pension board and the city council that the retirement date for employees be changed from 65 years of age to "rule of 78" which was determined by adding the years of service with the city to the age of employee. An example would be a 53-year-old employee with 25 years of experience. The employee group insisted that only a small fraction of the employees would avail themselves of the new retirement requirement. The city manager was not so sure that was the case.

The city manager asked the human resources director to analyze the number of employees that would be eligible to retire early under the proposed rule of 78. The analysis conducted by the human resources department by sampling the information contained in the HRIS system revealed that the number of employees that currently eligible to retire early about 20% of the entire work city workforce. The city manager was pleased the number was not too substantial but asked the human resources department for an additional sensitivity analysis to determine how employees would be eligible to retire under new rule in the 3, 5, 7 and 10 years and what kind of employees were eligible to retire under the new rule. While the number of employees able to retire under the proposed new rule did not increase appreciably, the human resources department determined that most employees that could retire under the proposed retirement rule were all the city's high skilled workers such as engineers, architects, accountants, nurses, urban planners, and lawyers. It was further determined that about 50% of these skills workers would be eligible to retire under the new rule immediately.

The city manager was disturbed that many highly skilled workers would be immediately eligible to retire and begin collecting retirement pay. These employees would then secure new employment with surrounding governmental entities resulting a huge brain drain in the city organization. The city manager immediately lobbied the city council to oppose the retire age rule change but to no avail. The city council approved the retirement age change and within months the substantial numbers of city highly skilled employees started filing for early retirement under the new rule of 78. This many retirements resulted in the pension becoming under-funded due the large under of early retirements that necessitated the issuance of pension bonds to plug the funding gap in the city pension fund. The city also lost a great deal of the institutional knowledge possessed by all these experienced city employees.

Summary

There are many differences between public, private and non–profit organizations, which impact how HRIS collects data used throughout the organization and how the data is reported and analyzed. In the next chapter, the history and evolution of HRIS will be discussed in relation to how HRIS has to account for different types of employees as well as the nuances of capturing, utilizing and reporting data for public and non-profit organizations. While private organizations have some requirements for federal and state data to be kept on employees, public and non–profit organizations typically have more complex human resources data requirements. As will be discussed in the next chapter, the evolution of HRIS is related to the advancement of software technology as well as the formulation of federal and state reporting requirements.

References

Acharyya, R. (December 17, 2017). *Careerizma*, Retireved on December 31, 2017. Differences between Government (Public) Sector and Private Sector Jobs - Careerizma.

Tarkia Arun, Zoho. (June 19, 2020). *A complete guide to choosing the right HRIS for your organization*. Retrieved on December 31, 2020. A complete guide to choosing the right HRIS for your organization I HR Blog I HR Resources I HR Knowledge Hive I Zoho People.

Basic. (2020). *Leave management*, Retrieved on December 31, 2020. Leave Management I Track Unplanned Absences I LOA Tracking. basiconline.com.

BLR. (2020), *Unions: What you need to know*. Retrieved on December 31, 2020. Unions laws & HR compliance analysis. blr.com.

Susan Heathfield. (November 1, 2019). *Human resources information system (HRIS), The balanced career.* Retrieved on December 31, 2020. What Is a Human Resources Information System?. thebalancecareers.com

Indeed. (April 17, 2020). *The most common types of employees and how they are different* Retrieved on December 31, 2020. The most common types of employees and how they are different I Indeed.com

Jenns N. (September 25, 2017).. *HR Zone, 8 Things HR Departments need to know about immigration law*, Retrieved on December 31, 2020. 8 Things HR Dept. Must Know About Immigration Laws I HRZone.

Prachi Juneja (2020). *Management study guide, training & development and HRIS applications, training & development and HRIS applications.* managementstudyguide.com

Ari Kopolus, HRIS & talent management. (August 16, 2016), Employee connect, retrieved on December 31, 2020. HRIS & talent management - employee connect HRIS.

Lucerna. (2020a). *Five ways a HRIS can help ease compliance worries.* Retrieved on December 41. 2020. 5 Ways a HRIS Can Help Ease Compliance Worries – HR Payroll Systems.

Lucerna, (2020b). *HRIS benefits administration.* Retrieved on December 41, 2020. HRIS Benefits Administration - HR Payroll Systems.

Raines, C. (March 6, 2019). *Small business chronicle, private sector vs. public sector employee rights*. Retrieved on December 31, 2020. Private Sector vs. Public Sector Employee Rights. chron.com.

Shannon Sanford. (2020) Finance A Lot.com. *Public pension vs. private pensions: What is the Difference*. Retrieved on December 31, 2020. Public Pension vs. Private Pension: What's the Difference?. alot.com

Erik van Vulpen. (2020). *Analytics in HR. What is a human resources information?* Retrieved on December 31, 2020. System What.

Zeepedia. (2020). *Strategic planning and HRIS*. Retrieved on December 31, 2020. STRATEGIC PLANNING AND HRIS: HRs Strategic Role Human Resource Information System Common HRIS Functions Human Resource Management Business Human Resource Management. zeepedia.com

ZingHR. (2020).. *Key HRIS Features that can transform your organization*. Retrieved on December 31, 2020.

The Theory of How HRIS Should Work

7

Key Points of the Chapter

- High-level viewpoint on what HRIS can potentially do for an organization.
- Discuss how HRIS stores data along with data entry controls
- Gains for the organization and employees using HRIS.
- Costs considerations for implementing and maintaining HRIS.

What Can HRIS Accomplish for an Organization?

HRIS enterprise software is a tool that enables an organization to retain official records, process personnel updates, promote the recruiting process, allow for data for analysis to retain personnel, comply with local, state and federal reporting mandates and allow for the seamless ability to pay employees correctly as well as process terminations. As stated by Karikari, Boateng and Ocansey:

> Human Resource Information System (HRIS) is a computer-based system that is used to manage the administration of HR processes and procedures. Its purpose is to become more efficient in providing better information for decision making [5] [6] . Mayfield, Mayfield and Lunce [7] added that the "functions of HRIS comply with organizational interests in maintaining and managing the human capital based on the organizational vision and the strategy of achieving that vision". This contributes to effective decision making which may guide spending of human resources in an organization. (Karikari, Boateng and Ocansey, 2015)

Each task associated with what an HRIS is designed to accomplish is complex and has many pitfalls if the HRIS software is unable fulfill the needed organizational capabilities for these roles. As stated by Troshani, Jerram and Hill:

> Furthermore, HR/HRIS are highly complex and driven by significant regulatory requirements. The impact of these requirements may be even more pronounced in the public sector

N. A. Valcik et al., *Human Resources Information Systems*, Management for Professionals, https://doi.org/10.1007/978-3-030-75111-1_7

> which is more open than the private sector for providing flexible employment opportunities for achieving work-life balance objectives (Taylor, 2010). (Troshani, Jerram and Hill, 2011)

An organization should see the HRIS enterprise software as an interactive tool and should not to be used as an "electronic file cabinet" where documents are just merely "retained for legal purposes."

Prior to Y2K, many enterprise software systems in public organizations were designed to operate from mainframe hardware with a non-GUI interface. This made accurate data entry by HR personnel as well as other administrative personnel difficult and time-consuming. For example, if an administrative assistant was responsible for inputting data into HRIS for a new employee, would the administrative assistant be trained well enough to not only put data in correctly but also resolve any unique situations that may occur during the data entry process? Training employees on an unforgiving mainframe interface can be extremely difficult for employees with a lower educational background or for employees who are not computer literate. In contrast, a more modern interface allows an improvement for data entry for employees who have less training or are not as computer literate. The older mainframe systems also tended to be designed with HR functions segregated or "siloed" from other enterprise systems (e.g. Finance, Facilities, Budget), which did not allow for data to be integrated across organizational lines of business. For higher education institutions these types of issues are problematic since faculty data, for example, can be stored in several enterprise systems and which, if not integrated, may include incongruent or erroneous data for the same employee. Newer enterprise system platforms (e.g. BANNER, PeopleSoft) have an integrated architecture that uses the same data between multiple areas of functionality and ownership.

The purpose of any HRIS enterprise software is to reduce labor costs, enable reliable official record keeping, and to enable accurate data extraction for reporting and analysis purposes. This however requires an organizational culture that can use HRIS effectively. Traditionally, human resources personnel interface with people in the organization to hire individuals, provide and register them for benefits, work with them on career goals, contend with difficult personnel issues and terminate individuals from their positions, among other responsibilities. Over the years however, the role of HR personnel has changed with the advent of legal statutes and with increased technological cap. Gone are the days where paper personnel files were locked away in a file cabinet. The HR professional now has to be computer literate, understand reporting compliance to a variety of public agencies, and be able process payroll electronically. As stated by Beadles, Lowery and Johns:

> Frequently mentioned by the respondents was the need for more training on the system. They believed that additional and better training would lead to better results. Several of the responses also reinforced the notion that the system was being underutilized and that they were not taking full advantage of the capabilities. They believed that other applications were needed and that the system could be more effectively utilized with the addition of some other features that were not currently part of the system. So, the potential contributions of HRIS are recognized, but further advances are need before the potential can be realized. (Beadles, Lowery and Johns, 2005)

The biggest barrier to using HRIS is to transition the skillset of the HR personnel toward better technical skills and to work with data in addition to interfacing with individuals.

HR has traditionally been seen as an organization within the larger entity that works with personnel and seen as the face of the administrative component of a public organization working with employment. With new legislative mandates and reporting requirements, HR is now tasked with contending with data in a manner never previously contemplated by public organizations. The transition will not be easy for many public and non-profit organizations because many HR professionals began their careers before technology became mainstream. HR directors, vice presidents and other upper level administrators may not have experienced the age of HRIS as it is currently in the workplace. Therefore, that generation of administrators may have difficulty directing resources or understanding what personnel are needed to run and manage HRIS enterprise software effectively to truly gain the benefits for their organization.

Not having the experience, knowledge, skills or abilities of the technological age can be a liability for senior HR administrators who may not grasp the technology, which can lead to major staffing deficiencies. A quote heard from one senior HR administrator in regard to reporting responsibilities was the following: "We've never been asked to do these types of jobs before." While this may be the case, that does not mean HR should not have had those types of responsibilities the entire time. It is also an example of job abdication to another department. With job abdication also comes loss of power and control over HR functions and the ability for the department to be seen as credible or viable within an organization.

An effective HRIS enterprise software package, if properly supported, implemented and utilized, can be a very powerful tool for a public or NPO. If the data is input into the system properly, a wealth of efficiencies in business processes, accuracy and reporting can be realized. Additionally, the organization can plan effectively for the future by calculating salaries to determine encumbrances and salary commitments, merit increases and promotions, turnover rates by department or supervisor and retirement projections. To run an organization effectively, personnel cost is a key component of strategic planning. The majority of costs for most organizations are their personnel costs, which are followed closely by capital costs. To provide key upper administrators with personnel information is critical for the decision-making process. Without personnel information upper administrators are making decisions using non-collaborated statements or using a political decision-making process to justify or make specific policy decisions.

Traditionally public and non-profit organizations have been held less accountable than their private industry counterparts since there is no board of directors and government funding were once at higher levels than they are currently. With the reduction of funds, public organizations and non-profit organizations must now to operate in a for-profit mode with regard to finances and resources. Adoption of viable HRIS enterprise software is critical for allowing upper level administrators to plan and analyze the organization's financial status and to identify future issues the organization might face.

For public organizations with union employees, HRIS allows for data to extracted and analyzed to see what terms are viable during the negotiation of annual contracts. During the negotiation phase, some positions and areas of operation can be identified for labor relations expansion while other areas of operations and positions may be obsolete due to new requirements and technology upgrades now needed by the organization. While some states have recently seen the political power of unions diminish (e.g. Michigan, Wisconsin), other states have large union representation that can significantly impact public organizations due to their political influence and stature within the state (e.g. New York, Illinois and Washington). If a public organization does not maintain accurate information in HRIS or the information is not captured completely, the labor negotiation can be fraught with tension, distrust and possible legal actions if violations are perceived with fair labor relations activities.

How Does HRIS Store Data?

As stated earlier, the days of keeping paper records are largely a thing of the past. In modern times, almost everything can be processed and stored electronically or kept in an electronic format. While there are many advantages to processing and storing records electronically, there are a few drawbacks that can occur that administrators should be aware of when contemplating the impact of HRIS to the HR profession. One of the more significant impacts upon an organization is transitioning from paper records, forms and files to an electronic format. Unless the organization is new, there will most likely be a large volume of existing paper files for historical personnel records.

Record retention laws vary from state-to-state, but for legal purposes certain records will need to be retained longer than others in case of litigation on topics ranging from wrongful termination to discrimination issues. Every organization will need to come to a decision on how long personnel records need to be kept and whether those records should be transitioned to an electronic format. The cost of storing such records can be quite high since it occupies facility space to keep those records. However, converting paper documents to digital will also cost the organization in terms of labor hours. The Return on Investment (ROI) for the organization should be calculated to determine if paper records should be transitioned compared to simply keeping records until they exceed their legal retention schedule and can be destroyed.

The type of HRIS enterprise software will dictate how data will need to be stored and managed by the organization. In several public organizations, record keeping is still driven by a paper-intensive process. This situation can be due to public organizations being either entrenched with their current systems or being unable to afford a cutting-edge enterprise system. Public organizations must take into account that the licensing costs for the software is just one part of the overall costs for HRIS. Besides the software licensing, there are costs with migrating data stored in an older system to a new system, which can also include transitioning paper records into an electronic format. Migration costs can be exorbitant for an organization if the organization lacks personnel with the appropriate knowledge, skills and abilities to convert data to a newer system. This would require the organization to hire consultants, which can cost anywhere from $200 to $400 per hour based on the skillset required for a consultant to work on the project (2018 dollar amounts).

Once the migration has occurred, there are costs associated with validating the data, which, depending upon the size of the organization, can take a considerable amount of time if there are thousands of records to verify. The other costs associated with an HRIS transition are personnel training/re-training costs, potential personnel hiring costs, hardware costs and facility costs. There may also be costs associated with building custom applications and processes into the new HRIS software to accommodate requirement set by the public organization's regulatory agencies (e.g. state and federal reports). For example, when UT-System component schools (e.g. UT-Arlington, UT-Tyler, UT-San Antonio, UT-El Paso and UT-Dallas) migrated to PeopleSoft, there were certain fields and table structures that had to be customized to conduct required reporting on personnel for the Texas Higher Education Coordinating Board (THECB). These fields are standard with PeopleSoft and would have to be added to the HRIS enterprise software that was delivered. Anytime an upgrade to HRIS enterprise software occurs, steps have to be taken to assure those customizations will not disappear when the update has completed. Data that is stored in customized fields will need to be backed up to secure storage to ensure data has been retained properly in case there is a problem during the upgrade process.

What Data Entry Controls Should be in Place?

The old saying of "Garbage In, Garbage Out" is very accurate even with the most modern HRIS software packages. However, there are many mechanisms that can control data entry and "clean" or edit the data in HRIS. One mechanism is the development of edit checks, allowing functional users to identify potential problems in HRIS and correct the data. Once the data is corrected, the edit checks are rerun to ensure the data is "clean" thus ensuring the data is consistent and accurate. A second means to control data entry is to use drop down menus or other controlled data entry where the functional user performs the least amount of typing possible to prevent errors from occurring. In systems such as PeopleSoft, the user is often provided a look up field that only allows the user to see and select valid data entry choices. The final mechanism utilized is either through a file upload or a connection to another database with validated data. These are the primary mechanisms used to control data in HRIS enterprise software.

What do Organizations Gain from Using HRIS?

Organizational gain from using HRIS can have a positive impact on how the organization is managed. Without HRIS, an organization would have a technological shortfall on even the simple task of paying employees or recording their sick time. Most public organizations' biggest expenses are salaries for employees. For such a large expense, an organization should have a mechanism or method to collect, store, report and analysis on salary data. How does an organization plan effectively without adequate data to inform the upper level decision-makers?

Personnel data is also critical since salary data and benefit data is linked to financial expenditures and budget items within the organization. Personnel data allows decision-makers to assess if salaries are at market value for particular jobs, whether the organization has money for raises, and if so who should be targeted for those raises as well as whether the organization is staffed appropriately with the knowledge, skills and abilities that are required. For example, how does an organization know which employees are to be laid off during tough financial times without facing potential lawsuits for violation of Equal Employment Opportunity statutes?

HRIS systems are a conglomerate of different electronic systems, the sophistication and price-tag of which is dependent on the specific organization, which provides the HR manager and even line managers with real-time data which can be housed until practical HR decisions need to be made. For instance, specific employee demographics such as their skill-set, training, and even compensation can be stored in electronic systems until this data is needed, such as in the event of requiring information about performance when constructing an annual review. This access to real-time data gives HR managers the flexibility required to adopt new models of human resources or simply to improve communications with a high-volume employee population in a manner that is both accurate and effective. (IceHrm, 2020).

The most positive aspect of HRIS involves dramatic technological improvements that provide HR managers with more high-tech tools for data storage and data manipulation. For example, organizations which have historically-struggled with their payroll systems would likely find HRIS systems a vital tool for improving the delivery of compensation, accuracy of payouts, and the ability to upgrade payroll information at short notice in a real-time environment. HRIS systems devoted to payroll allow employee information including insurance information, government-mandated payroll withdrawals, and the ability to automate what had traditionally been a complicated and labor-intensive HR function. Some governmental and non-profit units simply prefer to outsource payroll function to a third party using their HRIS systems to alleviate time constraints on the HR professional. "Payroll is function that can be outsourced in public, nonprofit and private sectors. Just keeping up with the regulations can be challenging for all types of organizations. Outsourcing and linking these external efforts with the extranet can give HR professionals more flexibility and the ability to monitor and regulate the efforts of the outsourced payroll partner. (hibob. 2020).

Improvements in relational databases which link separate HR functions gives organizations more data storage and the ability to cross-link employee data with business-related data. Relational databases provide opportunities to store a virtually limitless amount of data on employees. The data and memory capacity of these data systems also gives new flexibility for data storage and retrieval in a way that is relevant to the business' technological needs or HR focus. Implementing new HRIS systems can often lead to reducing the human resources expenditures on an annual basis which a constant need to all entities in these fiscally stressed times. (Majumder, 2016).

Automation of many HR roles is another superior benefit of implementation of HRIS systems as it "reduces time and costs for routine HR tasks such as benefit enrollment, vacation requests, and approvals and forms distribution. From a labor perspective, automating the HR function in these areas will free up a great deal of time for the busy HR professionals and allow them to focus on the more human-oriented aspects of job role including better interpersonal relationship development or even the provision of training. The role of HR professional continues to become more complex each day, demanding a dynamic, multi-tasking individual with the skills necessary to create a more rewarding organizational culture and business environment. Automation as a benefit of implementation creates positive outcomes for the HR manager by allowing them more time to devote to more important, strategic-minded organizational issues including coaching and staff development. (Tallyfy, 2021).

HRIS systems also maintain the ability to enhance the organizational culture of an organization as various social networking capabilities can be incorporated into a unit's existing extranet or intranet. Such systems provide "a social tool to collaborate, communication and make real strategic decisions about the management of people. Companies that maintain intranets can link multiple databases with the employee job role, such as allowing them to discuss events with managers or colleagues in real-time, avoiding the need for face-to-face interventions in the workplace. This provides a new type of flexibility to the contemporary organization where social networking becomes a commonplace means of communication with internal and external stakeholders. Employees, in more sophisticated networking systems, can even access their own personal files and update their skills profile after completion of mandated training programs to keep HR information up-to-date and fitting of actual employee competencies and skill levels. These types of systems can be accessed, and the data manipulated for performance analyses or other skills-related assessment objectives that require accurate employee data.

An effective HRIS delivers self-empowering tools that elevate employee engagement and becomes an integral part of a maintaining a more productive and satisfying workplace culture. A "desirable" workplace culture has many defining traits that inspire employee engagement. HRIS technology plays a vital role in inspiring engagement by:

- Enabling better communication and information sharing with integrated features such as: organization blogs, real-time polls, surveys and help desk
- Improving access and visibility to key organizational metrics critical for evaluating and planning

- Delivering functionality that enables more productive and collaborative processes such as: goal setting, performance evaluations, absence management and employee direct access

HRIS must provide intuitive tools that enhance user experience while promoting the desire to comply with process, communicate, and collaborate more willingly. Empowering managers and employees with self-service is a prime benefit of any HRIS strategy. The ability to "self-serve" to manage basic information like employee profiles or to request and track absences promotes employee engagement based on empowerment and productivity value. Cumbersome or paper intensive processes leave employees feeling less engaged to comply and may even detract from an otherwise positive organizational culture. An HRIS that provides intuitive, user friendly tools for every day processes are an extension of a progressive "employee first" culture and can positively impact an employee's perception of their organization's culture and values. Most importantly, it makes work life a lot more productive and satisfying. Consider the positive impact that a progressive, technology enabled workplace has on employee engagement compared to an organization that does not. Engaged employees are proven to be more productive, connected to the goals of the organization and more likely to stay. Technology like that of an HRIS plays a key role in any progressive organization's strategy to enhance culture and promote employee engagement. (Pivotal Solutions, 2020).

The time saved on compensation programs is yet another major benefit of HRIS, as programs such as base pay reviews, incentive compensation, and equity-share programs consistently require a great deal of labor-intensive effort on behalf of the HR manager. Line managers, as well, can contribute to the effectiveness of these electronic systems by having a data record to input their own assessments on individual employee productivity and ability to meet objectives which gives the HR real-time, 360-degree feedback mechanisms to give a more accurate and timely employee assessment. The HR generalist, in an organization without sophisticated HRIS, typically spends up to half of their job role-related time working and upgrading compensation programs for multiple level employees. A substantial reduction in manual effort related to compensation systems gives the HR professional new flexibility in being a more visible and dynamic contributor to employee relationship management. A public sector or nonprofit sector organization that invests in an HRIS much document the savings that are going to generated by the adoption of such technology.

Automated Onboarding

First, an HR Analyst or IT Analyst will need to compare the amount of time that it takes to onboard an employee with the current system with the new HRIS process. Then an assessment will need to be undertaken to consider how often employees are onboarded in the organization.

Automated onboarding can also boost the organization in other ways:

- Engagement - When employees believe their organization's onboarding software is effective, they are five times as likely to report high levels of engagement, commitment and job satisfaction (Cable, Gino, & Staats, 2013; Meyer & Bartels, 2017).
- Retention - Effective onboarding software boosts new hires' confidence in their decision to join your organization, reducing turnover by as much as 30 percent. (Greenhouse, 2020)
- Performance and Productivity - Effective onboarding software decreases time-to-productivity by 33 percent. (Greenhouse, 2020)

E-Signatures

Documents and forms are an indispensable part of every HR department, but tracking all those signatures can be time consuming—not to mention the headaches of lost paperwork or signature bottlenecks. However, e-signature software can save an average organization many hours and you need to determine the savings for your operation.

E-signature software offers a few other benefits as well:

- Efficiency - E-signature software reduces signed document turnaround times by as much as 90 percent. (Greenhouse, 2020)
- Employer Brand - Using e-signatures can attract top talent, as 92 percent of young professionals would prefer to work for an environmentally friendly company. (Greenhouse, 2020)

Time Management

Without time-off management software, HR professionals have to keep track of employee vacation time using some version of a manual spreadsheet. Not only is this process incredibly time consuming, but it also leaves the organization at risk for inaccurate time-off tracking. Whether by accident or on purpose, an average employee takes up to three unreported days of PTO a year when their organization has poor tracking capabilities. But with an HRIS, you could eliminate the cost of unreported PTO. The other benefits of effective time-off management software include:

- Efficiency - Automated time-off tracking helps you better manage employee absences, (Navarro & Bass, 2006), which cost businesses about six percent of annual payroll.
- High Performance - When employees enjoy effective time-off management software, customer satisfaction levels increase up to 10 percent. (Greenhouse, 2020)

Employee Self-Service

Perhaps the biggest time-consumer in an HR professional's busy week is the endless stream of employee questions, whether they are about benefits administration or changes in personal information. Employee self-service HR software gives employees the ability to find answers to their own questions and manage their own personal information. This takes a huge burden off HR and can reduce the amount of time required for administrative tasks significantly. Using an employee self-service system in your organization provides other benefits as well:

- Efficiency - Employee self-service software allows HR to serve 10 percent more employees. (Greenhouse, 2020)
- Competitive Advantage- Self-service boosts your organization's performance,
- making those with such software about 50 percent more likely to achieve Best-in-Class status. (Greenhouse, 2020)
- Performance & Productivity- 72 percent of HR generalists that use employee self-service in their organizations reported a lighter workload. (Greenhouse, 2020)

Cost Savings with HRIS

When an analyst adds all the time and money savings together, the benefits of an HRIS can be made clear to the elected officials, appointed officials and the public. However, it is not just about time and money. An HRIS sets HR professionals free from worrying about the day-to-day operations and helps them take a more strategic role in the organization by addressing turnover, boosting engagement, creating culture, and more. (BambooHR, 2020).

Empowerment as an outcome of implementing HRIS is yet another benefit of choosing such a system to power the HR job function. HRIS technology can give the line manager a more value-added role in the organization by allowing them access to employee data in a real-time environment. Empowerment is a concept of motivation in which the manager or employee is given new opportunities to flex their creative and innovative selves and also organize their own work functions without senior-level management intervention. There is considerable focus today on aspects of diversity and job role empowerment in the organization as a means of boosting staff and managerial motivation to perform. Rather than using policies and processes to coerce managers to rely on the expertise of human resources experts in the organization, such systems give managers new opportunities to take on additional responsibilities regarding the management of employee-related data. A more motivated and objective-focused organization can lead to productivity improvements, thus the flexible and self-serving nature of some HRIS technologies can lead to a better organizational culture that is motivated to exceed expectations.

HRIS and Employee Empowerment

Creating a culture in which employees are empowered has shown to be a key contributor to employee job satisfaction and contentment, which can result in lower turnover. Empowering employees can also help to increase productivity, as employees no longer must wait for management or HR professionals to make changes. HRIS can make it easy for management to empower employees with less risk.

Encourages Empowerment from the Start

Employee candidates may feel empowered right from the start when HRIS is used for recruitment. Employee candidates may be able to submit and view the status of an application without breaking anyone's routine or placing awkward phone calls. This can not only help employees to feel empowered right from the start, it can help managers to see how employee candidates act when given greater autonomy, which can help to make sure only the right people are chosen for the job.

Puts Employees in Charge of Their Information

Simply being able to view and make changes to their own information can make employees feel trusted. Waiting for managers or HR to make key changes to information about tax withholdings, beneficiary information, or personal information can be frustrating for employees that need those changes. Allowing employees to view schedules and make time off requests can also help employees to feel that they have more control over their working life and routine.

Can Help Make Employees More Autonomous

If certain features and functions are used in HRIS, employees may be able to access information about upcoming projects, future training and development, and other necessary daily aspects of the job. By being able to access this information without having to communicate with managers, employees can work more autonomously, getting started right away instead of waiting for the back and forth. If learning management systems are used, employees can determine when the optimal time to work on training courses is, saving time and possibly improving compliance.

Fosters Communication Among Peers

When communication among peers and between management and employees is allowed through HRIS, it can help employees to voice opinions on more topics more often. Employees may be able to learn about upcoming events, make suggestions, and provide feedback to peers about past work. The open communication lines can help employees to contribute more directly and feel that their voice matters.

HRIS Lowers Risks Associated with Empowerment

Feedback and 360-degree reviews from customers via HRIS allow management to see how employees are performing with the increased empowerment. This lowers the risks associated with employees abusing empowerment by slacking off and compromising revenues or productivity. Management has a window into employees' worlds that makes employee empowerment much more realistic than it may have been in the past for many industries.

Helps to Recognize Employees for Empowered Behavior

After using HRIS to view employees' productivity with the greater levels of autonomy and empowerment, managers can also more easily recognize employees for good results using HRIS. Simply communicating to say, "Good job!" can help employees to feel more valued. Managers can also communicate about rewards or incentives for empowered behaviors and great results. (Lucerna, 2020).

Online HRIS tools also provide new motivational outcomes as they allow employees to update their basic demographic information, review organizational policies, request time off, and even review internal job postings without having to rely on HR expertise. The software can act as an internal communications tool, which empowers employees to take a more active role in updating their skills profile. HR managers, due to their complicated demands, may be unaware that an employee has developed extended skills through training intervention, thus this employee could be a more positive candidate for future job promotions. Self-service systems allow the employee to access and manipulate this data in a way that is meaningful to their growth expectations in relation to job promotion. These outcomes can result in improved employee morale and increased efficiency. Motivated employees will not only be more dedicated to meeting organizational objectives, they will be more content. This can create open, communicative cultures that are predisposed to accept employee self-service systems. From a cultural perspective, self-service employee database systems can enhance teamwork, job role performance, and build better human capital for the organization. (Vulpen, 2020).

Avoiding Risks with HRIS

The costs of not using HRIS can be significant. Lack of accurate, accessible data can impact decision-making by upper administrators. While some decisions can be relatively minor, other decisions can have far reaching impacts upon the organization in the form of legal repercussions, budgetary issues and fiscal solvency. For public and non-profit organizations in particular, human resource issues can be complex and fraught with legal peril throughout the process of hiring and termination of employees. In the case of layoffs, for example, selecting which employees to terminate can be challenged legally if layoffs do not have in a framework that is legally defensible. For example, if a public organization reduces employees that are predominantly in a particular demographic or salary range, the organization could face an EEOC suit filed by an employee who was laid off. Before performing staff reductions, the decision-makers should have a complete picture of which employees should be laid off, why they should be laid off and should avoid terminating employees who are all of a particular race or gender.

If a public or non-profit organization is going to provide a limited pool of funds for raises, it is critical that the organization have not only a process in place, but also accurate information underlying those decisions to determine not only who gets a raise, but also how much of a raise is to be given. Organizations that do provide raises then have to determine what type of raises are going to be given, either a market -based adjustment on salary or a merit - based pay increase. For those public organizations that use a merit base pay increase, there will need to be data behind each employee's performance to determine whether they deserve a raise and to benchmark their performance against other employees in the organization.

Salary raises tie into an organization's budgetary outlook and can determine how well the organization is able to retain talented employees. Public and non-profit organizations often are at a disadvantage to the private sector market in regards to salary, so it is imperative to have data to provide upper administrators an understanding of what the capacity of an organization has for offering increases in salary to key employees. Without the ability to leverage data from HRIS, upper level administrators will be unable to determine what the average salaries are for certain employees that have seniority and excellent performance reviews to counter potential job offers from private sector areas. Not having data in HRIS software may also leave the public organization vulnerable to poaching from other public or non-profit organizations.

For public and non-profit organizations that have unionized employees, the lack of a viable HRIS software solution, can put the organization in a weak position when negotiating with the union for salaries and benefits. Without having accurate data, the upper level administrators for a public or non-profit organization will be at a disadvantage and can damage the organization financially if an optimum deal is not realized. These types of situations can leave the organization in financial distress.

Case Study: Paper, Rock, Scissors

In theory, HRIS should make an organization more efficient and more effective. However, that is only possible if HRIS is implemented by an HR office that is willing to change business practices to match the capabilities of the system. One vendor makes it well known that it is not just about purchasing an installing the system, it is also about changing HR business practices to match the manner in how the HRIS is designed to operate. In theory everything should be conducted by an electronic means and no paper should be used in any aspect. In theory every executive should be able to obtain their own reports without a person or programmer assisting them in any aspect. In theory there should be minimal data cleanup with only a minor amount of errors or data entry to be performed by an HR department.

However as one public organization discovered, the theory does not necessarily match the initial sales pitch nor does reality match the implementation. As one public organization found out additional systems and interfaces had to be constructed and implemented to make HRIS work as the initial vendor stated, and then only to a point could the system be completely automated. The public organization had to develop an interface that would work for leave of absence reporting and how to build in new processes on how to route approval to the supervisor for individuals to have time off approved. The new method was actually more labor intensive for the supervisor than the old previous paper method and thus there was pushback since the supervisor ended up doing more work.

Reporting for the public organization actually ended up being a massive cost since the organization had to develop all of the dashboards, their own data warehouse and personnel still had to provide reports to the executives. In this manner nothing truly changed except for the manner in how the reports were compiled and delivered to the upper administration. For self-service, while this sounds like a more efficient method in getting data into the system, there were a number of errors introduced into HRIS since there were no data entry controls on the form that was interfacing with HRIS. Thus, a number of personnel had to perform clean up duties on the data, which again cost the organization a good portion of funds. So while HRIS in theory can make an organization more efficient and effective, the correct planning has to be in place before implementation begins to make this theory (or at least part of it) a reality. The other aspect that needs to be stated is that HR has to be willing to change its business processes to match how HRIS functions and works with the data.

Summary

There are aspects to HRIS that are important especially how the functional users are to interface with the system, how data is recorded into the system and how to establish controls to prevent erroneous data from being input into the system. While this aspect may appear to be simple in practice, it is one of the more potentially damaging factors for attempting to maintain data integrity. Without sufficient data integrity, all functions for an organization's HRIS is theoretically at risk of experiencing a lack of functionality for their organization and the employees will have a lack of confidence in any data in their HRIS. The next chapter will focus on these functional areas and how those areas relate to HRIS.

References

BambooHR. (2020). *HR software*. Retrieved on December 23, 2020. HR Software | People Data & Analytics | Hiring | Onboarding | Compensation | Culture | BambooHR Software.

Beadles, I. I., Aston, N., Lowery Christopher, M., & Johns, K. (2005). The impact of human resource information system: an exploratory study in the public sector. *Communications of the IIMA, 5*(4), 6. Retrieved from: https://core.ac.uk/download/pdf/55332428.pdf

Cable, D. M., Gino, F., & Staats, B. R. (2013). Reinventing employee onboarding. *MIT Sloan Management Review, 54*(3), 23.

Greenhouse. (2020). *Calculating the ROI and benefits of HR software*. Retrieved on January 20, 2021, Calculating the ROI and benefits of HR software|Greenhouse. https://www.greenhouse.io/guidance/calculating-the-roi-and-benefits-of-hr-software

Hibob. (2020). *The guide to planning your HR strategy*. https://www.hibob.com/guides/your-hr-strategy-checklist/

HRIS for Employee Engagement and Culture. (2020). Pivotal solutions, Mississauga, Ontario, Canada. https://www.pivotalsolutions.com/hris-for-employee-engagement-and-culture/

IceHrm. (2020). HRIS. Implementation challenges. February 5, 2020.

Karikari, A. F., Boateng, P. A., & Ocansey, E. O. N. D. (2015). The role of human resource information system in the process of manpower activities. *American Journal of Industrial and Business Management, 5*(6), 57490. Retrieved from: https://www.scirp.org/html/9-2120583_57490.htm

Lucerna. (2020). *6 Ways HRIS helps with employee empowerment*. https://www.hrpayroll-systems.net/6-ways-hris-helps-employee-empowerment/#:~:text=%20%20%201%20Encourages%20Empowerment%20from%20theHRIS%2C%20employees%20may%20be%20able%20to...%20More%20

Majumder, S. (2016). March 22. 2016. *6 Components of human resources information systems (RHIS)*. Medium.com, https://medium.com/@realtynewsIndia/6-components-of-human-resource-information-systems-hris-39d239cb1714

Meyer, A. M., & Bartels, L. K. (2017). The impact of onboarding levels on perceived utility, organizational commitment, organizational support, andc. *Journal of Organizational Psychology, 17*(5), 10–27.

Navarro, C., & Bass, C. (2006). The cost of employee absenteeism. *Compensation & Benefits Review, 38*(6), 26–30.

Tallyfy. (2021). The Benefits of Automating Human Resources Operations to Transform Your Business. Retrieved on June 15, 2021. https://tallyfy.com/automating-human-resources/

Taylor, J. (2010). "Qld Health must stop system docking pay", May 28, available at: http://zdnet.com.au/qld-health-must-stop-system-docking-pay-339303504.htm (accessed July 29, 2010), ZDNet.com.au

Troshani, I, Jerram, C, & Hill, S. R.(2011). Exploring the public sector adoption of HRIS. Retrieved from: https://www.researchgate.net/publication/220672409_Exploring_the_Public_Sector_Adoption_of_HRIS. Accessed 10 Dec 2020.

Van Vulpen, Eric. (2020). What is HRIS? a HR practitioner's guide. AIHR analytics. https://www.analyticsinhr.com/blog/human-resources-information-system-hris/

The Functional Areas Utilizing HRIS in a Public Organization

8

Key Points of the Chapter

- What areas use HRIS and how are these functional areas interfacing with HRIS.
- The different types of capability sought after by different functional areas.
- Understanding how the organization has to operate in an integrated fashion with HRIS.

HRIS is like the tentacles of an octopus reaching out from a centralized system to touch multiple business processes, compliance reporting and decision making within an organization. A small public or non-profit organization can probably manage to do business using a homegrown system to house their HR system, or can outsource those functions to a specialized vendor to handle certain organizational aspects. However, an organization with a certain threshold of employees will need some type of HRIS system that is standardized. Throughout this chapter the functional areas of a public or non-profit organization will be discussed and reviewed on how those areas interact with HRIS.

Human Resources

The main driver of the HRIS enterprise application is human resources. Every organization differs on how human resources is structured, staffed and functions within the organization. With some organizations, human resources is limited in the scope of their responsibilities and how they function. In other organizations, human resources are staffed to encompass a greater functional role over multiple areas (e.g. payroll). How human resources perform and function has changed over time. Prior to the computer age human resources were focused primarily on hiring procedures, recruitment, termination of employees, organizational human resources policies, providing employees with benefits and working with human resources issues that

N. A. Valcik et al., *Human Resources Information Systems*, Management for Professionals, https://doi.org/10.1007/978-3-030-75111-1_8

occurred within the organization. In other words, human resources were primarily focused on working with people and keeping paper records when it was necessary. With the advent of the computer age, the function of human resources has changed and expanded. Instead of contending with personnel issues, human resources are now also tasked, in a number of organizations, with inputting in data into HRIS as well as determining how data will be coded, who has access to HRIS and if data should be input at the centralized core human resources department or if individual departments should be responsible for inputting information. With the advent of HRIS, human resources now needs to determine how individual employee data will be input into the system or if a paper form will be utilized to enable human resources to control how employee data is input into the system.

How human resources functions within the organization is dependent upon the technical abilities of human resources personnel in human resources. Employees with a higher level of technical ability will increase the department's involvement with the integration of HRIS functions and their business processes while the presence of less proficient employees will require a greater role from information technology in how data in HRIS is coded, data entry security and reporting. The other aspect to human resources is how involved the department is with compliance and operational reports. In some organizations standard compliance and operational reports are deferred to human resources, in other organizations human resources participation is very limited. The more advanced an organization is with their technology and data integrity, the more self-service analytics can come into play which also limits how much work human resources does with reporting.

Human resources that have converted to paperless personnel evaluations will also need to be involved in how those personnel evaluations are administered as well as who has access to those evaluations. Human resources will need to provide oversight to how the evaluation forms are constructed and provide training for managers, supervisors and employees in how to use the paperless evaluation forms. Human resources will need to determine how these personnel evaluations will be used and how they will be tied to merit raises or promotions. For retention purposes, performance evaluations can be used to determine which employees need to be retained and which employees may not be advantageous for the organization to retain long term.

Recruiting and Staffing The HR professional will work with the hiring managers within an organization to develop an action plan for the hiring of a diverse workforce. This may include, but may not limited to: sourcing for candidates in a creative manner; posting open jobs; screening resumes and applications; conducting telephone interviews; scheduling the in house interview; providing a tour of the facilities to the final applicants; conducting the appropriate background checks; recommending the appropriate compensation package; making the offer and preparing the offer letter and benefits information; conducting the new employee orientation program; and making sure that all new hires are enrolled in the company's benefit programs.(Lucerna, 2020).

Benefits Coordinates with the benefit brokers to annually review all employer-sponsored benefit plans for renewal and compliance; conducting open enrollment educational meetings with employees; making sure that employees are enrolled and terminated from each benefit program with each vendor, as appropriate; assisting managers with accident investigations and the coordination of workers' compensation; completing the OSHA logs, as needed and posting when required; and tracking all paid time off, to include the paperwork for the Family and Medical Leave Act (FMLA) and other related benefits. (Lucerna, 2020).

Compensation Assists hiring managers with the writing and updating job descriptions and maintaining them annually; reviewing salary survey data to make sure that the company is paying employees competitively within the market; maintaining internal hierarchy with regards to pay; developing and maintaining a salary administration plan for the organization; making recommendations with regards to pay, merit increases, salary structure maintenance, etc.; writing and recommending variable pay plans; making sure that the organization is compliant with the various wage and hour laws; implementing and maintaining a creative performance evaluation system for all employees. (iEduNote, 2020).

Employee Relations The HR Generalist is one who maintains confidentiality with all employment-related matters within the organization. He/she promotes an "open door" environment with all employees and is an active "listener" to their needs and concerns without projecting a bias opinion or taking ownership for their issue. He/she works with management to proactively resolve employee relations issues, conducts investigations and makes recommendations for resolution. He/she works with management to document disciplinary actions and makes recommendation with regards to nonmonetary rewards and recognition. The HR Generalist is actively involved in employee terminations and understands the unemployment claim and appeal process. Most conduct exit interviews with terminating employees and provide information with regards to the continuation of benefits after employment. (Mayhew, 2017).

HR Compliance The HR professional makes sure that the organization is compliant with all employment-related laws and requirements from a federal, state and local perspective. This may include making sure that the appropriate posters are posted and up-to-date; preparation and maintenance of all employee policies within the employee handbook; employee file maintenance; Employment Eligibility and Verification Form I-9 maintenance; and completion of all verifications of employment, reference checks, etc. for past and present employees. (Lucerna, 2020).

Organizational Design Strategically assists the management team with furthering the mission, vision and business goals of the organization through a solid organizational structure is paramount. The HR professional will maintain all organizational charts; make recommendations as to changes within the structure that would benefit the organization; understand how to manage the "white space" on the organizational charts; tracks turnover rates and reasons; develops career ladders within job classifications; is involved with succession planning, and promotes active employee engagement activities throughout the organization. (Junelja, 2015).

Training and Development Recommends and may create and conduct training and development programs for the entire organization to include: anti-harassment and discrimination avoidance, diversity, customer service skills, business communication skills, and so on. Works with managers to create and implement on-the-job training opportunities for all employees. Tracks all training programs and employee participation and follows up with managers and employees to measure utilization of skills learned as well as evaluating additional training resources or needs.

While the functional areas, as listed above, are the primary HR-related areas, there are others tasks within each area that could be added depending upon the organization. What competencies are represented by an HR Generalist? Fundamentally, it requires someone who likes people. However, the most important competency is one who is able to recognize a problem and bring creative solutions to management. The ability to work independently as well as within a team environment is essential and the ability to pay attention to detail while utilizing excellent verbal and written communication skills is required. The ability to maintain confidentiality, be a good listener and possess strong coaching and counseling skills are all a given. Most managers would tell you that a strong HR Generalist also has the ability to motivate and train employees at all levels. CEOs, Presidents, CCOs and CFOs want someone who is able to recognize that HR is not a cost center and is able to strategically provide a value add to the bottom line financial results of the organization. (Deutsch, 2015).

Payroll

Payroll is critical to any organization whether it is a private industry, public or non-profit Organization because employees have to be paid or else an organization ceases to function. Payroll is a functional area that can be structured to operate either as its own entity, under human resources, or under the financial/budgeting area of the organization. The bulk of what payroll does for an organization is to ensure pay checks are correctly issued to employees, salary amounts are correct, taxes are deducted correctly, and benefits accounted for in each payroll cycle. Additionally, payroll may also be responsible for ensuring sick and/or vacation time, which is also known as paid time off (PTO).

There are several challenges that Payroll must face to ensure that employees' pay checks are issued correctly. These challenges include if the organization maintains specialized payroll schedules (nine-month contracts paid out over 12 months, for example), issues additional pay stipends, if the employee has more than one job code or role, and if the employee is on paid or unpaid leave. Another challenge is if the employee is paid out of multiple accounts (e.g. state, restricted, designated, auxiliary). A number of the described examples can occur with higher education institutions that have many different types of employees. Furthermore, public and non-profit organizations with a unionized workforce may have different payroll requirements (e.g. step pay) that have to be accounted for differently than with non-union personnel.

Strategic Planning / Reporting

Almost all public and non-profit organizations have a department that contends with reporting and/or analysis. These units may be responsible for performing complex analysis, compliance reports, operational reports or completing requests required by external entities (e.g. state agencies, federal agencies, surveys, media). These departments usually employ personnel who have technical backgrounds, programming experience and have a working knowledge of HRIS and the business processes that govern how data is input into the system. Planning and reporting departments may also have a secondary responsibility of performing audits on the data since having inaccurate data would impact the reporting process and potentially the decision-making process for upper administration. Planning and reporting departments often have access not only to HRIS but also financial, facilities, and, where applicable, student information systems. This allows them to consider multiple data sources for reporting and auditing purposes. In essence, planning and reporting departments allow the organization to comply with reporting requirements and provide operational intelligence for the upper administration.

Veterans

Organizations that employ or serve veterans need to be able to track veteran status for a variety of purposes. Compliance reporting is one area of concern for certain organizations that must report statistical information to government agencies. Additionally, there are specific regulations that mandate public organizations report information for employees who wish to claim veteran status or for those individuals who are dependents of veterans. Often organizations have issues with identifying veterans from the dependents of veterans in their HRIS applications. This is usually not because the HRIS applications cannot accommodate the codes, but is due to the personnel in the organization not understanding (or foreseeing) how the data should be input. Incorrect coding creates issues for programmers and analysts attempting to extract and analyse the date for compliance or operational reporting purposes.

Social Justice/Diversity

At most public and non-profit organizations, a department exists for social justice or diversity. These departments exist to ensure that recruitment efforts attempt to improve diversity and retention of traditionally under-represented groups. To facilitate these efforts, demographic data on employees and job applicants must be available so that a successful diversity plan can be developed. The upper administrators need to have data to implement any plan or obtain buy in from whoever is providing oversight (elected or appointed) to the public or non-profit organization.

Budget and Finance

The budget and financial departments of public and non-profit organizations use HRIS information for a wide variety of purposes, including verifying the budgeted salary for a person or position to reimbursing employees. Finance can utilize data from HRIS to calculate and forecast payroll for the upcoming months and to compare actual expenses to budgeted to project shortfalls in fund balances. The budget and finance areas can also use information from HRIS to determine how much a department should receive for the upcoming fiscal year based on mandated increases to benefit or salary amounts. These variables are usually stored in HRIS based benefits selections made by employees while salary amounts are derived from the payroll system. Therefore, it is critical that budget and finance have access to HRIS and understand the data to be used in forecasting.

Information Technology

Information technology can be known by several names within an organization: information services, IT, enterprise applications etc. Information technology has the role of supporting HRIS, which includes installing upgrades and software patches. The role of information technology can be expansive dependent upon how large the organization is and how much control the organization wants to allow information technology to obtain. Information technology's role within the organization for HRIS is critical since that unit is responsible for the software itself, the hardware, the network and the security. This is an expensive cost because it is not just the costs of the licensing for HRIS, but also the hardware, the infrastructure and most expensive of all, the personnel.

The personnel costs for running and maintaining an HRIS application will usually be high since personnel have to be technical and more skills are needed for certain HRIS requirements. For example, a database architect could be extremely expensive compared to a web programmer. This is not only due to the costs of acquiring someone with those skills, but also the limited number of people with those credentials and the, among those, a smaller number willing to work in the public sector when more lucrative jobs await them in the private sector. Therefore, when a public or non-profit organization is budgeting for an HRIS application, the personnel costs as well as the fixed costs should all be taken into account.

Provost or Vice Chancellor (Higher Education Institutions)

Provosts and Vice Chancellors are the senior administrator at higher education institutions that primarily oversee instructional, curricular, and research efforts as well as admissions, records, libraries, and, in some cases, information technology. Faculty and their deans ultimately report to the Provost, and there are many rules, regulations and standards regarding faculty management. In institutions that have unionized faculty, these standards provide an additional layer of information that need to be tracked due to any collective bargaining agreement (CBA) entered into between the faculty union and the organization.

How faculty information is tracked can vary widely throughout the country as well as the type of information that is tracked. For institutions with tenure systems, certain data must be recorded for tenure and post-tenure reviews. In addition, faculty members who are in institutions that manage faculty rank must have data on file to determine promotion to an upper rank (e.g. Associate Professor to Professor). While some institutions have stand-alone systems to record such information, other institutions rely on HRIS to track this type of information.

For most universities and colleges, the HRIS application has provisions to accommodate these types of data. However, for HRIS applications that do not have this type of provision, customizations to the enterprise software will be necessary. Reporting faculty rank and tenure information accurately to IPEDS (NCES federal agency) is mandatory for any institution that receives Title IV funds (financial aid). If this information is not reported to IPEDS accurately, there could be severe financial consequences to the institution from loss of federal financial aid to a downgrade in national rankings.

Supervisors

Supervisors will need to access HRIS if the organization wants performance evaluations and employee time approved electronically. If this is the goal of the organization, then supervisor training will need to be conducted and there will be a cost associated with supervisors taking time to perform data entry into HRIS. While there may be cost savings on some levels, there will be an expense as well that needs to be considered. The return on investment should be analysed to determine if the personnel savings in other areas is worth the expense of training and having supervisors performing these menial data entry tasks.

Administrative Assistants

Administrative assistants' roles have changed throughout the years in public and non-profit organizations. In the past, the administrative assistant was tasked to do basic clerical work, answer the phone and keep calendars. In today's environment, administrative assistance have to interact with not only HRIS, but also financial and, at higher education institutions, student information systems. The training and education requirements have increased dramatically for administrative assistants such that having a high school diploma or a GED is no longer adequate. Administrative assistants are now required to use HRIS to post vacant positions, participate in recruitment efforts, input personnel information on newly hired employees, process merit or promotion documentation, oversee payroll completion by employees, process retirement or termination documentation, manage union data, and reconcile accounts in addition to their traditional duties such as purchasing supplies and services for the department, scheduling meetings and travel plans for supervisors, and answering telephone or email inquiries for the department. This expansion of knowledge, skills and abilities requires that administrative assistants greater education and training than their counterparts in the past, but also that they will need additional on-job training to interact with HRIS.

External to the Organization – State/Federal/Individuals

There are a number of government agencies and individuals who need to have access to HRIS data. There is data that is protected by certain statutes from being externally released, and there is data that has to be reported to government agencies. Depending on the state or local statutes, HRIS data may also be requested through open records requests. These open records requests can come from a wide variety of individuals or organizations and can encompass everything salary information to who is employed with the organization to information on a group of individuals. HRIS data may also be requested in litigation cases. While these entities are not so much a function of the organization, they are in need of accessing the information for a variety of legal reasons.

Case Study: Some of our Faculty Are Missing
For years, a public state flagship university had been designated as a Carnegie R2 research institution due to how the data was reported to the federal government. The incoming president made being named a Carnegie R1 research institution their top priority and goal for the university. Being named an R1 institution would allow the university to compete for additional contracts and grants as well as being able to hire more prestigious faculty to support their research activities. The university hired a new Director of Institutional Research who quickly discovered a number of faculty were not coded

properly in HRIS and the university had been incorrectly reporting tenured faculty on the IPEDS HR report at a lower headcount than the university had employed. As soon as this issue was addressed and corrected, the university obtained an R1 status.

For years, the university had been hurting themselves by not accurately reporting faculty to the federal government. This translated to a potential loss of contracts and grants because the university could not compete for the funding. Additionally, this cost the university prestige, the possibility of hiring top notch faculty and could have potentially resulted in thousands if not millions of dollars in research funding bypassing the institution. Not only can this impact national rankings, this also influences what type of students want to attend the university for graduate school and hampers the university's efforts toward upgrading research facilities with external contracts and grants funding. Failure to accurately report faculty information hurt the university's reputation for years when, all along, the university had the resources to achieve R1 Carnegie status. The previous president's failure to achieve R1 status hurt their reputation unnecessarily. Without doing a thing, this president's successor was able to claim success in achieving R1 status for their institution simply because errors in faculty reporting were finally discovered and corrected.

Case Study: Waters Rising

The city issued a Request for Proposal (RFP) to select a new Network Preferred Provider Organization to reduce health benefits costs. The city was spending $200 million dollars on its workforce of 13,000 employees and 13,000 dependents. The city received two bids for healthcare benefits with one bid being 10% less the less than the current provider. The city was tempted to go with the new PPO network. However, the employees, especially the police and fire officers were opposed to the new provider as most of the police and fire employees lived very far outside the city and they claimed the lowest bidder did not have a sufficient network of hospitals close enough to most of their employees. The lower rank and file civilian employees did not have an issue with the potential new PPO vendor as most of those employees lived in the city or were living near the city.

The city wrote a program to search their HRIS data base to determine the addresses of all their employees. The city used their geospatial information system (GIS) to analyze the location of the provider network facility locations against the two systems that were bid to see which vendor had facilities closer to the largest amount of city employees and their dependents. This analysis was to determine if the city was going to replace the existing PPO network with the new network that was 10% cheaper than the current provider. The analysis showed that the 5000 police and fire personnel were well positioned near the existing PPO provider and the 8000 civilian employees were better served by the new low bid vendor.

After much discussion, the city decided it was politically safer to use the HRIS information used with GIS resulting in all of the bids being rejected. This action resulted in the existing contract being issued a one-year extension, which was exercised by the city. In the upcoming bid cycle for healthcare provides, new bids would be developed with the existing address information generated from the HRIS system. This would ensure that the winning bid in the upcoming year would be evaluated against their ability to serve all the employees and their dependents. The new provider would be required to have network providers who were in the closest proximity to the most number of city employees while have a lower cost structure.

Summary

It is important to understand the different functional areas that interact with HRIS. Every department will most likely use HRIS in some form or fashion depending upon what role they have in the organization (e.g. hiring employees, payroll). HRIS is a hub for the organization to operate, and the departments have to operate within a sphere of parameters that allow for inter-operability with HRIS. These parameters have formal guidelines such as policies, procedures and legal statutes that have to be followed within the confines of certain restrictions. Then there are other informal aspects such as organizational culture, training, supervisors and the knowledge, skills and abilities of the employees themselves that influence how certain departments interact with HRIS. These parameters are important to understand for managers, supervisors and employees so that HRIS can be better utilized to its capacity for the benefit of the organization. The next chapter will discuss some of the potential obstacles to using and implementing HRIS faced by public organizations.

References

Kristen Deutsch, New focus HR, April 10, (2015). Retrieved on November 22, 2020. https://newfocushr.com/2015/04/13/the-functional-areas-of-human-resources/

iEduNote. (2020). *Compensation management, definition, objectives, importance*. Retrieved November 22. iedunote.com

Prachi Junelja. (2015). *Management study guide*. Retrieved on November 22, 2020, Systems considerations in the design of HRIS. managementstudyguide.com

Lucerna. (2020). *HRIS can help with payroll compliance management*. Retrieved on November 22, 2020. hrpayrollsystems.net

Ruth Mayhew, BizFluent, September 27, (2017). *Employee relations & human resources*. Retrieved on November 22, 2020. bizfluent.com

Obstacles for Public Organizations Using HRIS

9

Key Points of the Chapter

- There are several barriers that will be discussed to obtaining accurate data for public organization employees.
- Both technical and cultural issues can create barriers in obtaining accurate data for public organization employees.
- Several factors external to HRIS can create barriers in obtaining accurate data for public organization employees.

Need for Good Quality Personnel Data in the Public Sector

Data quality is defined in the literature as "a set of characteristics that data should own (p.1)" (Scannapieco & Catarci, 2002). Several scholars have provided various classifications for data quality. These include accuracy, timeliness, completeness and consistency (Ballou & Pazer, 1985; Scannapieco et al., 2005), meaningfulness, unambiguousness, and accessibility. The most detailed classification is provided by Wang et al. (1995), in which 25 different dimensions are used to classify data quality, of which accuracy tops their list. Given the importance of accuracy as a measure of data quality, this study will focus on the causes for inaccurate data in the public sector with a special attention on institutions of higher education.

Studies often discuss the challenges of poor data – resulting in reduced efficiency, lower performance, lower morale and turnover in organizations (Givan, 2005; Kahn et al., 2002; Pipino et al., 2002; Redman, 1998) – but are amiss to discuss what goes on from the time the data are input to receiving an output. If inaccurate data are produced, one is quick to point to the bad quality data. Garbage into a system leads to garbage out. Poor data quality is not the only reason; there are several other factors potentially leading to erroneous and inaccurate data. However,

N. A. Valcik et al., *Human Resources Information Systems*, Management for Professionals, https://doi.org/10.1007/978-3-030-75111-1_9

much of it remains as a “black box”, a mystery. Through this study, the authors unpack the various reasons for inaccurate personnel data from input to output.

Personnel data are critical for many public organizations for workforce planning, analysis, operational reporting as well as compliance requirements to local, state and federal entities (Abella, 1985; Caudle et al., 1991; Goodman et al., 2013; McCullough & Sims, 2012; Troshani et al., 2011). Human Resources data, for the additional reasons of compliance purposes, must be reliable and accurate. However, public organizations often must overcome several obstacles to realize analysis and reporting useful enough for upper level administrators to make policy decisions and accurate enough to comply with governmental agencies. Furthermore, since public organizations are funded by taxpayers, employees’ salaries, titles and departments can be disclosed as public information. Due to this level of transparency, it is imperative that salary data be as accurate as possible to avoid public backlash because salaries are perceived to be too high or too low. If inaccuracies are publicly revealed, this could trigger an audit and can result in poor public relations as well.

Public organizations are no different from their private or non-profit organization counterparts where employee hiring, retention and turnover are concerned. With a decrease in funding always being a possibility, public organizations need to be more flexible and adaptable in their employee recruitment and retention strategies. Operational data can be used to determine budgets for each department, salary raises for employees, hiring for diversity goals, turnover due to retirement, shortfalls in personnel requirements and loss of personnel through attrition from reasons other than retirement. During tough financial times or when the organization needs to re-staff with new or updated skill sets, personnel data can be used to determine if certain early retirement programs are feasible for the organization to utilize. Throughout this research, the authors will discuss the obstacles and possible solutions for an organization to obtain and effectively use Human Resources data toward these ends.

Barriers to Good Quality Personnel Data

There are several barriers resulting in poor quality personnel data. We classify these into Internal and External. Internal barriers are further classified into: (a) Information systems (b) Human resources culture (c) Organizational culture (d) Data ownership and (e) Reporting. External barriers comprise of (a) Legal mandates (b) Stakeholders and (c) Business Processes.

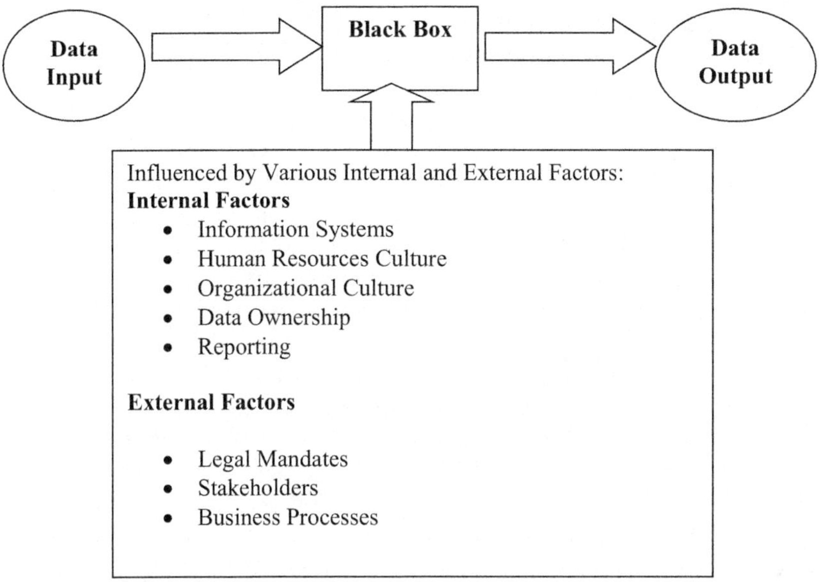

Internal Factors

Information Systems

With any type of large public organization, there will be a substantial enterprise information system for human resources. An Enterprise Planning System (ERP) is defined as "configurable information systems packages that integrate information and information-based processes within and across functional areas in an organization" (Kumar & van Hillegersberg, 2000, p. 23). While having their origins in the business world, ERP systems have gained popularity in university settings worldwide. Most popular ERP systems used in universities are Oracle, SCT Banner, PeopleSoft, and SAP. These systems make data accessibility and controls easier. Thus, the primary function of an ERP is to enhance efficiency of an organization by streamlining the decision-making process (Bingi et al., 1999; Li, 1999).

Organizations are thus choosing ERP systems over Human Resources Information System (HRIS) as they fully integrate all operations into one package. According to Ashbaugh and Miranda (2002, p. 10) "the value of ERP was to bring financials and HRMS under a single vendor and common technology standards" thus making HRIS a subset of the ERP software. HRIS is defined as a "technology based system that is used to acquire, store, manipulate, analyze, retrieve, and distribute pertinent information regarding an organizations human resources (Tannenbaum, 1990, p. 27). HRIS in the public sector is used mainly for information gathering and record keeping instead of transformational activities such as re-engineering of HR or strategic activities within the organization (Bamel et al., 2014; Kovach & Cathcart,

1999; Reddick, 2009). However, there are several challenges involved with ERP systems, the biggest being cost (Fui-Hoon Nah et al., 2001; Gibson et al., 1999; Holsapple & Sena, 2005; Kumar & van Hillegersberg, 2000).

Prior to Y2K, many of these information systems were not integrated with other systems such as finance, budget, facilities, and, in the case of universities, student information systems. Since these systems were stand-alone and isolated, the cultures within which these systems were "siloed" too. Each silo specialized in only their area of functional concern or expertise. Human Resources, for example, entered personnel information into the human resource information system unconcerned or unaware of what other employee data was being entered into the finance, budget, facilities or student information systems. Additionally, internal business processes during this timeframe still utilized paper forms with little or no electronic input from lower level employees who interfaced with the information system.

To keep information systems operational before Y2K, many organizations hired programmers that had already retired from the private sector to modify enterprise information systems so that their system would not collapse during the date change from 1999 to 2000. Programmers who supported these types of mainframe information systems tended to be an older generation of programmers that were accustomed and trained in programming languages that had become obsolescent (i.e. COBOL, NATURAL). Unfortunately, when large public organizations hired programmers to "patch" the older systems to remain operational, they inadvertently promoted the silo organizational culture. The personnel in functional areas such as human resources were not forced to change their business processes to work in an integrated fashion and thus entrenching the silos. Eventually, even these large public organizations were forced to transition to an integrated system when older mainframe systems became unsupported by the vendors. Unfortunately, this does not mean functional areas did not attempt to restructure the new integrated information system to match their older style of business processes. For many public organizations, this lead to turmoil because the new system was not compatible with older business processes (Al-Mashari et al., 2003; Davenport, 1998; Umble et al., 2003).

In many cases, public organizations pass through a series of transitions, which would involve retraining or replacing key personnel. With these types of transitions, an organization loses institutional memory, which can lead to gaps in organizational information and capability when older systems data are migrated to the newer integrated information system (Cain & Barata, 2001; Mnjama & Wamukoya, 2007). Additionally, vendors who sell an enterprise system do not customize an information system for a particular client without a great deal of expense. When the customer chooses an information system, they should choose one that will carry out the functionality of what the organization requires. Otherwise, the organization will need to restructure and embrace their business processes to fit the information system.

With the new advent of integrated information systems, the potential problems with data entry issues have increased. The first and foremost problem with data entry issues comes from employees who have the ability to self-report their own data. While there are many areas that can be audited by human resources and IT in the component (or module) of an integrated information system, other variables such as date of birth, gender, ethnicity, and, to a lesser extent, contact information (i.e. telephone number, physical address etc.) can become problematic. When data becomes an unreliable source of information for reporting, using the data for operational decision-making becomes untenable (Debbarma et al., 2013; Eckerson, 2002; Haug et al., 2011; Redman, 1998).

Additionally, public organizations will usually have different software packages for various business processes (e.g. payroll). These software packages will typically require additional modifications to the host information system to operate successfully. Since there is no federal mandate for public organizations to buy or use the same information systems and software packages, the combinations used by public organizations can be endless, rendering standardization among public organizations, particularly higher education institutions that are part of a larger system, nearly impossible. The type of information system chosen by an organization is often dictated by the following parameters:

1. Cost of the information system (what can the organization afford)
2. The capability of the employees of the public organization (can they support the information system?)
3. Business processes (how willing is an organization to change business processes to fit an information system)
4. Organizational culture (what politically can be supported in the organization)

These four factors will vary greatly among public organizations, resulting in an infinite number of combinations of information systems and software packages used for human resources data. Even with organizations that use similar information systems, the manner in which those systems are used can vary widely from one organization to another.

Human Resources Culture

The role of human resource administrators and employees is to conduct the following functions: hiring/recruitment, job analysis, employee planning and appraisal, training, compensation and benefits, and succession planning among others. Contending with data issues is another matter entirely. There is always a shortage of HR personnel who have information technology skills. Working with data requires human resources personnel to be more analytical when entering in data into an information system as well as ensuring the data is accurately updated when hiring an applicant or when an employee is promoted or changes job assignments (Ban, 2005; Mahapa & Chirasha, 2012; Pynes, 2004; Thite et al., 2012).

There is also the issue of how human resources is perceived by the organization itself. If the perception is not positive, this can lead to low morale within the human resources department, which can potentially lead to a high degree of incomplete or incorrect data being entered into the system. Departments that perceive (either correctly or incorrectly) that human resources personnel are incompetent will begin to question the credibility of those responsible for the data (Redman, 2013). An example would be a state auditor who declares that a university has no full-time faculty because they do not understand that universities consider faculty on nine-month contracts as full-time faculty. The auditor has lost credibility from university employees by not understanding the business processes they were sent to audit. The loss of political power can have several consequences not the least of which can result in departmental administrators finding themselves under increased scrutiny. Data produced by the department will be questioned because the organization has lost faith in the credibility of the department's data entry capability and the effectiveness of its business processes.

Often, human resources departments are dependent upon employees external to their department for technical support or analytical reporting requirements. Employees themselves are often responsible for inputting their own information into a human resources database. Variables that can frequently complicate information accuracy are ethnicity, address and educational background. In the modern age, obtaining an accurate address is becoming more problematic since employees (and universities' students), can conduct all of their business transactions online. Transactions that use to require a physical mailing address, such as maintaining benefits or issuing checks, are now conducted electronically. Thus, when an organization needs to use address information for operational analysis (e.g. GIS), the analysis can have gaps in the data, which results in incomplete results.

Another approach is to outsource data entry or entire human resource functions to outside vendors. Contracting human resources to outside vendors can pose several challenges as shown by Coggburn (2007) in the case study of Texas Health and Human Services outsourcing their HR functions to Convergys, a private firm. The different values and interests between public and private sector gave rise to several unanticipated problems. For example, eighty employees received warrants instead of paychecks and others received inaccurate payments. In another case in the mid-1990's, Nortel Networks contracted to a third party, which led to a host of data entry errors within the Human Resource system Resumix. These data entry errors necessitated the creation of an application built in Filemaker Pro designed to audit and clean the data and to produce profiles of new college graduate applicants who would receive multiple job offers from different departments. After the data was cleaned, the profiles generated were accurate over 67% of the time, which proved valuable for recruiters who could then pursue new graduates that fit the profiles provided by the hiring managers (Valcik, 2015).

Other examples of problematic information can range from employee health insurance to faculty rank and tenure attributes maintained by a department other than human resources. While this may in theory make life easier for human resources departments, this also makes them vulnerable to political forces that would isolate human resources departments and limit their involvement in policy decisions. Without the ability to extract and analyze the data accurately, the human resources department is operating blindly, which can severely limit their effectiveness and decision-making capacity on the organization (Beadles et al., 2005; Kovach & Cathcart, 1999).

As Daft would indicate, organizational life cycle will also factor into data integrity (Daft, 1995). With expanding public organizations, data integrity becomes a greater concern as more data entry is necessary to keep pace with new hiring, promotions and so on, all of which is dependent upon departmental input into the information system. Without participation by the departments, the gap between what is needed and what is occurring with data entry will widen and shrinking this gap will take more effort and more money.

Organizational Culture

"Because we have always done it this way." The quote identifies stagnation in a public organization. Stagnation or inertia can be a major obstacle if business processes are never re-evaluated or are deemed "good enough" by the public organization. This culture or mindset can be detrimental to any successful information system implementation (Kovach et al., 2002). Existing personnel and business processes will be difficult to alter with a new personnel information system. Instead of using the capabilities of the new information system, an organization is likely to use the new system like an electronic filing cabinet, which will not address current organizational inefficiencies.

There are several studies demonstrating how organizational culture can act as a barrier to the successful assimilation and integration of new technology (Fink, 1998; Gallivan, 2001; Gallivan & Srite, 2005; Lippert & Swiercz, 2005; Ruppel & Harrington, 2001; Tolsby, 1998). Tolsby (1998) describes a case study of the Norwegian Army's adoption of a new information system and found the organizational culture was a significant hindrance to the new system's success. The Norwegian Army's organizational culture encouraged leaders to avoid risk and take responsibility for their decisions. If Information Technology (IT) fails to account for the organizational culture when implementing an enterprise information system, the implementation will fail because the organizational culture itself was incompatible with the enterprise information system (Valcik, 2015).

Without motivation to input information correctly, the organization will see a drift in how data should ideally be recorded compared to how the data is actually being input into the information system. Data entry will remain a lower priority for the departments that do not understand why the data are important for organizational operations. This is in line with Agency Theory, which indicates that people will be driven by their own agendas to accomplish their set goals (Downs, 1967). While some departments require data to be accurate (which is their agenda), other departments view data cleansing or accuracy as a lower priority since they have different priorities. This decoupling "pushes" the organization out of alignment, which results in organizational drift.

With public organizations, there will always be some increase in organizational drift when new technologies appear for two reasons. First, existing employees will need to acquire new skills, which necessitates a learning curve that can be quite substantial for some employees. Second, new technology may require an organization to hire new employees. The hiring process can be time consuming. The new employees will then need to acclimate to their new organization, which takes additional time.

Employees who cannot, or will not, learn new technologies or adapt to a new organizational culture may be candidates for an early buyout or phased retirement program, which would benefit both the employee and the organization long term. However, to determine the true status of employee retention and hiring, accurate data are required. All of the issues identified operationally impact a public organization's financial wellbeing as well as their operational efficiency and effectiveness.

Data Ownership

In the organization, there must be a champion that will ensure the data being entered is correct and verifiable. The issue of data integrity comes down to data ownership and accountability (Redman, 1998; Vosburg & Kumar, 2001). In larger public organizations, there is sometimes confusion over what department should own certain data entry aspects. For example, should the data be entered by Payroll, Human Resources or, in the case of higher education institutions' faculty, the Provost's office? The question of data responsibility is an issue of organizational command and control issues with business processes. Additionally, the organization will need to ascertain which department in the organization will have responsibility to audit human resources data. In most public organizations, there is a department usually tasked with reporting responsibilities separate from the internal audit unit. Auditing human resources data can be conducted by either one of these units or by both working together.

Ownership of personnel data and determining who is responsible for keeping data current in the enterprise information system can be daunting (Chang et al., 2000). In many cases, an information system is seen as an electronic filing cabinet as opposed to being used as a tool to collect data and operationalize for the decision-making process. However, with the new ERP systems, data ownership is seen as the responsibility of everyone who has access to HR data. In the past, the IT department was solely responsible for maintaining the integrity of the data – this is certainly changing with evolution of integrated systems. According to Vosburg and Kumar (2001, p. 28) "Ensuring that all stakeholders of an ERP system understand their responsibilities with respect to maintaining data integrity will lead to a better quality system. Data that is a part of an ERP system belongs to an organization and not to any individual department or user." Despite the broad ownership that ERP systems offer, there are turf battles for data ownership and the politics of it can impact the quality of data (Demarest, 1997). Specifically, there are three types of power struggles and organizational control struggles: entities who want to have ownership and responsibilities, entities who are attempting to shirk ownership and responsibilities, and entities who are ordered to take ownership and responsibility for personnel data.

Ultimately, whoever is assigned to update such information will need to audit the data entry process to ensure data integrity. Without data integrity, the data will become unusable for accurate analysis, which in turn can lead to erroneous decision-making. An organization will need to determine if the entities responsible for entering and maintaining the data are truly the correct organizational component with the knowledge, skills and abilities to perform the task. Additionally, the organization will need to determine how the data entry process should be audited to ensure data integrity.

Reporting

Reporting and performing analysis of data has many potential pitfalls that analysts and administrators should be aware of when producing files or reports (Kaplan et al., 1998). Variables submitted according to certain criteria to a federal or state agency to achieve one policy objective might be translated and utilized in a completely different manner than for what it was originally intended. While federal or state agencies provide guidelines for the data they require, the definitions of those requirements may be open to interpretation. Certain variables, if not clearly defined by the state or federal agency, could be reported in many various ways depending on how different public entities initially captured the information. This will lead to data that is inconsistent if state or federal agencies attempt to compare organizations based on these types of data (Akbulut et al., 2009; Akbulut-Bailey, 2011). For example, a state agency may require a public entity to report contracted salary rates for employees. However, a public entity may instead report actual salaries paid, including part-time salary rates, because of the limitations of their enterprise information system. Thus, the state agency is assuming (incorrectly) that the amount being reported for salary is the contracted amount and may draw the erroneous conclusion that some individuals are grossly underpaid. The differences in reported and expected reported value allows drift to occur from the ideal to what is actually occurring. A public entity should assess what definitions are being used as well as how the information is being populated in the enterprise information system. This will allow for the information to be consistently stored and accurately extracted for reporting purposes.

Another challenge to data integrity is when employees add, delete or update their own information. It is virtually impossible to ensure the employee enters all data according to proper business procedure. Some data elements, particularly ethnicity, will be unverifiable due to how the employee categorizes themselves and because of federal and state statutes, which prevent the organization from requiring disclosure of certain information. Furthermore, if the data are not integrated across departments, it can lead to erroneous reporting with different departments producing different results for the same query (Guan et al., 2002).

External Factors

Legal Mandates

Legal mandates can pose an obstacle to an organization for obtaining accurate human resources data (Abella, 1985; Ashbaugh & Miranda, 2002; Givan, 2005). For example, federal law prohibits a public organization from requiring employees to disclose their ethnicity or gender. Additionally, information of this type is impossible to independently verify. Thus, a conundrum exists where public organizations are mandated to become more diverse but are not allowed to require employees to disclose the information necessary to determine if diversity efforts are working. According to EEOC (n.d) "Employers need to provide employees the opportunity to self-identify their own ethnicity. If an employee then refuses to do so, employment records or visual observation must be used" (EEOC, n.d.). This can further complicate reporting and data accuracy as HR is now left to guess the race or ethnicity of employees that choose to withhold their racial identity. Other information required by public organizations to verify legal dependents for benefits (e.g. marriage certificates) could possibly prove to be a point of litigation because marriage certificates frequently have religious affiliations printed on them, another protected category of personal information. As stated by the United States Equal Employment Opportunity Commission:

> "Pre-Employment Inquiries and Religious Affiliation or Beliefs
>
> Questions about an applicant's religious affiliation or beliefs (unless the religion is a bona fide occupational qualification (BFOQ)), are generally viewed as non-job-related and problematic under federal law.
>
> Religious corporations, associations, educational institutions, or societies are exempt from the federal laws that EEOC enforces when it comes to the employment of individuals based on their particular religion. In other words, an employer whose purpose and character is primarily religious is permitted to lean towards hiring persons of the same religion. This exception relieves religious organizations only from the ban on employment discrimination based on religion. It does not exempt such organizations from employing individuals due to their race, gender, national origin, disability, color, and/or age. Other employers should avoid questions about an applicant's religious affiliation, such as place of worship, days of worship, and religious holidays and should not ask for references from religious leaders, e.g., minister, rabbi, priest, imam, or pastor." (United States Equal Employment Opportunity Commission, 2015)

A public organization should be aware of the United States Equal Employment Opportunity Commission guidelines and ensure those guidelines are followed to avoid potential legal action from applicants and employees. Additionally, there are new initiatives regarding diversity and affirmative action in the workplace that require reports to comply with state and federal mandates. For public universities, the Integrated Postsecondary Education Data System (IPEDS), managed by the National Center for Education Statistics (NCES), requires colleges and universities to report salary, faculty/staff status by Standard Occupation Classification (SOC)

Code, ethnicity and gender on a regular basis. These reports are made public through NCES and can be accessed by the public (NCES XE "National Center for Education Statistics (NCES)" , 2015; Renn & Lunceford, 2004). Other state initiatives, such as West Virginia H.B. 439 (2015), use data reported by state agencies to determine comparative salaries for certain types of positions (West Virginia Legislature, 2015). Through the new state personnel database system (OASIS) and existing personnel reports, data are used by state agencies to determine how personnel at various levels should be compensated.

Stakeholders

In a public institution, there are several internal and external stakeholders a human resources department works with when collecting and reporting data. Internal stakeholders are usually employees in other departments who may see personnel data as simply a business process. The personnel that typically input information into an information system are secretaries and administrative assistants who are frequently tasked with inputting various departmental transactions and completing other accounting duties. These types of employees are mostly concerned with getting the information complete enough to satisfy the human resources department so empty positions can be filled or existing employees can be promoted. Other internal stakeholders at a public university are administrators, students, faculty, and alumni. However, personnel data can be of importance to external stakeholders as well. External stakeholders include citizens, parents, board members, legislators, funding agencies, community leaders, and employers.

Guan et al. (2002) argue that higher education is an ever-changing environment requiring leaders to make decisions that require sound data, which can then be presented to stakeholders who impact institutional direction and policies. However, studies indicate the poor utilization of data by upper administration. In an exploratory study of human resources systems in a large public university by Beadles et al. (2005), the authors found that over three-fourth (80%) of the HR directors agreed that the information produced was underutilized by the upper administration and only 40% agreed that the information system increased collaboration and coordination across departments and administrators.

Business Processes

Business processes can form an external barrier for human resources organizations if another government agency's processes will not integrate with the existing human resources information system. There may be an obstacle if a government agency requests information that is unobtainable due to the limitations of the current information system (Mahapa & Chirasha, 2012; Troshani et al., 2011). Business processes can also form an external barrier if one business process from a state agency conflicts with a federal reporting mandate. The information system may only be able to capture the information to comply with federal mandates, which causes an obvious conflict with the business process of the requesting state agency.

Salary is a good example of how information systems can be a barrier to providing accurate data. For example, a government oversight agency requires a state university to report salary of faculty on a contracted basis. However, the university captures only what is paid to the faculty member due to the limitations of the information system. Additionally, the oversight agency wants the information reported in twelve-month time spans when the university contracts faculty on a nine-month basis. Two conflicting business processes from different agencies have thus caused an external barrier for both agencies.

Organizational Interventions

The obstacles discussed can skew the quality of data, which will invalidate results from producing meaningful and actionable information. If the obstacles are not overcome by the organization, the data could be unreliable for the operational decision-making process. The positive benefit to having clean data are an organization can use the data to make informed decisions as well as use the data for strategic and operational planning. What can an organization do if their personnel data has issues in their information system? Several factors will determine whether an organization is able to correct the issues found in an information system: auditing, leadership, streamlining, and data entry controls.

Auditing

An organization can intervene by having regular audits in place to check for data integrity in the enterprise information system. An organization can also replace personnel with those who have the analytical abilities to develop a series of edit checks on the data, which can be sent to the functional areas to correct. If the organization is required to produce federal and state reports, it would be ideal to build in pre- and post-implementation audits to ensure data quality and accuracy (McCullough & Sims, 2012). This will allow the information to be corrected in the system before it is sent to federal or state officials for certification.

A public organization should assess its business practices at regular intervals to determine how human resources data are being collected and reported (Bargerstock, 2000; Nutley, 2000). Areas of operation that are vulnerable to, or have experienced, data entry issues should be reviewed as soon as possible so that data entry controls can be implemented to limit data entry errors. The data entry controls can include modifications to the user interface that will either validate when a user attempts to save a record or an application that checks for the validity of data that has been entered (i.e. address information). Many enterprise information systems now have the capacity to control free-formed data entry fields to limit data entry errors. That being stated, there is still a need to have business processes documented and evaluated to ensure the quality of the data.

The organization will need to evaluate its employees' knowledge, skills and abilities (KSA) versus the organization's KSA requirements per job position for operational purposes. It is important for the organization to understand the requirements of each job position and the performance level of each position in the organization. A thorough assessment will produce a gap analysis documenting present KSAs per employee (reality) versus organizational KSA requirements (theory). Meyer and Rowan (1977) describe this organizational occurrence as decoupling, a situation in which ideal operating parameters are compared to what is actually occurring in the organization, which results in organizational drift (Meyer & Rowan, 1977). Inevitably, there will be organizational drift between ideal KSA levels and actual employee KSA levels. An organization can attempt to close the gap between reality and theory, but, due to hiring laws, existing personnel, and available job candidates, there may be a limit on how much this gap can be reduced.

Leadership

Does the organization value the accuracy of personnel data? A better question might be which parts of the organization value accurate personnel data? Large, complex organizations often hold different values on personnel data within their own organization. Some departments may covet the information highly while other departments do not understand why the information is important or how the information impacts their areas of operation. Unless the organization's top leadership provides guidance as well as directive that such information is critical to organizational operations, the motivation to input, maintain and update personnel information will be minimal among the various departments (Bamel et al., 2014).

Support from the top leadership is documented as the most important factor for success in HRIS (Bamel et al., 2014; Kovach & Cathcart, 1999; Ngai & Wat, 2006; Razali & Vrontis, 2010; Tansley & Newell, 2007; Troshani et al., 2011). Without proper leadership in the appropriate areas of the organization, human resources data will most likely experience data integrity issues throughout the information system. Without organizational leadership to develop and implement mechanisms to insure data integrity, data standards and controls will be non-existent if the area responsible for data entry is not held accountable when or if data entry issues occur. A leader empowered to make organizational decisions in a positive manner is critical for accomplishing accurate human resources data. In contrast, a leader who refused to make organizational decisions in regard to human resources data or makes poor organizational decisions will be a liability to the organization.

If no one in an organization is assuming responsibility for or control of data entry and maintenance, leadership may be an issue. A good leader can reorganize their department or area and add additional resources to insure that data entry and maintenance are valued (Troshani et al., 2011). An effective leader can recognize the need to hire someone in the human resources department with technical abilities to analyze the data on a regular basis as well as perform audit checks and produce reports (McCullough & Sims, 2012). A human resource employee with technical skillsets can interface more easily with personnel inside the human resources department, information technology, and in other departments reliant upon personnel information.

An ineffectual leader will not acknowledge or address data entry problems. If the organization discovers it has an ineffectual leader, the organization has two choices. First, the organization can issue a directive to the current leader in an attempt to improve the situation. Good directives can make a difference if a leader is willing to change in a positive manner. Secondly, the organization can replace a leader if it is unlikely that new directives will make a positive impact on data entry or maintenance of data. An ineffectual leader may need to be replaced if they lack the knowledge, skills or abilities to restructure or address current shortfalls with data entry or maintenance of personnel data.

Streamlining Business Processes

When re-evaluating existing business processes, new methods or technologies can be utilized to increase efficiency or effectiveness of data entry processes in information systems. Often an organization will retain a certain business process because, at one point, this old process was logical or conformed to a pre-existing enterprise information system but now is no longer an effective or efficient method on the new enterprise information system. One common way to improve effectiveness and efficiency is to automate certain processes. Another common business process is converting paper forms to an online form, thus improving accuracy and the timeliness of the approval process (McCullough & Sims, 2012).

If data entry and data maintenance issues consistently occur within a particular department, an organization can transfer duties and data ownership to one or more areas of operation to reduce errors. Another solution could be recombining previously segmented ownership and duties into a single entity if the situation warrants an organizational change. A study conducted by Haug et al. (2010) found the lack of delegation of responsibility for data maintenance as the single factor impacting data quality.

Finally, the enterprise information system itself could be modified to use drop down boxes and validation tables for data entry personnel. If a data entry employee is presented with a small menu of viable options, invalid responses can be eliminated and data entry errors can be reduced. This approach also allows for a thorough audit to be conducted since the only answers that can exist are those on the validation table.

Data Quality

As with any organization, data quality can be a severe barrier to an organization's ability to mine data operationally or report data correctly for compliance. There are several areas of potential problems that create data quality issues. The HRIS software itself can be an issue if data entry points are not designed with limited open text fields. To control for data entry issues, one would want to have as many drop-down menus or lookup table choices for data entry points as possible. This limits how many data entry issues can arise in the first place. Another method that can prevent data entry issues from occurring is to have reliable data feeds from other systems (where possible), which in turn limits how much data entry is required by an employee. For example, location data can be fed from ArcSDE from GIS shapefiles of floor plans to provide room and building information to HRIS. This allows a drop-down menu or look up table for a user to select a valid choice instead of typing in a building code or room number that may not exist.

Other issues of data quality relate to training and documentation on HRIS. Without proper training and documentation, employees can very easily enter data incorrectly in HRIS, which follows the old adage of "garbage in and garbage out". This can be a severe issue to organizations wanting to use their HRIS software effectively to make operational decisions. If upper administrators do not have information that is accurate, their decisions may not be made on a sound basis leading to potentially serious consequences. Inefficient or ineffective business processes can also lead to a wide variety of problems for data integrity as well. If business processes are not correctly designed or documented, data integrity issues can arise, for example inappropriate use of HRIS variables or data recorded into inappropriate fields. If business processes are not documented, an analyst or programmer could extract the wrong data for a report, which will lead to erroneous analyses.

Reporting Data

A consistent problem with reporting data is discovering incorrect data in HRIS. Throughout this chapter we have identified issues leading to data integrity problems as well as identifying ways to correct those shortfalls. Another issue, however, deals with data definitions for the purpose of reporting and maintaining consistent data definitions for a long period of time. For example, if data is stored in HRIS in Year One by a particular definition and then the definition changes for Year Two, then a problem in consistent reporting occurs. Another problem that can occur is when fields have to be added or expanded to accommodate new variables for government reporting. This can create issue for legacy reports that continue to be used in a production environment. If variable names are changed or added in the HRIS table structure, any reports connected to those tables will have to be changed to ensure the programs run successfully.

Case Study: X Marks the Spot

A public organization wanted to use Geospatial Information Systems (GIS) to map where all of their employees resided so operational planning could be conducted with the organization's host city. The organization was the largest employer in the city and therefore roadways and other infrastructure were heavily used. The organization then assigned the task to a GIS programmer on staff and asked them to map down the employees residences. This proved problematic for multiple reasons. The main reason was having inaccurate or missing addresses in HRIS. It is impossible to map down to a GIS map an employee with no address or an incorrect address. One of the issues discovered during this task was that many employees did not provide an accurate (or provided a local) address for where they lived since so many business processes can be conducted remotely. This created a problem especially since many of these individuals lived in the city and provided only a post office box number. The second problem encountered was the GIS file itself. The satellite photo of the area did not have a number of newer roadways or addresses for the city, which prevented valid employee addresses to be locked down to a valid location. In certain cases, the GIS programmer had to manually add newer buildings (e.g. apartments and houses) to the satellite photo as a work around to show where employees resided. In this manner the GIS programmer was able to produce a map, but since the HRIS data was inaccurate or missing, only 75% of the employees could be linked to the GIS image. After this occurrence, the organization began to review data put into the self-service module in HRIS and had a piece of address validation software added to increase the accuracy for addresses.

Summary

While there are many "theoretical" aspects to using HRIS, populating data into HRIS or reporting data from HRIS, there will always need to be adjustments made to how the organization is going to use HRIS or how the system will be implemented. How HRIS is used by functional areas will differ from organization to organization since departments can vary in how they are structured, tiered or staffed. The staff will need to determine how HRIS will be utilized since the success of HRIS will depend largely on the knowledge, skills and abilities of the employees within the organization. If the organization chooses to outsource large segments of their HRIS, then the organization will lose more direct control on how their system is maintained and accessed. In the next chapter, the dangers and costs of migration to a new HRIS will be discussed as well as the considerations that need to be explored by the organization before an HRIS is selected and implemented.

References

Abella, J. R. S. (1985). General summary from equality in employment: a royal commission report. *Canadian Woman Studies, 6*(4), 5–7.

Akbulut, A. Y., Kelle, P., Pawlowski, S. D., Schneider, H., & Looney, C. A. (2009). To share or not to share? Examining the factors influencing local agency electronic information sharing. *International Journal of Business Information Systems, 4*(2), 143–172.

Akbulut-Bailey, A. Y. (2011). Information sharing between local and state governments. *The Journal of Computer Information Systems, 51*(4), 53.

Al-Mashari, M., Al-Mudimigh, A., & Zairi, M. (2003). Enterprise resource planning: A taxonomy of critical factors. *European Journal of Operational Research, 146*(2), 352–364.

Ashbaugh, S., & Miranda, R. (2002). Technology for human resources management: Seven questions and answers. *Public Personnel Management, 31*(1), 7–20.

Ballou, D. P., & Pazer, H. L. (1985). Modeling data and process quality in multi-input, multi-output information systems. *Management Science, 31*(2), 150–162.

Bamel, N., Kumar Bamel, U., Sahay, V., & Thite, M. (2014). Usage, benefits and barriers of human resource information system in universities. *VINE: The Journal of Information and Knowledge Management Systems, 44*(4), 519–536.

Ban, C. (2005). The changing role of the human resource office. In S. Condrey (Ed.), *Handbook of human resource management in government* (pp. 17–36). Jossey-Bass.

Bargerstock, A. S. (2000). The HRM effectiveness audit: A tool for managing accountability in HRM. *Public Personnel Management, 29*(4), 517–527.

Beadles, I. I., Aston, N., Lowery, C. M., & Johns, K. (2005). The impact of human resource information systems: An exploratory study in the public sector. *Communications of the IIMA, 5*(4), 39–46.

Bingi, P., Sharma, M. K., & Godla, J. K. (1999). Critical issues affecting an ERP implementation. *IS Management, 16*(3), 7–14.

Cain, K., & Barata, P. (2001). Information, not technology, is essential to accountability: Electronic records and public-sector financial management. *The Information Society, 17*(4), 247–258.

Caudle, S. L., Gorr, W. L., & Newcomer, K. E. (1991). Key information systems management issues for the public sector. *MIS Quarterly, 15*(2), 171–188.

Chang, S. et al. (2000). A Delhi Examination of Public ERP Implementation Issues, In Proceedings of International Conference Of Information Systems, 494–500.

Coggburn, J. D. (2007). Outsourcing human resources: The case of the Texas Health and Human Services Commission. *Review of Public Personnel Administration, 27*(4), 315–335.

Daft, R. L. (1995). *Organization theory and design*, 5th edition, ISBN 0-314-04452-3, West Publishing Company, New York. (Life Cycle)

Davenport, T. H. (1998). Putting the enterprise into the enterprise system. *Harvard Business Review, 76*, 121–131.

Debbarma, N., Nath, G., & Das, H. (2013). Analysis of data quality and performance issues in data warehousing and business intelligence. *International Journal of Computer Applications (0975–8887), 79*(15), 20–26.

Demarest. M. (1997). *The politics of data warehousing*. Retrieved July 21, 2015 from: http://www.hevanet.com/demarest/marc/dwpol.html

Downs, A. (1967). *Inside bureaucracy*. Library of Congress catalog card no. 67-18259, little Brown publishing company, Boston, MA.

Eckerson, W. W. (2002). *Data quality and the bottom line*. TDWI Report.

EEOC. (n.d.). http://www.eeoc.gov/employers/eeo1survey/faq.cfm

Fink, D. (1998). Guidelines for the successful adoption of information technology in small and medium enterprises. *International Journal of Information Management, 18*(4), 243–253.

Fui-Hoon Nah, F., Lee-Shang Lau, J., & Kuang, J. (2001). Critical factors for successful implementation of enterprise systems. *Business Process Management Journal, 7*(3), 285–296.

Gallivan, M., & Srite, M. (2005). Information technology and culture: Identifying fragmentary and holistic perspectives of culture. *Information and Organization, 15*(4), 295–338.

Gallivan, M. J. (2001). Organizational adoption and assimilation of complex technological innovations: Development and application of a new framework. *ACM Sigmis Database, 32*(3), 51–85.

Gibson, N., Holland, C., & Light, B. (1999). A case study of a fast track SAP R/3 implementation at Guilbert. *Electronic Markets, 9*(3), 190–193.

Givan, K. R. (2005). Seeing stars: Human resources performance indicators in the National Health Service. *Personnel Review, 34*(6), 634–647.

Goodman, D., French, P. E., & Battaglio, R. P. (2013). Determinants of local government workforce planning. *The American Review of Public Administration, 45*(2), 135–152.

Guan, J., Nunez, W., & Welsh, J. F. (2002). Institutional strategy and information support: The role of data warehousing in higher education. *Campus-wide information systems, 19*(5), 168–174.

Haug, A., Pedersen, A., & Stentoft Arlbjørn, J. (2010). ERP system strategies in parent-subsidiary supply chains. *International Journal of Physical Distribution & Logistics Management, 40*(4), 298–314.

Haug, A., Zachariassen, F., & Van Liempd, D. (2011). The costs of poor data quality. *Journal of Industrial Engineering and Management, 4*(2), 168–193.

Heeks, R. (Ed.). (1999). *Reinventing government in the information age: International practice in IT-enabled public sector reform* (Vol. 1). Psychology Press.

Holsapple, C. W., & Sena, M. P. (2005). ERP plans and decision-support benefits. *Decision Support Systems, 38*(4), 575–590.

Kahn, B. K., Strong, D. M., & Wang, R. Y. (2002). Information quality benchmarks: Product and service performance. *Communications of the ACM, 45*(4), 184–192.

Kaplan, D., Krishnan, R., Padman, R., & Peters, J. (1998). Assessing data quality in accounting information systems. *Communications of the ACM, 41*(2), 72–78.

Kovach, K. A., & Cathcart, C. E. (1999). Human resource information systems (HRIS): Providing business with rapid data access, information exchange and strategic advantage. *Public Personnel Management, 28*(2), 275–282.

Kovach, K. A., Hughes, A. A., Fagan, P., & Maggitti, P. G. (2002). Administrative and strategic advantages of HRIS. *Employment Relations Today, 29*(2), 43–48.

Kumar, K., & van Hillegersberg, J. (2000). Enterprise resource planning: Introduction. *Communications of the ACM, 43*(4), 22–26.

West Virginia Legislature, 2015. West Virginia H.B. 439.

Li, C. (1999). ERP packages: what's next? *Information Systems Management, 16*(3), 31–35.

Lippert, S. K., & Swiercz, P. M. (2005). Human resource information systems (HRIS) and technology trust. *Journal of Information Science, 31*(5), 340–353.

Mahapa, M., & Chirasha, V. (2012). An assessment on the uptake level of a fully integrated human resource information system (HRIS): A case study of midlands state university. *Public Administration Research, 1*(1), 121.

Massy, W. F., & Wilger, A. K. (1998). Technology's contribution to higher education productivity. *New Directions for Higher Education, 1998*(103), 49–59.

McCullough, R., & Sims, R. R. Implementation of an HRIMS at the Personnel Board of Jefferson County, Alabama: A case study in process reengineering. First published December 1, 2012. Research Article. https://doi.org/10.1177/009102601204100406

Meyer, J. W., & Rowan, B. (1977). Institutionalized organizations: Formal structure as myth and ceremony. *American Journal of Sociology, 83*(2), 340–363.

Mnjama, N., & Wamukoya, J. (2007). E-government and records management: An assessment tool for e-records readiness in government. *The Electronic Library, 25*(3), 274–284.

NCES (2015). "Institutes of Education Sciences – Annual reports", Retrieved on July 28, 2015. https://nces.ed.gov/annuals/

Ngai, E. W. T., & Wat, F. K. T. (2006). Human resource information systems: A review and empirical analysis. *Personnel Review, 35*(3), 297–314.

Nutley, S. (2000). Beyond systems: HRM audits in the public sector. *Human Resource Management Journal, 10*(2), 21–38.

Pipino, L. L., Lee, Y. W., & Wang, R. Y. (2002). Data quality assessment. *Communications of the ACM, 45*(4), 211–218.

Pynes, J. E. (2004). The implementation of workforce and succession planning in the public sector. *Public Personnel Management, 33*(4), 389–404.

Razali, M. Z., & Vrontis, D. (2010). The reactions of employees toward the implementation of human resources information systems (HRIS) as a planned change program: A case study in Malaysia. *Journal of Transnational Management, 15*(3), 229–245.

Reddick, C. G. (2009). Human resources information Systems in Texas City Governments: Scope and perception of its effectiveness. *Public Personnel Management, 38*(4), 19–34.

Redman, T. C. (1998). The impact of poor data quality on the typical enterprise. *Communications of the ACM, 41*(2), 79–82.

Redman, T. C. (2013). Data's credibility problem. *Harvard Business Review, 91*(12), 84–88.

Renn, K. A., & Lunceford, C. J. (2004). Because the numbers matter: Transforming postsecondary education data on student race and ethnicity to meet the challenges of a changing nation. *Educational Policy, 18*(5), 752–783.

Ruppel, C. P., & Harrington, S. J. (2001). Sharing knowledge through intranets: A study of organizational culture and intranet implementation. *Professional Communication, IEEE Transactions on, 44*(1), 37–52.

Scannapieco, M., & Catarci, T. (2002). Data quality under a computer science perspective. *Archivi & Computer, 2*, 1–15.

Scannapieco, M., Missier, P., & Batini, C. (2005). Data quality at a glance. *Datenbank-Spektrum, 14*, 6–14.

Tannenbaum, S. I. (1990). Human resource information systems: User group implications. *Journal of Systems Management, 41*(1), 27.

Tansley, C., & Newell, S. (2007). Project social capital, leadership and trust: A study of human resource information systems development. *Journal of Managerial Psychology, 22*(4), 350–368.

Thite, M., Kavanagh, M. J., & Johnson, R. D. (2012). Evolution of human resource management and human resource information systems: The role of information technology. In M. J. Kavanagh, M. Thite, & R. D. Johnson (Eds.), *Human resource information systems: Basics, applications, and future directions* (2nd ed., pp. 2–34). Sage.

Tolsby, J. (1998). Effects of organizational culture on a large scale IT introduction effort: A case study of the Norwegian Army's EDBLF project. *European Journal of Information Systems, 7*(2), 108–114.

Troshani, I., Jerram, C., & Hill, R. S. (2011). Exploring the public sector adoption of HRIS. *Industrial Management & Data Systems, 111*(3), 470–488.

Umble, E. J., Haft, R. R., & Umble, M. M. (2003). Enterprise resource planning: Implementation procedures and critical success factors. *European Journal of Operational Research, 146*(2), 241–257.

United States Equal Employment Opportunity Commission. (2015). Pre-employment inquiries and religious affiliation or beliefs. Retrieved on June 10, 2015. http://www.eeoc.gov/laws/practices/inquiries_religious.cfm

Valcik, Nicolas A. (2015). *Recruiting Analyst for NORTEL Networks*. 1996–1997.

Vosburg, J., & Kumar, A. (2001). Managing dirty data in organizations using ERP: Lessons from a case study. *Industrial Management & Data Systems, 101*(1), 21–31.

Wang, R. Y., Storey, V. C., & Firth, C. P. (1995). A framework for analysis of data quality research. *Knowledge and Data Engineering, IEEE Transactions on, 7*(4), 623–640.

The Costs of HRIS and Dangers of Migration of HRIS Data 10

Key Points of the Chapter

- Areas of concern for migrating from one HRIS enterprise software to a different HRIS enterprise software.
- Hidden costs of migration and maintaining HRIS enterprise software applications.
- Key aspects of migration plans to HRIS to take into account before implementation.

Costs of HRIS

In today's environment public and non-profit organizations have to be cautious funding enterprise software since budgets are tight and accountability for spending money has been increased in recent years. HRIS enterprise software is an expensive investment for any organization, but for medium to large organization, HRIS is necessary for compliance and operational purposes (Handrick, 2019). There are many costs and risks (e.g. security breach) associated with HRIS software, which organizations should assess before determining if one should be purchased and if so which one to select (CompareHRIS.com, 2021 and Leonard, 2019). With some public and Non-Profit organizations there may not be enough justification to purchase HRIS if the organization is small enough to operate without such a system (Leonard, 2019). There are also costs to the organization for not migrating to a new HRIS software package if the existing system is expensive to maintain and no longer supported by the vendor (Curic, 2017).

For organizations that are "given" software, there is a potential pitfall that any price waived could be exceeded by the costs of migrating to and maintaining the new HRIS software. As an example, one public university was "given" HRIS software, which appeared to be inexpensive to the institution when the decision was made, but ended up being quite costly upon implementation. Because the HRIS

N. A. Valcik et al., *Human Resources Information Systems*, Management for Professionals, https://doi.org/10.1007/978-3-030-75111-1_10

portion of the software was only used by four other institutions across the country, the software required numerous customizations that far exceeded the costs of buying another HRIS software package that would have been more functional for the institution in the long run.

Assessment of HRIS Migration Costs

An organization, especially a public and non-profit organization where funds are extremely limited, should perform an assessment to determine the following factors when deciding to purchase HRIS enterprise software.

1. Does the organization need HRIS enterprise software to operate?
2. If the organization already has HRIS enterprise software, can the existing software be upgraded or does it need to be replaced? Is the existing software no longer supported by the current vendor?
3. What type of HRIS software would most closely align with the operational and compliance requirements for the organization?
4. Does the organization have sufficient funding for the software license and the maintenance costs for the enterprise software?
5. Does the organization have the employees with the proper knowledge, skills and abilities to not only work with the new HRIS software but also to implement and migrate the existing data to the new HRIS software?
6. Does the organization have the proper infrastructure to effectively operate the HRIS software?
7. Does the new HRIS software require business process changes and security changes on who accesses the system?
8. Is there political buy-in from the key stakeholders for the new HRIS software chosen by the top organizational administrators?
9. Are there other similar organizations that would want to use HRIS as a combined service to reduce overall costs?
10. How accessible is the new HRIS software for reporting tools and what are the reporting tools to be chosen for using with the new system? Are those reporting tools capable enough to meet the organization's needs?
11. If consultants are needed for the implementation and migration project, what is the budget for those consultants and who will manage the consultants?
12. Will there be a project manager for the implementation of the HRIS software?
13. If there is a project manager, what is the project manager's role in the implementation for the HRIS software?
14. What is the project threshold for determining the end of the project?
15. What determines the success or failure of implementing new HRIS software?

If the organization is unable to answer any of these questions, the organization should wait before purchasing any HRIS enterprise software until these questions can be addressed. The organization should also understand there will need to be time allotted for implementation if events to not go smoothly, which will require more personnel time (and possibly consultant time), translating to more cost to the organization of implement software. Organizations should also understand that key stakeholders will require functional experts for the migration process and will likely use existing employees in this role, which will pull those employees away from their regular duties. How an organization contends with that issue in particular could result in employees leaving the organization or a reduction in productivity if they become overloaded with too many tasks.

The initial licensing cost of HRIS enterprise software can be very expensive; however, the licensing cost is only part of the overall cost of HRIS (Handrick, 2019). There is also a yearly license cost which is usually a percentage of the initial license, the personnel time associated with maintaining the database as well as the application itself, the hardware expenses, upgrading networking infrastructure, training costs, consultant contracts (if needed) and the cost of migration from an older HRIS to a new HRIS software. If the migration of data is not carried out successfully, costs can occur if salaries and benefits are not recorded correctly and employees litigate. Additional costs will occur if existing employees quit rather than learn the new system and the organization has to recruit and train new employees.

Creating a Viable Plan for Migration of Data, Functionality and Reporting

Once it is determined that new HRIS software is necessary, the organization will need to carefully plan how the migration is going to occur and what resources will be needed to ensure success of the project. Planning for a migration requires finding documentation on the existing HRIS software, completely understanding the functionality of the existing system and understanding how some of the variables may be used differently than what was originally intended in the existing system. How an organization will modify their business processes to work with the new HRIS system will be critical to a successful implementation (Gadhavi, 2015).

Data governance will be key to ensuring the data is consistent and accurate as data is migrated to the new system (Van Bergen, 2020). When performing data migration variables such as race and ethnicity should be documented thoroughly and planned before the migration occurs (Van Bergen, 2020). Correcting errors with demographic variables can be problematic if the organization tries to survey all employees to confirm their ethnic and racial demographics. Recent changes in federal and state regulations impact how ethnicity and race are to be reported for compliance purposes. What used to be a simple ethnic variable with six to seven categories has now expanded to two variables of race and ethnicity within multiple categories. Respondents with more than one category selected are now by definition multi-racial and have to be recorded differently than in the past. This can impact organizational diversity goals or can even make an organization appear less diverse if, for example, an African-American employee is now "two or more races". Inaccurate data in the old system will lead to inaccurate data in the new HRIS.

If the Human Resources department is using HRIS software application as an electronic filing cabinet, a successful implementation becomes much less certain especially if human resources lacks technically advanced employees in their department. The following questions should be asked during a migration:

1. What data fields in the existing system have corresponding fields in the new system?
2. How will data be audited when the migration is completed?
3. If data needs to be corrected, will the data be corrected in the existing system before migration or will data be corrected in the new system after the migration?
4. Are there resources available to run the existing system and new system simultaneously until the migration is deemed successful?
5. If the resources are not available, how long should you keep the existing system available in case the new system runs into problems while being brought into production?
6. Does anyone in the organization have the knowledge, skills and abilities to migrate the data from the existing system to the new system?
7. If no one in the organization has the skills to migrate the data, will a consultant be needed and how much will that add to the cost of implementing the new system?
8. How will data be moved from the existing system to the new one?
9. How much data will be moved from the existing system to the new one?
10. What data gaps exist where customization will be needed for compliance reporting?
11. What data gaps exist where customization will be needed for operational reporting?
12. What type of training will be offered to employees on the new system?
13. How much testing will be conducted by the information technology department and the functional areas?
14. What type of documentation will be available to employees for the new system?
15. How will the organization contend with gaps in the business processes if data is unavailable?

These are just some of the problems an organization needs to address when discussing a plan to migrate data from an existing system to a new system. Failure to do so runs the risk of increasing implementation costs as well as risking failure of the project. There also needs to be plans put into place to train personnel and to do post-implementation testing on any new system migration or implementation.

Additional Software Packages Plan for Integration

The migration plan also needs to account for other information systems that may be impacted by the implementation of new HRIS. For example, how will the new HRIS impact a data warehouse on the ELT (Extract, Load and Translation) for data feeds from the existing host system to the data warehouse table structure? What reports or operational areas could be impacted with a migration to a new HRIS software package? Some organizations use a separate recruiting software system to contend with applicants for job postings. How will existing recruitment software integrate with the new HRIS?

Running Two HRIS Simultaneously

An organization may want to have two HRIS software packages run simultaneously for insurance purposes (the existing system and the new system). Can two HRIS enterprise systems operate at the same time during implementation with the organization's existing resources? This leads to an issue of capacity. Does the organization have processing and network infrastructure capacity to operate the new HRIS software? This calculation should follow the vendor's recommendation according to how many individuals will likely be interfacing with HRIS and how many records, reports and external web interfaces the system is designed to operate with the organization's environment.

Shared Services

For shared services, there will obviously be more need for infrastructure than if an organization had its own HRIS software instance. While shared services may be efficient and economical, this arrangement may be problematic if one partner in the shared service is not receiving the service they perceive is needed, which can lead to a dissolution of any type of shared service arrangement (Reilly, 2000). Shared services can also be problematic if there needs to be different customizations of the software to fit the organizational needs at particular locations (Stevenson, 2019). While shared service arrangements can be beneficial, they can also have their pitfalls in terms of political turmoil, customizations needed for organizational software, depersonalization of service and the desire for operational independence with the organizations (Jacobs, 2014; Stevenson, 2019).

Personnel Requirements and Consultants

When a migration is about to occur, the organization should assess the personnel in their organization to determine if these employees possess the knowledge, skills and abilities required, or if the organization is going to have to train their employees with new skill sets. The other option is to hire new permanent employees into the organization, to use temporary employees or hire high-priced consultants. With consultants, the organization should definitely take care into selecting consultants that have the correct knowledge, skills and abilities for the job. If consultants lack the proper knowledge, skills and abilities, then the organization risks losing time and money without any gain to the organization. If properly employed the organization's employees can benefit from learning new skills and techniques from consultants, which will benefit the organization even after the project is completed. The other aspect to using consultants is that the organization must be willing to terminate their original consultants and hire new consultants in if the situation changes or bottlenecks appear where skill sets are needed. The organization should provide consultants enough notice out of professional courtesy if they will not be retained for the original expected time since the consultants may have other opportunities for work.

Additional Issues with Consultants and Independent Contractors

When an ERP or HRIS is installed or a migration occurs, it is common for consultants and independent contractors to be hired to provide additional manpower and skilled expertise with both the old systems and the new systems for implementation. While consultants and independent contractors can provide a number of benefits to an organization, but there are also some potential disadvantages as well that organizations should take into account when hiring consultants and independent contractors. The first issue is that consultants and independent contractors are expensive for an organization to hire, so if an organization needs them for a particular project, make sure there are specific tasks for them to complete that the organization lacks in their current employees or those contractors will free up valuable employees within the organization to work on other critical projects.

Secondly, make sure the consultants and independent contractors document anything they are working on for the project and that the knowledge is transferred to the organization's employees before the contractors leave the project. Third, consultants and independent contractors will need supervision. Just because these types of contractors are supposed to be experts in certain areas or are supposed to complete certain tasks does not mean they do not have to be supervised, they most certainly need oversight.

Fourth, understand that consultants and independent contractors are not necessarily loyal to the organization that is temporarily employing them, they are there for a paycheck. Any work assigned that is not completed in a set time period can and will be billed to the organization. Lastly, do not assume that the consultants and independent contractors know more than the employees in the organization, they may need guidance from the employees in the organization to accomplish tasks assigned to them (Reilly, 2000).

Case Study: "We Need a Bigger Boat!"

A public organization had implemented a migration from an older mainframe system to a new server-based HRIS enterprise software, which was also a shared system with other similar public organizations. The HRIS was also being migrated along with the financial system to provide an integrated system. While this was a significant change for the organization, it also brought significant issues since the organization struggled with consultants who were brought by the parent state agency in to work on the project and the employees had limited experience with the new HRIS software.

Additionally, the employees of the organization had been attempting to migrate from the older mainframe HRIS software for a number of years before the state agency chose another vendor and ordered a halt to all of the work the employees had already put into the migration. This resulted in a loss from anywhere between $10 to $20 million depending upon the source of information even though the new HRIS migration was being touted as a "cost saving measure" since it was a shared service initiative. The second vendor also lacked buy-in from key stakeholders who were not involved in the decision to adopt HRIS enterprise software from a different vendor. When the new vendor's HRIS software was selected, a number of employees left the organization, were terminated or retired. This left the organization with low morale; lack of institutional knowledge and a number of business processes that were not changed to fit the new system which resulted in severe problems with how the HRIS software operated.

When the new HRIS software went live, employees who were actively employed (1) did not receive paychecks (2) did not receive their full pay (3) were over paid or in some cases received pay after they had left the organization and (4) were being dropped from their benefits along with their dependents. An employee at this organization was paying for full medical and prescription benefits for himself and his spouse. This employee had been with the organization for over 15 years and had been consistently paying benefits for his spouse over that period of time. This employee was vacationing at Cape Cod and planning to go kayaking with his spouse when the spouse suddenly discovered they were no longer covered by the organization's medical plan. The employee quickly called the payroll manager (the third one in 9 months) who stated they had reinstated benefit coverage in the system. Since the employee was not sure if the coverage was active for his spouse, they cancelled the kayak trip. 2 weeks later, after they returned from vacation, the employee and his spouse learned that a great white shark was spotted swimming behind a kayaker off the coastline of Cape Cod. While nothing might have occurred during the employee's kayak trip, if he or his spouse had been injured and then discovered their medical coverage had been dropped during the HRIS migration, the organization could have faced possible litigation for mismanagement of medical benefit coverage. These are the types of situations organizations must be careful to avoid during HRIS migration. Not only does the organization risk litigation if something goes wrong, it can also suffer a severe loss of credibility when benefits are dropped and paychecks are incorrect.

Summary

While sales representatives during their initial sales pitch make it seem like all contingencies have been accounted for, this is far from the truth. The software package for HRIS is always generic and, for public organization, there will likely be many changes that need to be addressed in the HRIS architecture and functionality. While public organizations may have a mandate to keep their new system "vanilla" upon implementation, this rarely occurs because regulatory reporting requirements by state and federal agencies requires additional information and capability. Additionally, there will always been some overlap and gaps created between different individuals and departments attempting to implement the HRIS in their organization. This can be caused by different knowledge, skills and abilities of the individuals employed in the organization to the organizational culture influencing how the implementation for HRIS is going to proceed. The next chapter will discuss unique issues facing non-profit and public higher education institutions in relation to implementing and utilizing HRIS.

References

CompareHRIS.com. (2021). *Justifying the costs of a new HRIS or HCMS*. Retrieved on January 6, 2021. https://www.comparehris.com/hris-justification/

Curic, L. (2017). *How much does a human resource information system cost?*, Jungo HR. June 14, 2017. Retrieved on January 6, 2021. https://www.jungohr.ca/blog/how-much-does-a-human-resource-information-system-cost

Gadhavi, M. (2015). *Key challenges & guidelines for a legacy HR & recruitment software migration, Radix*. September 16, 2015. Retrieved on January 6, 2021. https://radixweb.com/blog/key-challenges-guidelines-for-a-legacy-hr-recruitment-software-migration

Handrick, L. (2019). *What is an HRIS/HRMS: definition, cost, features and providers*. January 7, 2019. Retrieved on January 6, 2021. https://fitsmallbusiness.com/what-is-an-hris-hrms/

Jacobs, K. (2014). *Can shared services provide a quality HR service?*, HR Magazine. June 23, 2014. Retrieved on January 6, 2021. https://www.hrmagazine.co.uk/article-details/can-shared-services-provide-a-quality-hr-service

Leonard, K. (2019). *Advantages and disadvantages of human resource information system, Chron*. February 12, 2019. Retrieved on January 6, 2021. https://smallbusiness.chron.com/advantages-disadvantages-human-resource-information-system-2107.html

Reilly, P.. (2000). *HR shared services and the realignment of HR*. The Institute for Employment Studies. ISBN 1-851840298-5, Report 368, IKON Office Solutions plc, Brighton, United Kingdom.

Stevenson, M. (2019). *Pros and cons of human resources shared services, HR exchange network*. May 7, 2019. Retrieved on January 6, 2021. https://www.hrexchangenetwork.com/shared-services/articles/pros-and-cons-of-hr-shared-services

Van Bergen, E. (2020). *How to plan and execute a successful data migration, SuccessDay*. August 7, 2020. Retrieved on January 6, 2021. https://successday.nl/how-to-plan-and-execute-a-successful-data-migration/

Higher Education Specific HR Issues 11

Key Points of the Chapter

- Higher education has many unique aspects as a public organization that HRIS has to take into account for capabilities and functional areas.
- Faculty data has unique characteristics since they can potentially be paid out of different types of accounts.
- Different types of faculty have to accounted for on state and federal reports.

Higher education institutions have many unique employment caveats, which create difficulties even for the best HRIS applications. While most public, non-profit and even private organizations have straightforward employment guidelines, which is not the case with higher education institutions. Unlike a private corporation, a higher education institution will usually have several different missions and roles requiring a mix of different employees when compared to other organizations. Higher education institutions can be involved not only with instruction of students, but also research activities, public service and extension services. This does not include higher education institutions with major athletic programs and specialized contracts for coaches paid from the non-profit organization's account (boosters). The HRIS software of an institution will need to be flexible enough to capture contractual information since these are both personnel documents as well as official documents.

Hiring employees requires HRIS software capable of storing multiple documents for search committees, provide an electronic process to contend with job applicants and capture demographic information on applicants to satisfy federal and state reporting regulations. While most HRIS packages are constructed for straightforward job recruitment in private, public or non-profit organizations, higher education institutions have certain positions (e.g. faculty), which require a number of documents for a search committee's review. Complicating factors exponentially would be a higher education institution that has a hospital attached to its organization.

N. A. Valcik et al., *Human Resources Information Systems*, Management for Professionals, https://doi.org/10.1007/978-3-030-75111-1_11

Positions such as medical doctors, nurses, medical technologists and so on all require specialized licensing. The HRIS database must be able to house certification and licensing data for compliance purposes. In addition to faculty and staff, higher education institutions also employ student workers, interns, visiting ranked faculty members, temporary workers, researchers and graduate assistants who all have a unique job title, their own job responsibilities and can vary on when and how long they are employed for the institution. This provides the organization a mix of employees that is not comparable to other public or non-profit organizations.

What Is a Full-Time Employee?

Unlike most organizations that have a 40-hour work week with a standard 12-month annual payroll, higher education institutions can vary widely on how employees are paid, what accounts they are paid from, what roles they have (which can be more than one), how many months are full-time employment as well as holding specialized assignments (e.g. tenure). At one state public research university in particular, a state auditor was performing an audit on faculty data and made the statement, "All of your faculty are part time." It had to be explained to the auditor that a nine-month contract was in fact standard and that all tenure/tenure track faculty were indeed full-time on nine-month contracts. The auditor's statement unfortunately reflects the general knowledge base of what most state employees and the general public understands – a lack of understanding about how faculty are employed or how faculty operate. Even employees in public higher education or non-profit organization institutions often fail to comprehend or understand the nuances on how personnel at higher education institutions operate or are recorded by HRIS.

Unions in Higher Education Institutions

Adding further complication is the fact that higher education institutions can also have unionized employees who may have certain negotiated rights from more than just one union (e.g. faculty, facility workers, police officers etc.). These negotiated contract terms all have to be input and tracked into an HRIS application capable of handling union data. To negotiate favorable terms for the organization, the higher education institute should have the data as accurate as possible to ensure before negotiations they are on a level playing field with union representatives. Without having accurate data, the institution is placing itself at a severe disadvantage at the negotiation table.

Command and Control Issues

Information on faculty can be controlled, input and reported from more than one department. Often, determining which department controls and validates faculty information can be more political than pragmatic. The greatest power struggle can often be between human resources and academic affairs. If there is tension between these two functional areas, this could lead to greater distrust and it will create a schism in the organization. The chief academic officer, who often holds the title of Provost or Vice Chancellor, often welds greater political power at a higher education institution because they command more personnel who are employed directly in the core business of the institution. The Provost or Vice Chancellor is often second in command to the President or Chancellor of the institution. The Provost will usually have a great deal of influence on how faculty data is tracked and recorded at the institution, which may mean an additional system to HRIS if the HRIS application is perceived to be unable to capture as well as report faculty information.

Faculty – Tenure Status

In theory, tenure allows a faculty member the academic freedom to perform research or instruction in the classroom without risk to their employment. Over time, this status has changed into essentially a lifetime appointment without risk of termination even though infractions by a faculty member are beyond academic freedom issues. This is due to fear of litigation and bad publicity in addition to protecting fellow colleagues in "the guild". In more recent times, tenure has been questioned on its validity in public higher education institutions, particularly as there are other legal precedents that protect freedom of speech.

Post Tenure Review

Governments as well as some institutions on their own initiative have emplaced post-tenure review procedures that enable the institution to terminate tenured faculty members over performance issues. While not common, there have also been institutions which have eliminated the tenure system altogether (Gittleman, 2015). That being stated, the number of tenure and tenure-track faculty is still utilized to establish institutional research status (e.g. Carnegie Research status), national rankings and academic reputations by program (e.g. Nobel laureates among faculty). These surveys and rankings use the IPEDS HR Survey to compile their metrics for a number of categories. Because faculty rank and other merits are evaluated by external entities, reporting this information correctly on federal and state reports takes on enormous importance. In some states, financial incentives have been tied to high producing faculty (e.g. National Research University Fund (NRUF))(The University of Texas at Dallas, 2018). If faculty data is incorrect, these incentives could potentially not be realized.

Faculty Workload

Faculty workload is additional information collected on faculty that reflects the percent of time the faculty members spend on their various responsibilities. For external reporting to IPEDS, this is critical information to determine what categories to place the faculty member in to ensure information is correctly reported. Faculty can be categorized in five different areas: instruction, research, public service, administrative, and academic support. On the IPEDS report, tenure and tenure-track faculty at research institutions, for example, can be categorized in instruction, research, and public service roles. For the purposes of faculty evaluations and tenure review, the ability to assess faculty workload correctly can impact job performance and promotion.

Tenure-Track Status

Tenure-track faculty is a unique category among higher education institutions with regard to the type of information that must be collected to conduct a tenure review for the purpose of awarding or denying full-tenure status. Every academic department and institution sets different qualifications for achieving tenure. For some teaching institutions, tenure can be granted by achieving a stellar teaching record and publishing a couple of articles for professional journals. For intensive research universities, attaining tenure could require a threshold of grant funding, number of published articles in specific journals for their field as well as national or international recognition in their field (e.g. Member of a National Academy). What confuses the process more is the fact that faculty rank (e.g. Assistant, Associate and Full) do not necessarily correspond to being “on-track” for tenure. However, a tenured professor at most institutions will not be under the rank of an Assistant Professor with very rare exceptions. Usually, if a faculty member does not attain tenure after their review, they are demoted to a lecturer and are given a year before their contract is not renewed. Tenure and tenure-track promotions and the tenure review process require an HRIS application that can record and extrapolate all data necessary for the tenure review. An HRIS that cannot accomplish this will be unable to provide actionable data and it will be necessary to create a separate system to accomplish tenure review.

Faculty Contracts

Faculty contracts are another issue where HRIS can at times be problematic. A faculty member can be contracted a certain amount and yet be actually paid a lower or higher amount depending on what time was actually worked or if additional duties were assigned. A number of HRIS applications will not be able to capture this information unless HRIS is customized to capture this data. If additional duties are assigned (e.g. department chair, program head etc.) this amount and the additional duty will be recorded on the contract. However, some institutions will only put their base faculty salary on the contract. How often a contract is signed will be another factor, which can vary from institution to institution. Some institutions use yearly contracts, some create new contracts when a major change occurs (e.g. tenure promotion) and some institutions have no set policy to when contracts are issued. Keeping an HRIS database up-to-date with the latest contract amounts and terms can become problematic if there is no systematic method or business process for contractual information.

Administrative Appointments for Tenured Faculty

Faculty with dual appointments can prove to be fairly complex for HRIS applications that were designed for private industry. Many institutions have tenured faculty members in administrative positions (e.g. President, Provost, Dean etc.) and pay them from an administrative job title linked to an account for administrators. The problem lies in how to keep a tenured faculty member's academic position information when they are not being paid from those accounts by their academic department. One method that can be used, dependent upon the type and vendor of HRIS, is to input 0% full-time equivalency (FTE) into the budget/salary information to serve as a placeholder while their administrative position is 100% FTE in HRIS. This allows the information to be retained for their academic status for reporting purposes while allowing accurate salary information for their administrative appointment to be reported or compiled in summary statistics. For reports such as IPEDS, it is necessary to capture academic rank and tenure for full time administrators. Otherwise, the institution runs the risk of under reporting their tenured faculty. As discussed earlier in the chapter, this can hurt the institution in multiple ways.

Other Nuances in Faculty, Staff and Student Pay

Most HRIS software is built with private industry in mind: a simple payroll with few exceptions on how employees are paid, an assumed 40-hour work week, 12 months a year from a single account or cost center. One-time employee bonuses might be the one area that is unique to private industry rather than federal, state or local governmental organizations. However, in higher education institutions, stipends can be given for multiple reasons. A stipend can be given for faculty members performing extra duties (e.g. Department Chair), a staff member can be provided a stipend for teaching a course, moving costs can be provided in the form of stipend for new employees, or, in rare cases, upper administrators (e.g. President, Provost) may be provided perks like parking or cell phones through a stipend. One institution in particular coded the President's salary as only $60,000 per year when in actuality it was closer to $360,000 per year. The $300,000 was funded by endowments and did not include perks such as a car allowance, house allowance and golf course allowances, which were coded as stipends. If a programmer were unaware of how these stipends were coded, they would not include the special codes to calculate the correct salary and benefit amounts.

Length of Contracts

A nuance that is particular to higher education institutions is the option provided to their faculty to receive their nine-month contracted salary over a 12-month period. This creates a number of problems for many HRIS software packages since this is a unique situation for higher education institutions and, in some cases, public school districts. Most universities and colleges also have lecturers that may instruct only once a year for a particular term or semester. Since these lecturers return every year, there is a disincentive to formally terminate their employment, and privileges like email and parking, only to reinstate them every year. Furthermore, these lecturers, although they instruct during only one term, might also be working on publications or research for the university throughout the year. If short contract lecturers are repeatedly purged from HRIS and reinstated, reporting those faculty members correctly becomes somewhat of an issue.

Accounts Paid out to Salaries

Higher education institutions are also unique in how they pay employees, particularly with regard to dedicated or fund accounting. For example, state or public accounts (also known as cost centers) are fairly flexible and can be spent on a number of operational areas while restricted funds are denoted for research activities, designated are fee driven funds for a particular purposes and auxiliary funds are usually derived from sales revenues (e.g. food services, merchandise etc.). Some staff and faculty members can be paid out of more than one account since they can be working on a contract or grant in addition to receiving state funds for the balance of their salary for performing instructional duties. In addition, some faculty members are paid from endowed chairs, which consist of donated funds generating interest to pay for a faculty member's salary. Endowed chairs can have millions of dollars provided to an account from a donor, which is usually named in honor of the donor. These chairs are seen in academia as being prestigious and usually are quite lucrative for faculty members who are paid from those types of funding mechanisms. Again, HRIS will need to be customized to capture these funding mechanisms in order to tie in a particular faculty member to a specific chair.

Multiple Institutions, Schools or Departments

In very rare cases (e.g. Nobel Prize laureates) there could be a faculty member shared with another institution. In these cases, the faculty member is usually tracked by the percentage of what the institution is paying the faculty member. This arrangement is more common when a faculty member is conducting research at a medical school in addition to their academic department. At The University of Texas System, for example, several UT academic universities are located near UT medical schools where faculty members can easily commute to both institutions. Since the academic and medical schools exist within the same system but are not affiliated directly with each other, it is important to report accurately to the state agency exactly what each institution is paying the faculty member to avoid over or under payment. More commonly, faculty shared among multiple departments or schools within the same institution can create issues for HRIS if there is no home department for the faculty member. When attempting to implement Responsible Center Management (RCM), it is imperative to know what departments or schools the faculty member is based to determine what the school or department is expending in salary versus what revenue the unit is generating. Otherwise it would be extremely difficult to determine how to apportion the budget for the upcoming fiscal year.

Self-Reported Data

For compliance and operational reporting, it is important to gain buy in from faculty and staff for inputting their own data into HRIS. The disadvantages to self-reported data are numerous. First, the employees must want to input their demographic information into HRIS. This activity may or may not require training dependent upon how easy the HRIS software is to use. Secondly, the employees may not put the demographic information into HRIS if, for example, they self-identify as a different race or ethnicity than how others perceive them. Third, employees are not legally obligated to report their demographic data. With upper administrators tasked with determining their organization's diversity, this can become problematic and makes analysis of the organization's current ethic and race makeup difficult to determine.

Case Study: How Many Faculty do we Have?

A regional public university has just hired an Executive Director of Institutional Research. The university is a middle sized institution with around 12,000 students who are undergraduate and graduate students with around 500 tenure, tenure-on-track and non-tenured faculty members. This is considered a medium sized faculty, which should not be very difficult to keep track on how many are hired, terminated and retained. Upon arrival the Executive Director realizes there are several different databases with faculty information. When discussing this issue with their supervisor, the supervisor states, "The President would really like to know exactly how many faculty are employed at the university."

The university has PeopleSoft for its ERP system, a separate faculty database for credentialing and a data warehouse. None of the three systems are correct or can be used for reliable reporting for the upcoming accreditation visit. In all three systems the rank, tenure status and even who is an actively employed faculty member is inconsistent. There are presently no data feeds between the faculty credentialing database (Faculty 180) and PeopleSoft, which leads to inconsistencies in the data. These inconsistencies are an issue for the federal IPEDS HR Survey that has to be compiled and submitted to maintain federal compliance and maintain federal funding as well as the state report.

The Institutional Research staff uses SAS to compile a series of edit reports as well as a master file and audits for the information from all three systems to flag down inconsistencies. Once the inconsistencies are identified then the Institutional Research staff goes to the functional areas as well as the Dean of each school to verify what information is correct and what information is incorrect.

Upon review the Executive Director discovers that the data warehouse, contrary to statements made by the IT staff, utilized dynamic, operational data instead of static data for official reporting. In short, the data warehouse has been improperly designed and improperly managed for a number of years. The Executive Director meets multiple times with parties in the Provost Office, IT and Human Resources along with their staff members to resolve the issues. The first step to resolving the issue is to determine what the official system of record will be for that information. In this case it is determined to be PeopleSoft, which is the HR system of record. A person is then trained in the Provost Office to enter the information into PeopleSoft along with Faculty 180 to allow for consistency. Once the information has been entered into PeopleSoft, a SAS program is developed by Institutional Research to extract the reports for IPEDS HR Survey as well as the state report on staff. The program has a series of edit reports built into the programming to allow for questionable or errors to be sent to the functional areas for correction. Once the data issues are addressed, the program is rerun to produce the state and federal reports. After these actions are taken, the institution is able to produce the number of faculty who are tenure/tenure-track accurately for the first time in years. Equally important, the static files used to produce the state and federal reports are now stored in the data warehouse where that data can be retrieved consistently for a given time frame.

Summary

How to enter data into HRIS for faculty and staff is essential for federal reports in higher education institutions. State and federal agencies want a better record of what their employees are being paid to do, how they are paid and, most importantly, what funds they are paid from for their employment. In public higher education institutions, some tenured and tenure–track faculty tend to have the perception that they are not mere employees but are the institution itself. However, the reality is that faculty at public institutions are state employees and as such will have their job performance assessed just like any other state employee. Faculty can have their salaries reported to public media under open records requests since they are paid from taxpayer revenue streams. Therefore, it is imperative that salary data for faculty and staff in public organizations is accurate before this information is delivered to the media. To accomplish this task, HRIS must be configured to capture all faculty information, including information unique to the higher education setting.

References

Gittleman, Sol, 2015. *Tenure is disappearing. But it's what made American universities the best in the world.* The Washington Post. October 29, 2015. Retrieved on August 15, 2018. https://www.washingtonpost.com/news/grade-point/wp/2015/10/29/tenure-is-disappearing-but-its-what-made-american-universities-the-best-in-the-world/?utm_term=.e7ff9d13ccda

The University of Texas at Dallas. (2018). *National University Research Fund.* Retrieved on August 15, 2018. https://www.utdallas.edu/nruf/?WT.mc_id=HomePageFeature

Conclusion – What Have we Learned? 12

The key purpose of this book is to examine the need for accurate personnel data, identify barriers and provide solutions to supply good quality data that can be used for sound decision-making. Good quality data are the backbone of any organization and impacts institutional decision-making capacity, which in-turn impacts policies at all levels of an organization (Strong, Lee, & Wang, 1997). Thus, the importance of accurate human resources data cannot be underestimated. The data can be used for operational and compliance purposes since public entities are responsible for reporting employee data to the federal and state agencies. Any sizable public organization will need to have an information system to manage human resources information. However, there are several challenges in getting good quality data as indicated by this research. HRIS in the public sector is often used for data collection and storage more than for strategic decision-making (Beadles et al., 2005; Kovach & Cathcart, 1999). According to Guan et al. (2002, p. 174) "what is needed in developing effective information support for institutional decision making is a 'paradigm shift' that re-conceptualizes information systems as critical to decision making."

There is very limited research in the public sector that examines the issue of data accuracy within the human resources function. Public sector organizations across local, state and federal levels are increasingly relying on personnel departments for data related to workforce planning and analysis, recruitment, professional development, performance evaluation, payroll, retention, and attrition (Troshani et al., 2011). To meet these demands in an efficient and cost effective manner, public sector organizations are looking to information systems to automate existing processes. HRIS is most commonly used in public organizations, but due to its limitation of fully integrating all operations into one package, larger organizations (e.g. public universities) are switching to ERP systems. Despite the move to more powerful systems, there continue to be challenges faced by human resources departments, which this study highlights. Furthermore, having access to good quality data can improve the competitiveness of public sector organizations as they continue to vie

N. A. Valcik et al., *Human Resources Information Systems*, Management for Professionals, https://doi.org/10.1007/978-3-030-75111-1_12

with the private sector for talent (Davidson et al., 2007; Light, 2000; Lyons et al., 2006).

Unfortunately, there are only a limited number of information systems commercially available to public organizations. All information systems will have limitations and almost all will need to have modifications made to be compliant with state, local and possibly federal reporting guidelines. There will never be a generic information system that functions as a one-stop information system workable for every public organization. Every public organization is responsible for reporting to state and federal agencies with other public organizations needing to report information to county governments or municipalities. When state or federal agencies compare data files from public organizations, the variables may be very different from one organization to another since the definitions and manner in how the information system is configured can be different. Having consistent definitions and data entry protocols are important to ensure data accuracy across public organizations. Furthermore, having leadership that is committed to promoting a culture of maintaining data accuracy and accessibility is key to improving organizational performance and decision-making.

What Are the Trends within HRIS?

In the future, it will not be uncommon for public sector employees' to completely interface with technology for HR services. Existing HR portals provide a one-stop shop for meeting employee needs related to performance, training and development and compensation. The challenge is to integrate the HR systems with wider data across departments for making strategic decisions that advance the agency and help recruit best talent. However, as public and Non-Profit Organizations have tighter budgets, investment into HRIS will be limited and migrations will not occur until an organization has to make a change either due to data breach or business processes needing additional capabilities, or if the HRIS software becomes unsupported. The costs of HRIS will continue to increase for both the licensing and the annual yearly costs for maintaining the license. To reduce those costs a number of vendors have developed new HRIS applications to run more effectively on the "Cloud". The Cloud is essentially allowing the vendor to host the application on their servers. While this does have some cost saving advantages and some efficiency gains (e.g. patching servers and software), there are also so consequences to using Cloud based systems. These negatives would be a loss of control for the organization over their HRIS application and possibly the loss of being able to access the HRIS application with reporting tools the organization wants to use. Additionally, an organization has to rely on the vendor for security of the organization's data. If a data breach occurs it is the organization that will suffer consequences primarily with public relations. The vendor may well be liable, but how will the stolen data impact the organization financially? The costs are insurmountable, the massive OPM data breach of about 22 million employees cost the Department of Defense approximately $132 million, and the General Services Administration (GSA) sanctioned an additional $500 million to agencies to access for data monitoring, data breach and protection services (GSA, 2015; Miller, 2015). Thus, issues of cybersecurity will be front and center for human resource professionals as they are essential to maintaining sensitive employee and organizational data.

Cybersecurity

There are several challenges that public managers have to be aware of as they adopt human resource information systems, one of the biggest being cybersecurity. The adoption of technology though a difficult task is usually the first step in the implementation cycle; often, organizations do not spend time and resources updating their software, thus, exposing their data to security holes that are vulnerable for attack by cybercriminals. These challenges were discussed in chap. 5. Moving ahead, organizations must not only focus on integrating software, but also updating the software on a regular basis (Kruse et al., 2017). Threat to data vulnerabilities are rising since majority of the employees are now working remotely due to the COVID-19 pandemic. While the pandemic has opened the doors for hiring global talent that is not limited by geographic restrictions, it does place added responsibility on the employer and employee to protect the data on individual devices. Protecting data and its access on government owned devices operated by individuals from remote locations is a priority in these times. Migrating data to Cloud services that can be accessed by employees and citizens is a conversation that is gaining momentum since the pandemic (Baksh, 2020). Federal policy has to keep up with rapidly changing technology and the threats that arise from it. Organizations must continue to foster a culture of safety where employees are encouraged to report phishing emails and practice good data hygiene to reduce data vulnerabilities (Wiggins et al., 2020). Training of HR staff and employees on protocols of cybersecurity should be provided on a regular basis and further be made part of the onboarding process of new employees. Additionally, university education has not kept abreast the rising needs and demands of the field of cybersecurity. Moving forward, public administration and policy schools should create interdisciplinary curriculum that meets the rising demands of the future workforce. Certificate programs or specializations can be created in areas of HR and cybersecurity. Challenges with data security are further amplified as the public sector continues to outsource its IT services (Benaroch, 2020).

Outsourcing

Outsourcing of services is another extension of organizations attempting to save costs by not employees, but instead opting to use contractors where time can be bought yearly (or in some cases less) and the organization does not have to pay benefits. The organization also does not have to show contractors as employees to elected or appointed oversight for the organization. To the public and stakeholders alike it appears the organization had reduced overhead in the form of support for the organization in overhead. This will continue to be a trend since budgets are being reduced and software prices keep increasing. The money eventually has to be reallocated to cover either the license or the costs to support the system. Another manner in reducing costs is to have several like organizations go into a shared services model. This shared service model can combine several organizations on one HRIS applications and database. In theory this should be cost effective to have an HRIS application hosted in this manner. In reality however, political power and control heavily dictate what organization is to receive how much support from the hosting system. In addition, specific software applications needed by the organization can be problematic in how those specific software applications are merged with the HRIS application of a particular organization. The cost of staffing can cause the costs of the HRIS applications to increase at an exponential rate. As privatization and contracting of HR services increased in the public sector (Battaglio, 2015; Coggburn, 2007), private organizations have access to confidential HR data placing the responsibility for protecting these data on both the employer and the contractor. Public organizations outsourcing HR services to a private contractor cannot abdicate its responsibility of maintaining data security; while on the other hand, the contractor cannot assume that the public organization shoulders the entire responsibility of protecting sensitive personnel data. Both organizations must work in tandem to safeguard important employee and organizational data.

Over-Centralization Shared Services– (System Offices Combining Databases)

With the Shared Services model, this can create efficiencies and reduce costs. However, there are also several drawbacks to having a shared service model. The first is that security has to extremely tight in order to prevent hacking from gaining access to the database and breaching the firewalls for confidential information. The more organizations who are sharing the database structure, the more information can be compromised if a breach occurs, thus impacting more organizations. A second Shared Services drawback is potentially individual organizations lose control and access to their own data.

Whether HRIS is onsite at a third party vendor's location or in "the cloud", essentially on a server farm with clusters, the risk of an organization not having direct support or enough support to run operations is a very real problem. Shared service models also have an issue with utilizing third party software from different organizations attempting to use one shared data structure (database) with a vanilla user interface. This can cause issues when attempting to place patches on HRIS or provide updates to HRIS. In many cases it has been argued that the Shared Service model depersonalizes Human Resources personnel. If an organization (or organizations) transition to a Shared Service model and the migration does not go smoothly or as planned, it can be extremely difficult to rectify the situation to have accurate information in the Shared Service database. A Shared Service model also requires cooperation among all parties involved with the Shared Service and agreement on how certain business processes are going to be implemented as well as how certain variables are going to be coded so that reports can be consistently extracted for accurate analysis.

Changing Workforce

The changing workforce will place greater emphasis in several areas of HR from recruitment to performance management to work-life balance. More number of minorities, women and mixed race identities are entering the workforce. Additionally, the workforce is generationally very diverse. While the baby boomers (born between 1946–1964) are approaching retirement age, reports suggests that they are delaying their retirement due to better life expectancy, rising cost of healthcare, the desire to better retirement savings, which is impacted by the changes to social security and the 2008 economic recession and the 2020 COVID-19 pandemic (Epstein, 2019; Vernon, 2019). By 2024, baby boomers between the ages 60 to 78 will be among the fastest growing generation in the workforce compared with any other age group (Toossi & Torpey, 2017) (Fig. 12.1).

Millennials (born between 1981–1996) comprise the largest proportion of adult population (ages 24–39) across any generation; they have surpassed baby boomers in 2019 according to data by the U.S. Census Bureau (Fry, 2020). The projected population by each generation from 2019–2050 is shown in Fig. 12.2.

With several generations in the workforce, the level of comfort with the use of technology is varied. This comfort with technology might also reflect in the expectations that millennials and generation Z (born post 1996) may have from their organizations. Younger generation emphasize the need for work-life balance and thus prefer working from home/remote location. While majority of the workforce is working remotely during the pandemic, the future landscape of work might be

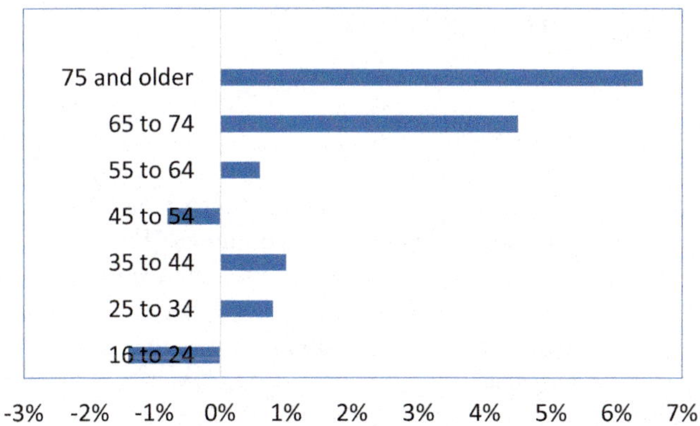

Fig. 12.1 Annual growth rate in labor force, Projected 2014–24. (Source: U.S. Bureau of Labor Statistics)

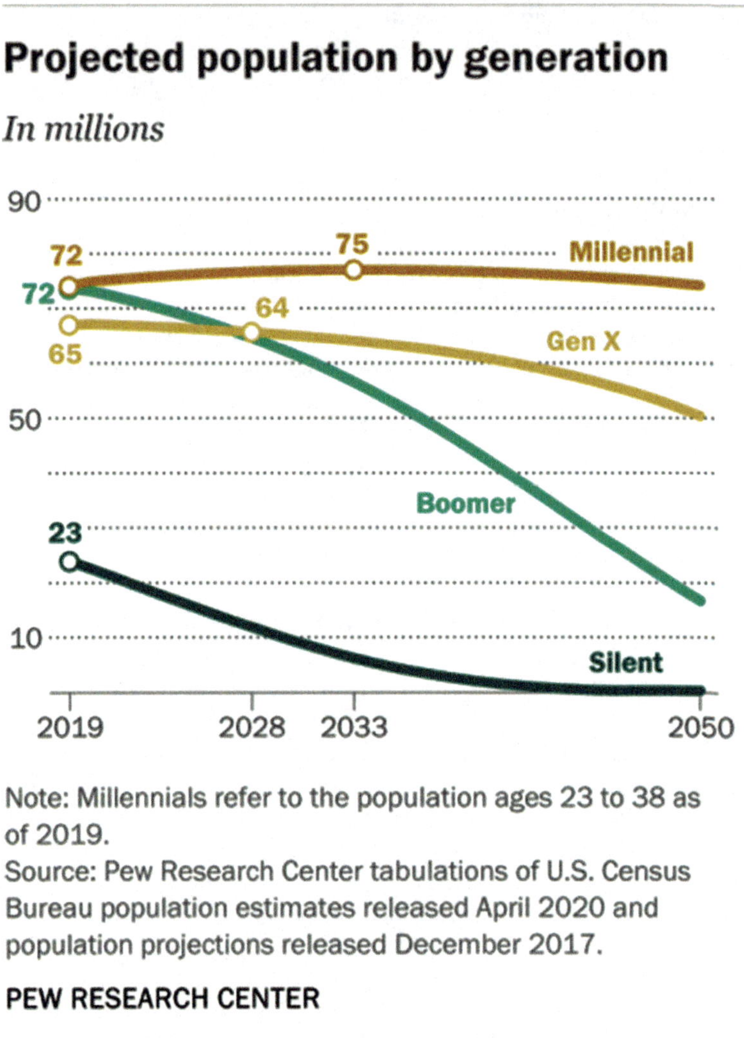

Fig. 12.2 Projected population by generation

altered from this experience, further changing the role of HR and HRIS. In an increasingly technologically loaded work environment, HR has to find ways to engage employees and ensure they remain motivated and are not subject to mental stress that can arise from isolation due to working online. Thus, HR has to be aware of the advantages and downsides of managing a workforce that is increasingly becoming diverse and virtual.

Case Study: Carry on my Wayward Son

Never assume a system is working correctly and that a public organization is never too big to fail. There are certain aspects of HRIS that are extremely complicated that can be missed by the organization's personnel. Every public and non-profit organization should strive to obtain the best applicants when jobs are posted. Great organizations also strive for those applicants to be from a diverse applicant pool. However, the organization has to do due diligence to ensure the system is working correctly to accept the applicants' information and documentation. For organizations that are extremely bureaucratic in nature, the application process can be onerous and time consuming. This alone can cause good applicants to apply for positions that have a more streamlined business process.

To illustrate a point we will take an applicant who will be called "Anne". Anne is a highly educated and experienced worker in a highly desirable professional field, which most public organizations would want Anne to apply with them. Anne has worked private industry for many years and saw a position she wanted to apply for with a large public organization. Anne put in the application, her transcripts, references and many other forms required for applying for the position. Once Anne put in her application, she received an electronic notice that all of her materials were attached for the position and that she was a valid applicant. Anne determined who the hiring manager was and called the hiring manger to verify the status of her application. Anne was then informed by the hiring manager that her transcripts were missing from the application. Anne stated that the transcripts were attached to the position and that she could log in and see the transcripts in HRIS. The hiring manager stated she did not know what was going on and was going to contact the HR department since it was now past the closing date.

Anne then decided to take the initiative and call the HR department herself. The organization transferred Anne several times before she finally got in contact with the appropriate HR person overseeing the application process. The HR person stated they could only see one of the transcripts through their screens in HRIS and that the job would have to be reopened and that Anne would have to reapply a second time. Anne pointed out that all of the transcripts were in the HRIS before the deadline. Anne logged in and tried several different ways to load up the transcripts in different formats to see if the HR person could see the transcripts. After several efforts, the HR person stated, "I cannot see them. Can you just email me your transcripts?"

The question should now be how many applicants were rejected on false grounds when their materials were actually in the system before the deadline? How do applicants see an organization who has an HRIS operating in this manner? What type of credibility and reputation does this cause for the organization? Does this prevent the organization from hiring good candidates?

These are all valid questions, which can be positively or negatively influenced by how an HRIS operates for an organization. To have a viable HRIS is valuable for an organization, but to have one that is flawed can be a severe liability.

Summary

Throughout this text there have been a number of topics raised on the value and importance of HRIS. While public organizations over a certain size have to use HRIS, they should also be aware of the consequences of not having a viable HRIS in place. The consequences can be quite severe if the data are not captured correctly for a number of reasons that have been discussed throughout the chapters. It is important for organizations to plan appropriately and have the appropriate staffing in place for HRIS. Unless an HRIS is extremely limited in capability, no organization enjoys migrating to a new HRIS with all of the expenses and hardships these actions can incur. However, it is inevitable as technology evolves and the world becomes more complex that newer HRIS platforms will be developed and deployed. HRIS is rarely implemented as a cost saving measure and should not be seen to be a cost saving measure. HRIS should be seen by upper administrators as a necessity to operate as a public or Non-Profit organization. The upper administrators should also understand that to successfully implement HRIS they must invest the right resources.

References

Baksh, M. (2020). *Cyber defenders*. Nextgov. Retrieved December 15, 2020 from https://www.nextgov.com/assets/cyber-defenders-ng-q3-2020/portal/

Battaglio, R. P. (2015). *Public human resource management: Strategies and practices in the 21st century*. Sage Publications.

Beadles, I. I., Aston, N., Lowery, C. M., & Johns, K. (2005). The impact of human resource information systems: An exploratory study in the public sector. *Communications of the IIMA, 5*(4), 39–46.

Benaroch, M. (2020). Cybersecurity risk in IT outsourcing—Challenges and emerging realities. In R. Hirschheim, A. Heinzl, & J. Dibbern (Eds.), *Information Systems Outsourcing: The Era of Digital Transformation* (pp. 313–334). Springer.

Coggburn, J. D. (2007). Outsourcing human resources: The case of the Texas health and human services commission. *Review of Public Personnel Administration, 27*(4), 315–335.

Davidson, D., Lepeak, S., & Newman, E. (2007). *Recruiting and Staffing in the Public Sector: Results from the IPMA-HR Research Series*. Retrieved July, 28, 2015 from http://unpan1.un.org/intradoc/groups/public/documents/ipma-hr/unpan027173.pdf

Epstein, G. (2019). *Baby boomers in no rush to retire*. Barron's. Retrieved December 23, 2020 from https://www.barrons.com/articles/baby-boomers-in-no-rush-to-retire-51557948765

Fry, R. (2020). *Millennials overtake baby boomers as America's largest generation*. Pew Research Center. Retrieved December 24, 2020 from https://www.pewresearch.org/fact-tank/2020/04/28/millennials-overtake-baby-boomers-as-americas-largest-generation/

General Services Administration (GSA) (2015). *GSA awards BPAs for identity monitoring, data breach response and protection Services*. Report retrieved December 19, 2020 from: https://www.gsa.gov/about-us/newsroom/news-releases/gsa-awards-bpas-for-identity-monitoring-data-breach-response-and-protection-services

Guan, J., Nunez, W., & Welsh, J. F. (2002). Institutional strategy and information support: The role of data warehousing in higher education. *Campus-Wide Information Systems, 19*(5), 168–174.

Kovach, K. A., & Cathcart, C. E. (1999). Human resource information systems (HRIS): Providing business with rapid data access, information exchange and strategic advantage. *Public Personnel Management, 28*(2), 275–282.

Kruse, C. S., Frederick, B., Jacobson, T., & Monticone, D. K. (2017). Cybersecurity in healthcare: A systematic review of modern threats and trends. *Technology and Health Care, 25*(1), 1–10.

Light, P. C. (2000). The empty government talent pool: The new public service arrives. *The Brookings Review*, 20–23.

Lyons, S. T., Duxbury, L. E., & Higgins, C. A. (2006). A comparison of the values and commitment of private sector, public sector, and parapublic sector employees. *Public Administration Review*, 605–618.

Miller, J. (2015). *DoD's share of the OPM data breach: $132 million*. Retrieved December 19, 2020 from: https://federalnewsnetwork.com/workforce/2015/08/dods-share-opm-data-breach-132-million/

Strong, D. M., Lee, Y. W., & Wang, R. Y. (1997). Quality data in context. *Communications of the ACM, 40*(5), 103.

Toossi, M & Torpey, E. (2017). Older workers: Labor force trends and career options. Career Outlook, . https://www.bls.gov/careeroutlook/2017/article/older-workers.htm

Troshani, I., Jerram, C., & Hill, R. S. (2011). Exploring the public sector adoption of HRIS. *Industrial Management & Data Systems, 111*(3), 470–488.

Vernon, S. (2019). Redesigning retirement and human resource programs to support longer lives. *Benefits Quarterly, 35*(3), 17–16.

Wiggins, M. W., Auton, J., Bayl-Smith, P., & Carrigan, A. (2020). Optimising the future of technology in organisations: A human factors perspective. *Australian Journal of Management*. https://doi.org/10.1177/0312896220918915

Index

N. A. Valcik et al., *Human Resources Information Systems*, Management for Professionals, https://doi.org/10.1007/978-3-030-75111-1

Printed in Dunstable, United Kingdom

66798727R00118